An Irish Banking Manifesto

About the Author

From 1973 to 1990 Tim McCormick worked in investment banking in Dublin (originally Northern Bank Finance Corporation, later National Irish Investment Bank and now part of Danske Bank) and for the following twenty years ran financial courses with the Irish Management Institute. He continues to work in the financial industry as a consultant. He is the author of *Strategic Cost Reduction: How to Cut Costs without Killing Your Business* and has written over 20 articles for *Accountancy Ireland*, several of which focused on banking issues.

AN IRISH BANKING MANIFESTO

The Views of a Disenchanted Former Banker

Tim McCormick

The Liffey Press

Published by
The Liffey Press Ltd
Raheny Shopping Centre, Second Floor
Raheny, Dublin 5, Ireland
www.theliffeypress.com

© 2015 Tim McCormick

A catalogue record of this book is
available from the British Library.

ISBN 978-1-908308-67-2

All rights reserved. No part of this publication may be
reproduced or transmitted in any form or by any means,
including photocopying and recording, without written
permission of the publisher. Such written permission must
also be obtained before any part of this publication is stored
in a retrieval system of any nature. Requests for permission
should be directed to The Liffey Press, Raheny Shopping
Centre, Second Floor, Raheny, Dublin 5, Ireland.

Printed in Ireland by Sprint-Print

Contents

Part Three:
Culture, Competition and Culpability
– Revealing the Root Causes

Part Four:
Devising Solutions – The Rugged Road Ahead

Foreword

Shane Ross

It is rare to discover an ex-banker who can pen prose. It is even rarer to unearth an accountant who can entertain. Tim McCormick, a former member of both professions, has mastered both skills as an author.

Of all the books written so far about the Irish banking crisis, this one has the greatest authority. There have been narratives, academic works of distinction and tabloid tales of wrongdoing covering the catastrophe. But this book is different.

Tim was a banker when banking was prudent and reputable. He left National Irish Bank (NIB) in Dublin in 1990 to pursue a career teaching at the Irish Management Institute. Many years later, when offered a lucrative return to the same bank, he declined. It was a wise decision.

His decision to turn down a return to banking gave him the authority to write this book. It is written from the unique perspective of one who practised banking with a view to risk management, not short-term profit. Tim McCormick, unlike those who followed him in Ireland's big banks in the nineties and noughties, did not become rich from banking. Instead, he watched aghast from the sidelines.

While the biographical anecdotes are enlightening, the analysis of the reasons for the crash are convincing. Tim concentrates on the flaws of the bankers rather than other culprits in the crash, partly because that is where his expertise combines with his horror of developments, but also because that is where he believes the lion's share of the blame lies. He does not spare the politicians, the regulator or the developers but – as he says in the final chapter – he wants the book to 'contribute to opening up a debate on the need for real change in the industry'.

It surely will. And no industry needs it more. Nor indeed has any industry been indulged more than banking and bankers, despite the gaping flaws in its governance.

Tim traces the beginning of the crisis as far back as 2000 when he shows how the property bubble developed in Ireland. Bankers abandoned high standards and embraced risk. 'Groupthink' took over. Worrying global trends of softer regulation were accompanied by an emphasis on short-term profits and the infamous bonus culture. Board members, big beneficiaries of ballooning fees, saw no evil. They were in denial. Ireland was no exception to this trend. But with a banking sector far too big for our small island economy, we suffered disproportionately.

While the wrongs which the narrative exposes are useful because there is no area where Tim is afraid to tread, this book is not merely a lament about the wrongs of the past. Nor is it another polemic. It offers hope for the future. One of its most novel contributions is its 'Manifesto for Reform'.

This is the difficult bit, but Tim, with all the dedication of a man who has seen his once noble vocation decline into a haven for the greedy, attacks the crusade for renewal with an energetic zest. His final chapter spells out a charter that current bankers would do well to acknowledge. While sceptical of their willingness to listen, he spells out Six Guiding Principles.

Chief among his demands for the future are an end of the emphasis on short-term profits, which he rightly fingers as a cause of the cultural contamination. He wants to restore traditional lending standards, not just in the housing market but in corporate banking. He wants to ensure that customers are no longer targets for the wrong products and that bankers are fined – no longer indulged or even rewarded – for mis-selling. Reform of bankers' exorbitant remuneration is a *sine qua non*. The author refreshingly suggests that directors should serve no more than five years in such powerful positions. More radically, he proposes that members of his former profession, the battered auditors, be given the same short-term appointment.

Hell is likely to freeze over first, as the two bastions (the boards and the politicians) of Ireland's business establishment regroup. The current willingness of the government and the directors to appoint the usual suspects to the boardroom gives little hope that there is any appetite for reform. Quite the opposite. They are regrouping.

That does not mean that this book will not provoke debate. It is a more than useful contribution to the debate raging over Irish banking. Tim McCormick will not win any friends among his former colleagues in banking or accountancy for his invaluable work. But he must not be ignored. He has no axe to grind, simply offering a mature judgment on a profession that has descended into the financial gutter.

Shane Ross is an independent TD representing Dublin South. He is the author of *The Bankers: How the Banks Brought Ireland to Its Knees*.

Acknowledgements

I have been assisted by a wide variety of people who have been kind enough to read the text and make their suggestions, which have proved invaluable. These include several former bankers: Willy Cotter of Bank of Ireland, John Carroll of UIB and my former colleague at NIIB, Maurice O'Brien. Outside of banking suggestions came from Dermot McAleese, Emeritus Whately Professor of Political Economy at Trinity College Dublin and former director of the Central Bank, actuary Dr Ronan O'Connor, former spatial planner Mary Warren Darley, journalist Stephen Ryan and my IMI colleague Ruth Handy. I was helped also by two members of my family: my brother Simon, a solicitor, and my son Myles, a recent economics graduate. Others who provided extremely useful advice have chosen to remain anonymous.

I should also like to mention Daisy Downes, editor of *Accountancy Ireland*, who has published over twenty of my articles, either on the topic of banking or cost reduction over the last five years, and also Chartered Accountants Ireland, which published a book on Strategic Cost Reduction, containing some banking illustrations, which I co-authored, permitting me to try out my ideas to a wide audience.

On a broader front I have been influenced, not only by the official reports in different countries, but also by a range of academics, economists, bankers, journalists, regulators and diverse other commentators who have written on various aspects of banking and finance, mostly on global rather than Irish issues. Over a hundred of these authors and their works are listed under 'Selected Further Reading'. Often their views or opinions are necessarily recorded rather succinctly in the interests of brevity, but references in the text to their writing should enable interested readers to follow up their ideas in greater detail.

Finally, I would like to offer my thanks to Shane Ross, who kindly agreed to write the foreword to the book. As an independent politician, a long standing commentator on banking matters and a former stockbroker, he provides an unrivalled expertise on the topic of this book. Also, I wish to thank my publisher, David Givens of The Liffey Press, without whose guidance the book would never have seen the light of day.

To all of the above I would like to express my most sincere gratitude. Any remaining flaws or mistakes are, of course, entirely my responsibility.

Anyone else who wants to express their views to me on any aspects of the book, positive or negative, is welcome to contact me at: timmccormick@eircom.net.

Acronyms and Glossary

AIB
Allied Irish Banks, 99.8 per cent owned by the State

Anglo or Anglo Irish
Anglo Irish Bank, acquired by IBRC and placed in wind-up

BoI
Bank of Ireland, 14 per cent owned by the State

Central Bank
The Irish national bank that supervises Irish banks and implements monetary policy in Ireland

Celtic Tiger
Term used to describe Ireland during period of high economic growth from 1994 to 2007

Contagion
The process by which risks are transmitted from one financial institution to another

Creative accounting
Improper use of accounting techniques to improve the appearance of a company's Balance Sheet and Accounts

Credit Default Swap
A derivative used to transfer the risk of loan default from one financial institution to another – they can be employed for insurance or speculation

Derivative
A synthetic financial instrument whose value is derived from and dependent on the value of one or more assets or events

EBS
Educational Building Society, acquired by AIB in 2011

ECB
European Central Bank, responsible for supervision of banking in the Eurozone

Efficient markets
Markets where prices reflect rationally all public information

Examinership
Irish insolvency procedure, largely comparable with UK administration provisions, allowing for a restructuring of debts under the control of the courts

Financial Regulator
Authority under the aegis of the Central Bank with responsibility for banking regulation

Fractional banking system
Banking where a small proportion of capital is retained to meet withdrawal of deposits

FSA
Financial Services Authority, the UK Regulatory Authority, disbanded in 2013

Gearing
Relative amount of debt in the capital of a business, commonly measured by the ratio of Debt : Equity

Glass-Steagall Act
1933 US Act, enforcing the separation of the activities of commercial banks and securities firms, largely repealed in 1999

Groupthink
The tendency to accept the consensus view without question or debate

IBRC
Irish Bank Resolution Corporation (now in liquidation)

IFRS
International Financial Reporting Standards

IFSC
International Financial Services Centre, located in Dublin

IMI
Irish Management Institute

INBS
Irish Nationwide Building Society, acquired by IBRC

INSEAD
International business school with campuses in France and Singapore

Insolvency
A business is insolvent when it cannot pay its debts, as they fall due – it is also insolvent, when its liabilities exceed the value of its assets

Interbank market
The wholesale money markets, where banks lend to one another

Irish Life and Permanent plc
Formerly a building society and life assurance company, but now basically a bank, 99 per cent owned by the State – its subsidiary, Permanent TSB, was a major source of tracker mortgages

Leverage
US term for gearing

LIBOR
London Interbank Offer Rate, the cost of available funding for varying time periods used as the basis for setting many interest rates

Liquidity
Availability of cash

Loan impairment
Amount of a loan deemed to be irrecoverable

NAMA
National Asset Management Agency, the 'bad bank' created by the Government.

NBFC
Northern Bank Finance Corporation, Irish merchant banking arm of Midland Bank

NIB
National Irish Bank, acquired by National Australia Bank and subsequently by Danske Bank

NIIB
National Irish Investment Bank (formerly NBFC)

Oireachtas
Irish parliament, consisting of Dáil and Senate

Overtrading
Excessive growth, causing a business to run out of cash

Pillar Banks
AIB and BoI, the two banks deemed by the Government to be fundamental to Ireland's economic recovery

Ponzi loans
Loans advanced where neither capital nor interest can be paid from cashflow and repayment relies on rising values of the underlying assets

Provisions
Amounts of capital set aside for loans considered to be irrecoverable

Shareholder value
The value of a business, usually measured by its stock market valuation

SME
Small and medium sized enterprise

Subprime lending
Loans to customers who have an impaired credit history or do not meet normal credit criteria

Swaps
A transaction where two counterparties exchange the cashflows of one party's financial instrument for the cash flows of the other party's financial instrument

VAR
Value at risk, a statistical model for measuring the potential loss in value of an asset or a portfolio from 'normal market risk' over a specified period

Window dressing
Legal, if sometimes dubious or misleading, accounting techniques used to improve the appearance of a company's financial statements

This book is dedicated to the Irish taxpayer, who bears and will continue to bear the cost of the banking debacle, but in particular to my children – Myles, Conor, Patrick and Tara – who may join its ranks, if they remain in the country on the completion of their education.

Introduction

Sometime in the late 1980s, while employed by a Dublin bank, I had occasion to go to London on banking business, the details of which I have long since forgotten. I do, on the other hand, recall the lunchtime conversation. I was dealing with senior British bankers who wore well-tailored suits and drove expensive cars.

One of the bankers quizzed me about Irish banking and particularly the mortgage market there. I had to deny any expertise, as this was not my field of lending. Nevertheless I thought that I understood the basic principles. Building Societies tended to lend over a period of about twenty years, based on up to 3.5 times the main income up to two-thirds or maybe three-quarters of the value of the property. Prudence generally dictated that these limits should not be exceeded to ensure an orderly repayment.

The banker somewhat scornfully told me that such ideas were very much out of date. He explained that people needed to live in London and new accommodation was limited. Prices could not fall, although they might level off temporarily. Income multiples were considered to be inappropriate to assess repayment capacity. Banks were prepared to lend one hundred per cent of the cost or somewhat more to cover furnishings. If borrowers fell into difficulties, they could readily trade down market, so the risks were minimal.

I listened politely to views which ran counter to the lending principles I understood. Although I had not previously discussed lending with London banks, it all sounded eerily familiar. I puzzled

1

over the matter on the way back to the airport, when the answer struck me. I had heard a similar argument from Irish farmers some years earlier, advanced with equal confidence.

Farmers had told me that no more land was being made and that people needed to eat. Land could not fall in value from IR£4,000 per acre. The fact that in an era of high interest rates the interest alone might amount to nearly IR£800 per acre and that the gross yield from land was likely to be IR£100 to IR£200 per acre did not worry them. Small parcels of land could always be sold to service the loan agreement. The ensuing crash in land prices gave rise to much hardship.

The following day back in Dublin I rang my stockbroker and told him that London was in a massive property bubble. If I could short sell the market, selling first before buying back later, I could make a fortune. After considering the matter, he rang back to dissuade me. It was not possible to sell properties that you do not own. While it was possible to short sell property shares, his firm discouraged such a practice in general. Accordingly, I dismissed the idea.

Shortly afterwards the London property market did implode, as I had predicted, and homeowners there learnt about the horrors of negative equity, where the value of their home was exceeded by their borrowings. I smiled to myself and briefly thought of the fortune I might have made if I had managed to short sell the London property market. There was only one sure consolation for me: Thanks be to God that the madness of the London property market could never happen in Ireland!

Into Banking

I had some grounds for my optimism, for believing that Irish bankers would never succumb to the madness of British banks in dealing with the property bubble in the 1980s, if a similar situation were to arise. In my time the Irish banks had survived a major property reversal, when the Gallagher Group collapsed in 1982, but had come through with minimal collateral damage. There was an immediate impact on the market, confidence was lost and property prices fell. The banks incurred a serious loss from the failure of the business and depositors lost their money in the failure of the Group's in-house bank, Merchant Banking Limited. I was not involved in loans to the business, although my employer, Northern Bank Finance Corporation (NBFC), was and suffered a loss as a result. But the broader financial system, involving many banks of different sizes, proved to be robust and no other big developers were dragged down in his wake. Builders stopped developing for a time and maybe played more golf. But they and their banks remained solvent in the difficult years which followed, while their credit continued to flow in other sectors.

The other reason for my confidence in Irish banking standards was based on my experience gained in the industry over seventeen years. I had entered banking in 1972 in Dublin, the city in which I was born and was later to obtain an economics degree. I was anxious to return to Ireland, having spent four years away, qualifying as a chartered accountant in London and then obtaining an MBA from Insead in France. I joined NBFC, the relatively new merchant banking subsidiary of the British Midland Bank. With around 50 retail branches, Northern Bank had a relatively small market share of around 5 per cent in Irish banking, trailing far behind the leaders, Allied Irish Banks and Bank of Ireland, as well as its northern rival, Ulster Bank.

My initial work was in the field of corporate finance advice, mainly around corporate takeovers. Despite its small client base the bank had established itself as an important player in the field. After some years of interesting, varied and challenging work the level of activity dropped, along with the fortunes of the economy and the small Irish Stock Market. It was time to turn my attention elsewhere.

In 1980 the opportunity arose to transfer to corporate lending and there I was to spend the next nine years. Proposals came in all shapes and sizes, as well as covering a wide spread of industries. They could include Midland Bank connections, such as foreign multinationals setting up manufacturing plants, agricultural cooperatives, expanding supermarket chains, semi-state organisations, indigenous businesses with longstanding connections to our bank branches and, of course, builders or property developers. Some borrowers were highly sophisticated financially, while others had primitive accounting information. Usually the bank operated independently, but where the exposure was deemed large, it could join a syndicate with other banks.

The 1980s were not an easy time for banking, but business continued to be generated through the branch network. The Celtic Tiger had not yet been born. The decade started in the aftermath of the second oil crisis and ended in a downturn with some better times in between. Yet throughout the period there were few bad loans amongst the clients I managed. If the loan was sensible in the first place, if the credit was structured appropriately with ample protective covenants and then diligently monitored, then it should be fully recovered in due course. Naturally there was the occasional problem and twice it was necessary to appoint a receiver, when no restructuring was possible. But overall it was a good business, generating satisfactory margins and profits.

In 1987 Midland Bank, which had undertaken a disastrous foray into the US through the acquisition of Crocker Bank, divested itself of its Scottish and Irish subsidiaries, Clydesdale Bank in Scotland and the Northern Bank in both Northern Ireland and the Republic. NBFC had acquired a new and very different parent in National Australia Bank, a retail bank with a reputation for aggressive marketing of its products. While we were renamed National Irish Investment Bank, the future of the investment bank, with its emphasis on corporate and commercial lending, was unclear. Most employees welcomed the change. Midland had highly bureaucratic manual systems, which involved much tedious form filling, serving little apparent useful purpose. But if any forms were incomplete the proposition would be returned, which led to slow decision making. The procedures manual could take precedence over commercial common sense. While the Midland advertised itself as the 'listening bank', this was not always evident to those of us working in its Irish subsidiary.

When banks make acquisitions, particularly those overseas, there is always a concern that some awful problem is hidden away far below the surface, which when discovered can cause major embarrassment and entail substantial provisions for subsequent losses. I was approached to become head of the Irish group's internal audit department, reporting to London and ultimately Melbourne, as well as to the CEO and the bank board's audit committee. For a year, aided by a team of assistants, I checked out the main areas of risk, which were perceived to be treasury and corporate lending, rather than the branch network, where transactions tended to be of a much smaller scale and subject to regular audits.

Within a year the major risk areas and controls had all been scrutinised. No unexpected horrors had emerged and with some tightening of controls life continued. However, the future of the investment bank as a separate entity was becoming more doubtful. Since this was the activity which best suited my skills, so was my own future. Lending reporting lines were now conducted through a credit committee in Belfast and corporate lending seemed likely to be integrated more closely into the retail bank, a trend increasingly evident in other Irish investment banks. I was now a mid-career, middle aged, established banker, so a complete change would pose a real challenge for me, particularly in a difficult economic climate.

I decided to seek a prolonged leave of absence to allow myself time to find a new career outside of banking. The request was sympathetically received and I was offered leave of absence for five years. At the end of the period I phoned to check out my position. The salary on offer to me was much higher than I was earning, but the prospects were not promising and so I declined to return. Thus my involvement in banking had finished in mid-career at the start of 1990 after seventeen years, having spent considerable time in understanding how lending was conducted at that time.

Out of Banking and into Teaching

Shortly after leaving the bank I started running financial courses at the Irish Management Institute. I had always enjoyed teaching since I had worked as a volunteer in the then little known city of Bangalore, located in Southern India, after leaving school and entered my new profession with relish. IMI was the dominant provider of management training in Ireland and sought to promulgate leading business practice in all fields. Most of its business consisted of running short courses, either on an open basis or specifically for a particular organisation. In addition, it provided first and second level degrees, for which it combined with my alma mater, Trinity College. Outside of that it had an international business, building on its long standing reputation. I was engaged to work in all areas, adopting a somewhat unusual approach, since I could interpret modern financial theory from the perspective of a former banker, who had experienced it working in practice.

Throughout the period I only kept in touch with banking in a haphazard fashion. I did run diploma courses for senior managers in Bank of Ireland and courses for the Financial Services Industry Association, so I learnt of the changing competition within the industry. I ran treasury courses, but outsourced most of the teaching, since I lacked the specialist knowledge. I acted as tutor to senior managers writing masters' theses on their strategies for their financial institutions. However, although I ran lending programmes for banks overseas, I could not become involved in credit training for Irish managers, since this was an activity that Irish banks guarded closely.

Outside the IMI I gained some practical experience in financial services, particularly fund management. For almost a decade I acted as a non-executive director of a small, conservatively run, hedge fund, seeing the risk monitoring tools I had taught to undergraduates working in practice. I also had a long standing involvement over four decades with a religious organisation, which retained fund managers in London and Dublin, as well as running its own portfolios. But basically I remained an outsider in a rapidly evolving industry.

Disenchantment

My decision not to return to NIB proved to be fortuitous in the light of subsequent events. As I worked for IMI, NIB ran into troubled times. As will be discussed in Chapter 10, during 1998 RTÉ, the national television authority, armed with leaked internal bank reports, broadcast a damaging story about an insurance product. Deposits were invested in an Isle of Man policy, but then returned to the branch in an anonymous numbered deposit account, available to the customer. For a substantial commission customers were being assisted to evade tax. It further emerged that some bank branches had been systematically overcharging customers on their current accounts.

The Government appointed high court inspectors to examine the allegations. As a former head of audit, I was approached by them to testify. I readily assented, adding that I would dispense with legal advisors. I was never called and could not have been of much assistance, since the troubles arose after my time in the bank. The inspectors eventually reported[1] and confirmed the allegations and several senior managers were duly disqualified from acting as company directors. In 2004 the bank was sold to the Danish Danske Bank, which after a few years closed down the branch network before withdrawing from personal and small business banking.

In 2004, after fourteen years with IMI, I ceased working there on a full-time basis, but continued on as required. I became more involved in developing my consulting practice and my writing hobby. Cost reduction was an important topic for Irish managers and in due course I co-authored a book with a colleague on the subject, which was published by Chartered Accountants Ireland and later in New Zealand. Subsequently, I wrote regularly on this subject for *Accountancy Ireland*, while also addressing topical issues in banking, as the crisis unfolded.

When the banking crisis broke in 2008, I wrote in a Sunday newspaper that the banks had only themselves to blame for the problem, since they had abandoned their lending principles in the property bubble.[2] Banks in general had adopted a herd mentality in search of short-term profit. Irish banks were overly exposed to the property sector and it was difficult to know if they had made adequate provisions for loan impairment. They needed to look at their credit and risk management controls. In a further article I suggested that they should look also at their rewards system to see how much it had contributed to the problem. The bank guarantee, which had just been announced, was very onerous in view of its scale, equating to about €100,000 per head of the population and was likely to receive considerable claims.[3]

The views I expressed were far from the prevailing wisdom expressed by the banks. Shortly after I had blamed the banks on radio, in another radio interview Sean Fitzpatrick, the Chairman and former CEO of Anglo Irish Bank, attributed the problems to difficulties in the wholesale money markets, denied recklessness and refused to apologise. Not long afterwards the Irish banks collapsed under the weight of bad loans and fell in varying degrees under state control.

I was by now totally disillusioned by the practices of banking in the late twentieth and early twenty-first centuries. Equally, I could not stomach the defences put forward by the banks for the mess, since I considered the real reason to be terrible risk management. Banking, both in NIB and elsewhere, simply bore no resemblance to the industry I had left back in 1990. I was determined to discover how and why the change had happened.

My disillusionment turned to horror and disgust, in common with most Irish citizens, when in June 2013 I heard tapes of telephone conversations between senior managers in Anglo Irish Bank shortly before their deposits were guaranteed. The story quickly spread and the country suffered serious damage to its reputation abroad. It seemed that they were seeking a loan from the Central Bank of €7 billion, knowing that it could not be repaid, but should help them to stay in their jobs.

When the property bubble burst in 2007/8, I was astonished at the extent of the bad lending in an industry that I had believed I understood well. Somehow the nature of banking, its underlying culture and the values espoused must have fundamentally changed since my departure almost twenty-five years earlier. Perhaps from the outside I could see them more objectively and clearly than bankers closely involved throughout the period in the constantly changing competitive environment. Having a background in both the practice and theory of banking and finance I approach banking differently from most other commentators, who have never viewed the industry from the inside. My perspective is unusual, if not unique.

I have no axe to grind, but merely wish to uncover the deep roots of the problem and explain them in a manner intelligible to the general reader. Drawing on my experience and assisted by the available literature, this entails not only searching widely in the fields of banking, economics and accountancy, but also exploring cultural and ethical issues. My approach is to delve into the various challenges, both global and domestic, facing banking and to assess the response of the management in Ireland to them. More than six years after the Irish State was obliged to guarantee the deposits of the Irish banks many questions still remain unanswered. If the root causes are revealed, it should then be possible to plot a course to better and safer banking for the future by producing a manifesto for changes to the current system.

The Explanations to Date

Bankers were quick to provide an explanation for the crisis, refusing to admit their own mistakes, still less to apologise. It was the problem of illiquidity, caused by the freezing up of the wholesale money markets in the aftermath of the US subprime lending crisis, when interbank lending came to a halt, because of the uncertainty as to where the subprime mortgages had ended up. The Government bank guarantee was accepted as the way forward. After a time they urged the public to move on, advice which did not seem to apply to themselves, as all too often they clung on to their jobs. There was no question as to the solvency of the banks or reckless lending. The country required an explanation from an independent source.

The first report was commissioned by the Government in 2010. It requested the new and widely respected Governor of the Central Bank, Patrick Honohan, a former professor of economics at TCD, to investigate. The brief was to examine the performance of the Central Bank and Financial Regulator up to the granting of the bank guarantee. It was designed as part of a wider investigation into the systemic failure of the banking system and the necessity for the bailout.

The report was published promptly in May 2010.[4] It set out the macroeconomic background, the activities of the Regulator and details of the crisis management. Its focus was on answering why the dangers of the emerging financial imbalances which led to the crisis and how well the crisis was managed. The conclusions were damning. It blamed the Government's budgetary policy and undue dependence on the construction industry for unsustainable tax revenue. Heavy losses were inevitable when the property market turned, but warnings had been ignored. The banks relied too heavily on international finance, when these markets were awash with money.

It stated that while international pressures contributed to the timing, intensity and depth of the banking crisis, the underlying causes were domestic and classic, centred on the property bubble. It pinned the major blame on the directors and senior management of the banks for their comprehensive failure to maintain safe and sound banking practices, with lesser blame attaching to mortgage brokers, auditors and accountants. In particular, it pointed out that Anglo Irish Bank and Irish Nationwide Building Society were well on the road to insolvency at the time of the failure of Lehman Brothers in 2008. Lending standards had been allowed to decline to protect or expand market share, documentation was incomplete and unnecessary risks had been incurred. The report revealed that in December 2007 inspectors for the Financial Regulator, examining the five largest exposures of each of the five participating in NAMA, had found some serious deficiencies in credit assessment and an attitude of complacency at the banks.

The main focus of the report was, however, to be on the Central Bank and the Financial Regulator. The criticisms homed in on weaknesses in bank supervision, the approach to stabilisation policy and the failure to take effective remedial action. Senior bank staff failed to recognise weaknesses in the banks and also failed to gather the proper information. They failed to quantify risk, as well as being insufficiently intrusive and assertive in challenging the banks. The financial stability reports misinterpreted the Irish situation and too much confidence was placed on the reliability of annual stress tests. There were also communications problems. Public servants were too diffident and deferential, when intervention was required. During the crisis efforts should have been made to bolster bank capital. The report accepted that an extensive bank guarantee was needed, though the solvency problems were not appreciated. However, there could have been more international consultation, and leaving the senior management of two banks in place, when it should have been clear that the two institutions were well on the way to insolvency, was not questioned.

A further report was commissioned by the Government at the same time from two outsiders, Klaus Regling and Max Watson, both non-Irish senior public servants with experience of international financial markets.[5] It confirmed that, while the crisis bore the imprint of global influences, it was in crucial ways home-made. There had been an extended period of high liquidity and 'low risk premia', which meant that banks had mispriced risks. The boom needed to be seen in the context of strong expansion as Ireland caught up and surpassed average European living standards. Official policies and banking practices added fuel to the fire. Fiscal policy heightened the vulnerability of the economy. Bank supervisors were not called in to address complex technical problems and warnings from the Central Bank on macrofinancial risks were notable by their absence. Bank governance and risk management were deemed to be weak. Credit risk controls failed to prevent a severe concentration in property lending. The banks were overly dependent on the wholesale market for funding. Internal procedures were overridden. The report concluded that there should be a wide probe into the scope of bank governance, whether of a general kind or very specific lapses and whether auditors were sufficiently vigilant in some episodes. These matters required further investigation.

A third report in 2011, commissioned by the Government, was prepared by Peter Nyberg, a senior Finnish public servant with responsibility for financial markets, and published in March 2011.[6] It set out to evaluate how various institutions had contributed to the Irish financial crisis. It pointed to increased foreign competition in the Irish market. The risks were not understood and risk evaluation procedures were not implemented in Anglo Irish Bank and INBS, while governance at the banks fell short of best practice. There was a consensus to expect a 'soft landing' for the property boom. The auditors were described as silent observers, while the public authorities were termed the enablers. In particular it found behaviour of herding between institutions and 'groupthink' within them, so that policy was not adequately challenged. This last report produced little that was new for me or many others. I had identified groupthink as a factor almost two years earlier, when I pleaded for board changes in an article published in *Accountancy Ireland*.[7]

Critical histories have also been produced, which record the events leading up to the guaranteeing of deposits, especially an account by Shane Ross, both a journalist and a politician.[8] Other journalists recounted the salient historical facts relating to the failure of Anglo Irish Bank and Irish Nationwide Building Society. One further explanation came more recently from two other experts.[9] Antoin Murphy, an economist who had foreseen the property collapse, throws further light on the nature of the bubble, while Donal Donovan, a former IMF official, analyses the impact of tax reliefs and other Government policies.

Have all these reports and accounts of events provided a complete picture of what went wrong and what reforms of the system are necessary?

The Missing Explanation

Undoubtedly, there have been large volumes written now of the 'how' and a certain amount on the 'who'; there is still a piece missing, the 'why'. Clearly a full understanding of the death to the Celtic Tiger is essential to understand the problem. But the critical question for me is why banks behaved in the way they did. While some former bankers in London and New York have acted as whistleblowers, writing of their experiences and disclosing disturbingly bad practices, no Dublin banker has produced comparable revelations about Irish banking excesses in the Celtic Tiger era. Yet without a full understanding and analysis of the root causes of the debacle, how can anyone be sure that the system has been properly reformed and that the mistakes will not be repeated?

The current situation can be compared to the situation of a sports team which has suffered a dismal defeat. We have plenty of general information about the referee (the Financial Regulator) and the grounds staff who prepared the pitch (the politicians). There are still questions to be asked of the linesmen (the auditors and rating agencies), who could have assisted the referee. But what we totally lack is information on the team of bankers and why they performed so poorly. Yet we are told that the team members bear the primary responsibility for the fiasco.

There are glaring omissions in the official explanations to date, as a result of the restrictive terms of reference. The Honohan report stresses that the management and operations of the banks were not investigated in detail. Responsibility has not been pinned on any individuals and there is very little explanation as to how Irish banks fell from being amongst the strongest in the world to becoming the weakest.

There remains some possibility that further understanding may be gained from a pending official Oireachtas inquiry, conducted by politicians. It will focus on the origins of the crash over the preceding twenty years, issues leading to the build-up and night of the granting of the State guarantee in 2008, together with the role and influence of international institutions. It is expected to report late in 2015. However, there are doubts about its ability to compel witnesses to attend. Also, such inquiries have limitations in what they can discover, being restricted in making adverse findings about third parties. In 2014 it was finally launched in a welter of controversy about its terms of reference, independence and overall credibility.

My focus will be primarily on the main players, namely the bankers, rather than politicians and regulatory authorities, seeking to discover how and why they contributed to the debacle. I cannot point the finger at individual bankers, since I do not have access to the relevant information and I, like others, am restricted by the libel laws. In any event I would not wish to do anything which might prejudice the trials of certain bank directors, if and when they eventually take place. I will therefore concentrate on the team as a whole, rather than the individual players. What I can do is to provide the perspective of someone who was part of the system in the 1970s and 1980s long before the heady days of the Celtic Tiger. I will endeavour to explain how the banking system degenerated to its present low level from the viewpoint of a former insider, familiar with the workings of the system.

To set about this task in Part 1 I will look at recent developments in banking, not only in Ireland, but further afield. In Part 2 I will explain how banks produce profits, what causes them to fail, how lending was poorly performed, how cycles such as the Celtic Tiger develop and how risk spreads. Part 3 deals with soft issues around culture and values, competition, the conflicts for management, the crucial role of rewards and the ambivalent role of the State. Finally, in Part 4, I address ethical issues before pointing where banking in general, and Ireland in particular, needs to go, together with my explanation of the debacle and proposals to rectify the current dire situation. Readers may choose to skip over material with which they are familiar or find too technical. Some may proceed straight to Chapters 17 and 18, where I set out what I believe to be the real causes of the problem and my recommendations for reform.

Demands are still regularly made for a full explanation of how the financial crisis came about. The explanations to date seem to me to be woefully incomplete, since their focus has been almost exclusively on the property bubble, the economic difficulties which resulted and the failure of the authorities to act. Such approaches can only throw a limited light on the catastrophe, since they largely ignore important changes in banking internationally, which are central to understanding the problem of why bankers could behave in such an anti-social manner in managing risks. Unless these subtle and sometimes abstruse issues, which originated in investment banking over twenty years ago, are brought to surface and addressed, any solutions are likely to be flawed.

If this book can add anything substantial to what is known about the debacle and what reforms are necessary, I will have achieved my objective. But, even if I fall short of this ambitious goal, at least it will have cost the already heavily burdened taxpayer nothing. The deep rooted changes that I advocate may well prove unpopular with the banks, and many are likely to be strongly resisted by strong vested interests. But the problems need to be debated and resolved if a sustainable economic recovery is to be achieved. Confidence needs to be restored, based on the foundations of a sound banking system.

PART ONE:

Background to a Crisis

CHAPTER 1

The Irish Financial Crisis Revisited

The World Economic Forum is a global organisation which collects economic data. Each year it publishes its global competitiveness survey, a league table which scores various attributes of different countries.[1] In 2008/9 Ireland maintained its overall ranking at 22 out of 134 the countries covered. It slipped a few places in subsequent years to 29 before recovering to 25 in 2014/15. There is nothing remarkable in that, but what is truly remarkable is one of the underlying metrics, namely the soundness of the Irish banks.

In 2008/9 Ireland's banking strength at ninth place was up with the best in the world. The following two years it had dropped to 121 and 139, by which time it was rated last in the world, a ranking which it retained for the next two years, while new countries were added to the survey. In 2013/14 the country rose to third from the bottom, having overtaken Greece and Slovenia, before passing Burundi, Libya and Cyprus the following year to reach sixth place from bottom in the league table of 144 countries. This, by any estimation, is a rapid and precipitous fall from grace in an industry noted for staid and gradual transitions. 'Debacle' does not sound too strong a term to describe such a change.

The Origin of the Debacle

The US subprime lending crisis broke on a surprised world in August 2007. Panic rapidly spread throughout the world's financial system through a process of contagion. Since the loans had been

16

securitised, which meant that they could be sold on to other parties, nobody knew where they might have ended up and nobody knew whether to believe the denials by banks regarding their exposure. The result was that banks stopped lending to each other and the wholesale money markets in effect ground to a shuddering halt.

In fact, little or none of the bad US subprime loans had ended up in Ireland. This is not necessarily due to the skills of Irish bankers, but may be due to the small size of the Irish investment market, which had not attracted the attention of aggressive loan salesmen. Nevertheless, Irish banks experienced difficulty in attracting the funding necessary to continue business in an orderly manner.

The Emergent Crisis

In September 2008, a year after the subprime crisis broke, Anglo Irish Bank, a bank considered by the Government to be of systemic importance, teetered on the verge of failure. The State responded by taking the unprecedented step of guaranteeing all the deposits and senior capital of the six leading Irish financial institutions, amounting to €440 billion, or approximately €100,000 per head of the population. Its proud boast that this was a cheap solution to the problem proved hollow as ever increasing demands for capital were made. Eventually, the Government set up a 'bad bank', the National Asset Management Agency or NAMA, which took over the large property loans of the five Irish banks financing the developers at 'economic value', an amount generally in excess of their market value, thus providing much needed capital for the banks.

As NAMA took on these massive loans, becoming in effect the world's largest property company, the true horror of the fall in lending standards started to emerge. Five out of the six banks transferred substantial loans to NAMA, while the sixth one, Irish Life and Permanent, had provided no finance for developers but had serious funding problems of its own. The average discount on the face value of the €15 billion loans amounted to almost 50 per cent, reflecting how poor the lending had been. In due course NAMA paid €32 billion for loans of €74 billion.

NAMA's chairman accused the banks of 'reckless abandonment of the basic principles of credit risk and prudent lending', describing a 'litany of horrors' in documentation, which he was unsure whether to attribute to fraud or incompetence. Later he stated he was 'extremely disappointed and disturbed' at the behaviour of the five institutions. They were not using the full range of legal options open to them to secure income in respect of their troubled loans.[2]

The NAMA CEO pointed out that some borrowers had free cashflow over which the banks had not established a charge. Some had not been pressed to pay interest. Surplus funds were returned to developers on sale of assets, despite unfulfilled commitments elsewhere. He stated that major developers operated on a divide-and-rule basis, where they did not disclose the full level of cashflow to each of the lenders.

Nor was the EU sympathetic to Ireland's difficulties. Jose Manuel Barroso, President of the European Commission, stated bluntly in the European Parliament that the problems of Ireland were created by the irresponsible financial behaviour of some Irish institutions and by the lack of supervision in the Irish market.[3] The institutions directly providing the finance were not purely indigenous, but also included the overseas subsidiaries of UK and continental European banks. Perhaps some blame too must ultimately be laid at the door of those overseas banks and institutional investors which provided the funding to the Irish banks, without which the banks could not have expanded their balance sheets so rapidly.

The Cost and the Price to be Paid

With the recapitalisations in the spring of 2011 the enormous cost of the banking bailout became clearer. The capital required to recapitalise the six Irish banks amounted to €64 billion, which was roughly double the estimate of a year earlier and equates to more than two years of tax revenues. Including the overseas banks, the total losses exceeded €100 billion. It was, in the words of the Governor of the Central Bank of Ireland, one of the most expensive crises in history.

All of the six Irish banks were heavily dependent on life support from the European and Irish central banks, which provided funding of €140 billion. Anglo Irish Bank and Irish Nationwide Building Society were nationalised and placed in windup, while AIB became virtually wholly owned by the Government. EBS, or the Educational Building Society, was absorbed by AIB. Bank of Ireland, which had received €3.5 billion assistance, alone retained a degree of independence. The one bank which had eschewed financing developers and so avoided NAMA, Irish Life and Permanent, had lent aggressively in the housing market, was heavily dependent on interbank financing and mismatched its funding in offering 'tracker' loans. Bank of Ireland and AIB were proclaimed to be 'pillar banks' by the Government and Ireland's future seemed to largely rest in their hands.

Nor were many of the overseas banks in much better health. Bank of Scotland (Ireland), part of HBOS, offloaded the management of its loan book, as a prelude to withdrawal from the market. The branch network of NIB was closed down by its parent, Danske Bank, while the future of Ulster Bank, a subsidiary of the UK-based RBS, remained unclear, as its parent company sought to solve its own problems. The Dutch Rabobank retreated from the market, announcing that it was to hand back its banking licence in 2013, thereby closing down its branch network. Only the Belgian KBC Bank sought to expand its business.

From the moment the Irish Government provided the massive guarantee to the banks in September 2008, it was only a matter of time before the burden was passed on to the people. Slightly more than two years later, the Government was obliged to seek international assistance. The Troika, consisting of the European Union, the European Central Bank and the International Monetary Fund, offered a bailout package. But the terms were onerous, economic sovereignty had been lost and an era of severe austerity commenced.

Who Bears the Burden?

As Ireland slid into the Great Recession, the economic and social costs have been immense, but have been borne somewhat unevenly. While some senior bankers and public servants have retired on substantial pensions, many still retain their positions. Politicians too continue to enjoy generous tax-free expenses and large pensions after relatively short service. Some property developers have sought to have themselves declared bankrupt in more favourable jurisdictions than Ireland, while several seem to have successfully divested themselves of large assets to their family members or trusts, thus softening the blow of insolvency, which in any event no longer carries its traditional stigma.

Many members of the general public have been less fortunate. Unemployment has increased, along with mortgage arrears. Involuntary emigration, not seen for decades, has returned, as large numbers of highly qualified graduates and skilled tradespeople seek a new life abroad. Government cutbacks have severely impacted many people most in need and complaints about the quality of the health services in particular are widespread. Many pensioners find that their capital has been decimated and they can no longer rely on bank shares for an income, while the Government has levied pension funds in an attempt to raise much needed revenue and has reduced some pensioners' benefits. Efforts to charge greater costs on the private healthcare and education sectors have caused many to abandon the private sector and place an even greater burden on the overstretched public services. Unfortunately, everywhere the public, especially the middle class, are experiencing reduced income, higher taxation and new charges on property.

How has Irish business suffered? Many multinationals are able to avail of the 12.5 per cent tax rate in Ireland, but in practice pay much less with the assistance of legal, if in some quarters unpopular, international tax planning. They may even benefit from greater competitiveness from lower rates of pay, while lobbying for special tax concessions for their management. Some senior business figures may also escape extra personal taxes, since they have long since taken up residence abroad. But what of the unfortunate small and medium sized businesses, suffering from a serious fall in demand for their products or services, coupled with a severe shortage of credit?

Different industries have been affected in different ways. Retailers have suffered badly in the face of reduced consumer spending and high rents. Businesses associated with the construction sector have been hit hard. On the other hand, some sectors have prospered, such as some accountants and lawyers, particularly those with insolvency work or working for NAMA, while the legal system has incurred the wrath of the IMF for its high costs.

The SME sector has suffered from a lack of credit facilities. In its competitiveness survey, the World Economic Forum evaluates countries' ease of access to loans. In 2008/9 Ireland was ranked 19th in this category, comfortably in the top 20 per cent of the world. By 2014/5, after a modest recovery, the country still languished in 117th place, amongst the lowest 20 per cent in the world. The 27 countries beneath Ireland consisted of 12 from Africa (Angola, Ethiopia, Chad, Mauretania, Mozambique, Egypt, Sierra Leone, Burundi, Zimbabwe, Nigeria, Burkina Faso, and Libya), four from the Eurozone (Spain, Greece, Italy and Slovenia, three from the rest of Europe (Serbia, Hungary and Albania), three in Asia (Korea, Mongolia and Myanmar), three in the Americas (Costa Rica, Jamaica and Argentina) and two in the Middle East (Yemen and Iran). Many of these countries can point to war, political unrest, economic turmoil, currency instability or prolonged dire poverty as an excuse for their difficulties. Ireland's decline must be seen simply as a result of the weakness of its banks. Unfortunately, economic recovery will be held back until a reasonable flow of credit is available and consumer confidence restored with a properly functioning banking system.

CHAPTER 2

Weaning the Celtic Tiger –
The Evolution of Irish Banking

To understand fully the Irish banking debacle, it is helpful to understand how banking developed over the years. The evolution of Irish banking provides the local backdrop to the industry and context for the crisis, when it broke in 2007/8 before spreading globally.

Early Days

When Ireland gained its independence from Britain in 1922, it remained heavily dependent on Britain for its trade, both as a source of its imports and as a market for its goods, which were predominantly agricultural produce. It set up its own currency in 1927, but maintained a 1:1 relationship with sterling, in which it remained very much the poor relation. There ensued an era of protectionism and economic war with Britain, followed by an uneasy time as Ireland chose to remain neutral during the Second World War. Banking was conducted in a conservative manner by a number of small indigenous banks and two British banks – Ulster Bank owned by National Westminster and Northern Bank owned by Midland. The State tried to encourage new businesses and to this end set up two banks, the Agricultural Credit Corporation (ACC) to service farmers and the Industrial Credit Corporation (ICC) to service small and medium sized businesses.

The 1950s was a decade of high unemployment and large-scale emigration. The Government reacted by introducing two programmes of economic expansion, the first focussed on agriculture and the second on developing industry. The the state-owned Industrial Development Authority concentrated on attracting overseas investment, while domestic efforts were aimed at modernising industry to face wider competition. To assist the growth of exports the Government in due course introduced export sales relief, whereby profits from exporting were free of tax. The banks took advantage of this incentive to provide preference share financing, whereby exporters could pay out tax free dividends to the banks, which held these shares.

The 1960s saw the consolidation of Irish banking. Bank of Ireland acquired the National Bank and Hibernian Bank, while shortly afterwards Allied Irish Banks was formed by the merger of Munster & Leinster Bank, the Provincial Bank and Royal Bank. Bank of Ireland and AIB were to dominate Irish banking for the next forty years. In due course they expanded their geographic coverage to Northern Ireland and the UK, while also opening offices in the US. At this time too North American banks entered the Irish market as part of their global expansion. Citibank, Bank of America and First National Bank of Chicago were to provide healthy competition for corporate business in the years to follow with their emphasis on cashflow analysis, in contrast to the more security-based lending traditionally offered by Irish banks.

The State in 1972 also set up an agency to provide reconstruction finance, Fóir Teoranta. Its aim was to provide finance to businesses which were viable but unable to raise finance through normal commercial channels. Not generally regarded as a success, Fóir Teo was subject to political pressures in the guise of maintaining employment and often merely prolonged business failures at considerable cost before being wound up in 1991.

Expansion of Activities

The growth of banking received periodic setbacks. From the mid-1960s to the mid-1970s Ireland suffered three major bank strikes, severely disrupting the services of the retail banks. The banks were highly unionised through the Irish Bank Officials Association, which made big strides to improve the lot of its members. The chaos was worsened by the problems of a large business, Hibernian Shipping, which failed and whose employees had cashed their wage cheques with local traders, such as pubs and garages, thereby spreading its difficulties more widely. However, by the time of the third strike the union's hold was weakening and bank managers were able to provide a service with the aid of technology. Though it left a legacy of bitterness, there were no further strikes.

Irish banks had developed into consumer finance through hire purchase subsidiaries, but the 1970s saw the development of investment banking. These banks sought to attract graduates and professional people, particularly accountants, by offering competitive salaries. The retail banks had largely discouraged such recruitment, since the salary structures negotiated with the IBOA were based on length of service. The new banks provided corporate finance advisory work, portfolio management and treasury services. Their lending was based on wholesale deposits and funds raised on the developing interbank market, which provided funds based on DIBOR, the Dublin Interbank Offer Rate.

In addition to providing tax relief for exports, the Government introduced a 10 per cent rate of tax for manufacturing industry to attract foreign direct investment into Ireland. Other incentives included high levels of grants for capital investment and generous training grants. Banks then developed into leasing, since the law permitted the writing off of capital expenditure against tax in the year in which the expenditure occurred. Facilities could sometimes offer negative interest rates on leasing, since the bank could obtain the 60 per cent grant and 40 per cent tax relief in a year and so had little reliance on the lease payments. The leasing industry boomed, with facilities to finance small items of equipment, as well as major capital expenditure, such as aircraft. The reduction in corporation tax rates eventually reduced the attraction of leasing with the result that some independent leasing companies had insufficient profits to sustain their growth and eventually failed. Banks also developed other specialised forms of lending to provide subsidised rates of interest to manufactures in exchange for tax savings to the banks.

Traditional building societies, many mutually owned by their members, offered mortgages for house buyers on a conservative basis, usually up to 65 or 75 per cent of the cost up to three times income. The process was slow and it was usually necessary to take a lengthy bridging loan from a bank before the society had completed its security. In due course Bank of Ireland acquired the stock exchange listed Irish Civil Service Building Society, while Irish Permanent merged with Irish Life. All of the other societies eventually diversified away from their traditional business into more risky property finance.

The economy in the 1970s suffered several external shocks, in particular two oil crises which led to high inflation and high interest rates, severely curtailing economic growth. The Central Bank responded by imposing credit restrictions on individual lending institutions, thereby seriously curbing competition. Credit guidelines were removed In 1984 and thereafter banks were able to compete with each other freely.

European Influences

The year 1972 saw Ireland, along with the United Kingdom, enter the European Union. Membership had been overwhelmingly endorsed by a referendum and the Irish became enthusiastic EU citizens, partly because it lessened the country's dependence on Britain. It was also helped by the availability of grants and subsidised loans for agriculture, regional development and social purposes, which could be claimed by a small country with GNP per head well below the EU average. Initial fears that peripheral countries would lose out to the large central powers were confounded by events, greatly assisted by changes in technology and the development of the internet.

An inevitable result of EU membership was an increasing interest of European banks in Ireland. IIB, later to become KBC, a Belgian bank, was an early entrant, benefiting from a favourable tax treaty, which enabled it to use parent company profits to support tax-based lending in Ireland. BNP from France made a brief appearance and an investment bank, Paribas, teamed up with the Smurfit Group, a leading Irish industrialist, while ABN from Holland also entered the market. However, they were all at a disadvantage in the market for deposits with the resident banks which had large branch networks. Eventually, the Dutch Rabobank acquired the ACC and HBOS, Halifax Bank of Scotland, took over ICC, thus taking the Irish State totally out of banking until 2008, when it acted to rescue the financial system.

Still, in the 1970s Ireland was of limited appeal to overseas bankers. It was a small country with its currency linked to sterling, which had displayed a chequered record of economic growth. But in 1979 it joined the new Economic Monetary System, which was intended to produce a zone of monetary stability for the EU, while the UK remained outside. The EMS evolved into the ERM, the Exchange Rate Mechanism, which led to an overvalued currency for Ireland and it was forced to devalue in 1986. Ireland was still regarded by many as the 'sick man of Europe', with GDP per head only 69 per cent of the European average in 1987 and too small a market to be worthy of a major investment.

Irish fortunes were to change dramatically during the 1990s, and by 2003 GDP per head had risen to 136 per cent of the EU average.[1] In 1994 an American banker noticed the rapid growth and compared it with the fast growing Asian economies, coining the term 'Celtic Tiger', a name which quickly caught the public imagination, providing a welcome boost to national confidence. But not all visitors were impressed. Around this time I ran a course in Dublin for a group of Finnish bankers and when they heard an economist outline the problems with restrictive practices and poor labour relations, they expressed their disappointment. They had hoped for something very different from what they were experiencing at home. In due course Finland was to undergo a traumatic recession following the break up of the USSR, but with Nordic fortitude was to emerge again as a strong economy.

One particular development which did gain international attention was the creation of the International Financial Services Centre, established in 1987 in Dublin's Dockland. Kept totally separate from domestic banking, other than treasury operations moved there, it was designed to attract genuine financial businesses, rather than brass plate names commonly found in offshore tax havens. Its main attractions to overseas banks were generous tax allowances, a low 12.5 per cent rate of corporation tax and light touch regulation. It developed a large international aircraft leasing business, a substantial cross-border insurance industry and a major investment management back office centre, providing approximately 25,000 jobs, together with substantial work for professional firms in law and accountancy.

The Celtic Tiger attracted global publicity, drawing much favourable comment, as it left its lair to prowl on the world arena. Many small countries watched Ireland and sought the secrets to its rapid economic growth. It had embraced globalisation and had become a major beneficiary of the trend. At the height of the Celtic Tiger era it was possible to set up the country, with certain caveats, for others to imitate.[2]

The advent of the euro, the development of the famous beast and its ultimate demise will be addressed in Chapter 6. In the meantime it is worth relating problems which arose in Irish banking over the years.

Irish Banking Troubles

The troubles in Irish banking over the years have been well recorded in a critical manner.[3]

Ireland had its own small fringe bank, called Irish Trust Bank, which collapsed in 1976. Set up five years earlier by Ken Bates, an English businessman who is best known today for his past association with Chelsea Football Club, it had always been considered controversial. In 1973 the Central Bank, concerned with elements of Bates' past business career, attempted to prevent the bank advertising for deposits, which effectively would have closed it down. But Bates successfully resisted this challenge in the High Court and trading continued until its failure in a property market crash. Depositors had been attracted by high rates of interest and there were around 1,200, mainly small savers, owed £500,000 at the end. In an election pledge Fianna Fáil, the country's largest political party, undertook to bail out the depositors, despite opposition from the Central Bank, so ultimately the taxpayer picked up the bill.

In 1982, a few years after the failure of Irish Trust Bank, as previously mentioned, another small Irish bank, Merchant Banking, collapsed. This bank was closely associated with the Gallagher Group, a property development business and one of Ireland's largest private companies. Patrick Gallagher, a flamboyant young property trader and developer with strong political connections, had inherited the business at an early age and expanded it rapidly with large land purchases. Its downfall took with it the in-house bank, whose funds were used to finance property speculation. Approximately 600 depositors, many of whom were attracted by high interest rates, lost out since there was to be no State bailout. Gallagher ended up serving a prison sentence in Northern Ireland but, to the surprise of the liquidator who had detailed numerous breaches of company law, he was never prosecuted in the Republic.

A year after the failure of Merchant Banking, a much larger disaster struck, when the Private Motorists Protection Society collapsed in 1983. PMPS was part of the PMPA, the Private Motorists Protection Association, which insured over half of Irish motorists. The major asset of PMPS was a loan to PMPA, but it had also lent money to small investors, directors and employees to buy shares in the group. The group had been founded and run by Joe Moore, a former civil servant with strong nationalistic views and political connections, who wanted to compete with British insurers. He was considered to be a maverick in financial circles and managed the business in an autocratic manner.

I recall causing ripples when some time before the crisis broke I compared it with Vehicle and General, a UK cut price insurer which went out of business in 1971. PMPA sold low cost insurance, was slow to settle its claims, grew too fast and made unwise investments, drawing trenchant criticism from the economic advisor to the Government, Patrick Honohan, the current Central Bank Governor. Since the deficit of £223 million equated to about 2 per cent of Irish GNP, the business was too big to fail, so emergency legislation was enacted to permit the appointment of an administrator. Joe Moore litigated unsuccessfully, protesting that the insurance company was solvent before it entered administration. The problem was resolved by the introduction of a 2 per cent levy on all non-life insurance premiums. About 5,600 small depositors were owed £9.4 million, but were uninsured, eventually recovering their funds after 22 years.

An even greater insurance fiasco was to strike in 1985, two years after the PMPA collapse, when the Insurance Corporation of Ireland (ICI), the second largest non-life insurer in the country, ran into trouble. AIB, Ireland's largest bank, had acquired a minority interest in the company as part of its diversification in financial services, before hastily acquiring the remaining shares in 1983, when a large shareholding became available. Most of its business was conducted in London, where incredibly risky underwriting took place.

In March 1984 it was revealed that ICI had an enormous deficit and AIB was ceasing to fund it. Only four months earlier we had been informed publicly that all was well in the business. Now we discovered that ICI was threatening to collapse not only AIB, but also the entire Irish banking system. The Government felt obliged to intervene to take over the open-ended and unknown liabilities. As part of the funding plan the following year all the other banks were obliged to provide £7 million per annum. It seemed unjust to be forced to subsidise the major competitor in the industry. The Government could have forced AIB to sell off valuable major assets, such as First Maryland Bank, or at least taken options to acquire shares at a favourable price as the consideration for its rescue, but failed to do so. To cap it all the bank announced an unchanged final dividend. A protracted law suit took place with the auditors, which was settled after eight years, but no member of senior bank management resigned. The Taoiseach, Garret FitzGerald, later criticised the bank for allowing its duty to shareholders to take precedence over public responsibility.[4]

AIB was not the only Irish bank to experience problems with overseas investments. Its main rival, Bank of Ireland, relented to public pressure to emulate AIB and expand into the US. In 1988 it acquired First New Hampshire Bank after limited due diligence at near to the top of a local property boom. Unlike AIB, the Bank of Ireland CEO was obliged to resign. Over the next eight years it was forced to pump in hundreds of millions of dollars, before the bank was merged in 1996 and the remaining interest sold in 1998, along with another New England bank. The bank also experienced difficulties in the mid-1980s with property lending in the UK, leading to significant losses.

AIB was to become involved in many other publicised scandals over the years. One did endanger the bank's future, when it discovered its own rogue trader in Allfirst, its US subsidiary, formerly named First Maryland Bank. Like Nick Leeson in Barings Bank, John Rusnak used options to hide his vast foreign exchange trading losses, which had accumulated over four years. He generated false confirmations of transactions on his personal computer in a file openly named 'Fake Docs'. The bank was meant to operate a small proprietary trading book, where exposed positions were intended to take advantage of market anomalies, but limits were breached and the back office failed to obtain the relevant confirmations. For years neither senior management, nor the internal auditors, nor the external auditors unearthed the true situation. While the losses amounted to $691 million, AIB was strong enough to bear them, although it did reduce the group profit by 47 per cent in 1991. An independent inquiry found serious shortcomings in the operation of controls. Several of the local management lost their jobs and Rusnak ended up in jail.

The single biggest failure in Ireland came in 2008, leading to the recapitalisation of the German Depfa Bank. Originally a state-owned bank, it was privatised in 1990 and set up its headquarters in Dublin at the International Financial Services Centre, attracted by low rates of corporate tax and light regulation. It was acquired by Hypo Real Estate, a German mortgage giant, in 2007. The following year it ran into serious liquidity problems in the aftermath of the failure of Lehman Brothers in the US. It had underwritten large volumes of US municipal bonds, which it was obliged to buy back after downgrading by the rating agencies. Eventually, through a series of bailouts the German Government ended up with 100 per cent of Hypo Real Estate. The Irish Government and taxpayers fortunately escaped from paying out any compensation, since the bank had not become a separate subsidiary under the aegis of the Irish Regulator. Nevertheless, the country attracted much criticism over the years for its light touch regulation and had been unkindly dubbed by the *New York Times* in 2005 as 'The Wild West of Capitalism'.

The Warnings Overlooked

Where mistakes are made and disaster occurs, it might be expected that lessons would be learnt, so that any repetition could be avoided. Yet memories are short and often the mistakes are indeed repeated years later, while banks and regulators slip into a false sense of security. Prolonged economic growth can engender reckless banking, as amnesia or wishful thinking afflicts both the old and the young. Perhaps if the underlying reasons for reckless behaviour are better understood, systems can be put in place to mitigate, if not completely eliminate, such an appalling vista.

The collapse of small secondary banks indicated the dangers from loans imprudently granted to businesses associated with the directors. Merchant Banking demonstrated the perils of allowing a bank to devote its lending predominately to the property sector. Strong entrepreneurs with inadequate controls, such as Joe Moore, Ken Bates and Patrick Gallagher, drove the uncontrolled growth of PMPA, Irish Trust Bank and Merchant Banking. Depositors might learn that there is no guarantee that they can recover their funds when lending to unregulated entities. They were fortunate to be bailed out in the case of Irish Trust Bank and forfeited their deposits for many years in PMPS.

Larger banks can also experience problems, despite the existence of more sophisticated controls. AIB fell into jeopardy as a consequence of reckless underwriting by ICI, and to a lesser extent by the activities of a rogue trader, Nick Leeson. Bank of Ireland ran into trouble when it submitted to shareholder and media pressure to emulate the market leader, AIB, ending up in making a disastrous overseas acquisition. Following the strategy of the market leader may prove to be an unwise, if understandable, approach to competition, which was to haunt Ireland again in the recent property bubble.

Maybe the greatest warnings were in the field of regulation. The Central Bank learnt the importance of restricting credit growth, which they had successfully conducted in the aftermath of the first oil crisis. From the PMPA and ICI crises they learnt that financial institutions could become too large to fail. From the ICI rescue Governments discovered that they can suddenly be forced into making unpalatable and expensive decisions in the absence of the relevant information in a crisis, when a more considered solution might be found with greater time.

Irish banking should have learnt some lessons from its mistakes over the years, but essentially it was in strong, robust condition at the start of the twenty-first century, making its presence felt beyond Irish shores. Of course, Ireland need not restrict its learning to its own troubles. It can also learn from disasters overseas.

CHAPTER 3

Lessons from Overseas Banking Failures

While working in IMI and wishing to explain my work to my young son, I told him that I taught people about money. As something of an expert on the subject of pocket money, he quickly retorted: 'Don't be silly. There is only one thing you need to know about money and that is there is not enough of it.'

On reflection that is reasonable advice to banks experiencing financial problems. Banks, like other businesses, ultimately fail, not because they run out of profits, but because they run out of money. Banks take in deposits, which largely are recycled as loans. But if depositors fear that the bank has insufficient cash reserves, they may panic and demand repayment, thus causing a run on the bank, leading to its failure.

A fractional banking system, where cash reserves must be maintained as a minimum proportion of total liabilities, needs to be prudently managed to prevent such panics. Central banks set the rules for the safety levels of reserves to prevent any maverick bank from retaining insufficient funds to meet the demands of depositors. This creates a 'level playing field', so that banks can compete with each other on equal terms. The failure of any single bank should, whenever possible, be avoided, since it can lead to a loss of confidence by depositors, causing them to withdraw funds from other solvent institutions. Without confidence and depositors the entire system can fall apart. Aware of this dire possibility, banks have traditionally operated in a conservative and prudent manner.

An examination of failures around the globe might help to throw some light on the reasons for the collapse of the Irish banking system. In banking, just as in the animal world, it is the survival of the fittest and those institutions which fail to adapt may face extinction.

Northern Rock, Barings and Other British Failures

One day during September 2007, while driving in Dublin, I noticed a long queue, which led to the local branch of Northern Rock. I did not know it at the time, but I was witnessing a run on the bank, as depositors nervously sought to recover their money in a similar manner to what was happening in England.

Bank runs are something of a rarity in the UK. In fact, before the run on Northern Rock the last one happened in 1866 with the failure of Overend Gurney, allegedly the greatest discounting house in the world. It had invested heavily in long-term investments, such as railways, ships and shipyards, with the result that it only had £1,000,000 in liquid assets to cover liabilities of £4,000,000. Writing a year before the Northern Rock collapse, one commentator attributed the Overend Gurney fall to greed, ambition and overwhelming self-confidence, compounded by a refusal to admit mistakes or the imminence of disaster.[1] In 1878 the City of Glasgow Bank failed, leading to the bankruptcy of most of its shareholders, who were exposed to unlimited liability. In 1890 the Bank of England had to intervene to save Barings Bank after an unwise South American venture, but no significant British bank failed during the following century.

A year before the Overend Gurney failure in 1865 the Rock Building Society was founded, the forebear of Northern Rock. Its rise and fall are recounted by a career banker who joined them in 2005.[2] The building society grew mainly by acquisition before it demutualised and went public in 1997. It was admired by financial analysts, liked by its customers and respected both by its competitors and staff, who regarded it as an excellent employer. It had built up a substantial loan book with residential and commercial property investors in what was seen as the lower risk segments of the market. By 2006 it had become the fifth largest UK mortgage lender, writing 20 per cent of all new residential mortgages. Operationally it was considered efficient with below average arrears and a low cost to income ratio.

The bank was restricted in its deposit base, since it only had 76 branches in the UK. To finance its rapid growth it sought 25 per cent each from retail deposits and the wholesale market with the balance of 50 per cent coming from securitisation, a process whereby it sold on pools of mortgages to outside investors. This was a low retail deposit base in comparison with its peers, which typically funded over 40 per cent of their funding by way of deposits. It failed to buy insurance or arrange a standby facility in the event that liquidity dried up.

When the subprime crisis arose in the US investors globally shied away from securitised mortgages and the cost of funding on the LIBOR wholesale market increased relative to the Bank of England base rate, which adversely impacted the small margins which existed on the mortgage market. Yet the bank was still expanding rapidly and was unable to refinance its short-term borrowings. It became necessary to issue a profit warning. News leaked out that the bank was seeking emergency funding from the Bank of England, depositors panicked and the run commenced. The Government felt obliged to guarantee all the bank's depositors in September 2007.

A month later the directors were grilled by the House of Commons Select Committee. The bank was blamed for its funding policy, its reckless lending strategy and poor management. However, criticism was also levelled at the Bank of England for its monitoring and support systems. It had also been reluctant to adopt the more interventionist approach associated with the European Central Bank and the Federal Reserve in the US. It feared that this would constitute a 'moral hazard', which might encourage bank boards and management to take excessive risks in the expectation of being bailed out in the future.[3] Efforts to secure a takeover failed and the bank was nationalised a few months later.

The most spectacular other British banking failure had occurred in 1995, when Barings failed. Barings was a true establishment bank, where the Queen of England had banked and which had established its reputation with the flotation of Guinness' brewery over a century earlier. Its collapse was caused by foreign exchange dealings by a brash young trader, Nick Leeson, in its Singapore operations.

Incredibly, Leeson, the general manager, was placed in charge of both trading and the back office, a fundamental breach of internal control. By his own account he was encouraged to set up a local differences account, which he named 88888, a Chinese lucky number.[4] Initially, according to him, this was used to hide a modest trading error, which was quickly resolved, but went undetected. The bank was not allowed to indulge in proprietary trading on its own account, but rather was expected to arbitrage small differences between the Singapore and the Japanese Osaka stock markets, in addition to trading for clients.

Despite the prohibition the bank did, however, indulge in proprietary trading. In a culture of hard drinking and high living, traders continued to make periodic mistakes, which were less readily resolved. Mounting futures losses on the Tokyo stock market were hidden in account 88888 and growing deposits were needed to cover margin calls on the positions. Meanwhile, declared trading profits in Singapore started to contribute significantly to group profits, which for 1993 were declared to amount to approximately £100 million after payments of a similar sum in bonuses. This did not include the hidden loss of £23 million, which had gone undetected by the internal or external auditors.

Throughout Leeson claimed that he was urged to produce more trading profits required to pay the large bonuses of the senior management, including himself. In early 1995 the Singapore authorities advised Barings management of the existence of account 88888, pointing out that the bank had violated the exchange rules, which prohibits members from financing margins of their customers. London had transferred to Singapore massive amounts of funds to cover the bank's exposure, without satisfying themselves about the identity of the fictitious customer. The management and external auditors were persuaded by a document, forged by Leeson, as to available funds of over 7 billion yen or about £50 million.

Eventually, with increasing losses following the Kobe earthquake, Leeson could no longer continue the sham and fled. That weekend the Bank of England convened a meeting of all major banks to organise a rescue. The estimated losses started at £400 million, but later rose to £650 million. Short of time and more precise information, after a bid failed to materialise, rescue was deemed impossible and so Barings, the oldest independent British bank, founded in 1762, failed the week before the 1994 bonuses were due to be approved.

There were also disasters which were narrowly averted and other lesser failures. I can remember well the impact of the fringe banking crisis in my early banking career.[5] In 1973 the gross mismanagement of London and County Securities was exposed. Over the next two years many secondary or fringe banks got into trouble. Names included Keyser Ullman, United Dominions Trust, Slater Walker Securities and even the blue blooded William Brandt's. The major reasons were undisciplined lending into the property sector at high interest rates, inadequate funding and poor management. The Bank of England, keen to preserve the reputation of the City of London, brought together the leading banks and organised a lifeboat under a cloak of secrecy to avoid disorderly failures. The total amount of support over two years was estimated at £2 billion.

The Icelandic and Cypriot Comparisons

When the Icelandic banks collapsed in 2008, the wisecrack in the market was: 'What is the difference between the banks in Ireland and Iceland?' The answer: 'One letter and six months.' Was this a fair comparison?

The Icelandic saga contained its own peculiarities.[6] This small island, with a population of only 320,000 citizens, had traditionally survived on fish, wool and thermal power. Traditional conservative banking changed following the privatisation of the banks completed in 2002, when local oligarchs gained in varying degrees control over the three main banks. Quickly financial services became the leading industry, attracting bright graduates with large salaries. The total assets of the banking system rose from 96 per cent of GDP in 2000 to 800 per cent in 2006. The New Vikings expanded rapidly abroad, buying up foreign businesses, particularly British retailers, with large loans. The Government tried to stem inflation through high interest rates, but the banks responded by offering 90 per cent mortgages in low interest currencies, such as yen.

The collapse came in the wake of the US subprime crisis, when inter-bank funding dried up. Latterly they had obtained deposits by offering attractive rates in Britain, Holland and Germany. After the fall of Lehman Brothers in 2008 two of its main banks, Glitnir and Landsbanki, were nationalised. When it appeared that the Icelandic Government could not meet the deposit guarantee for small depositors, the British Government invoked anti-terrorist legislation to confiscate Icelandic bank assets in London, leading to the total collapse of the third main bank, Kaupthing, and the entire Icelandic banking system.

There are some parallels with Ireland. Both small islands grew oversized banking sectors, which expanded through some reckless lending. But, while Iceland's problems were international, Ireland's were essentially domestic. Also, Iceland was not part of the Eurozone and could devalue its currency. Its people, with their reputation for low levels of corruption, protested and demanded answers from their leaders.

Their approach to the crisis was very different from that adopted by Irish Governments. They allowed their banks to fail and thus penalised their bondholders, while devaluing their currency and introducing capital controls. Their unemployment remained low and some modest economic growth returned. However, they experienced a rapid rise in inflation and the cost of living, which caused considerable hardship for their citizens. Their difficulties were exacerbated by high interest rates, strict rules for taking currency abroad and onerous domestic mortgages, denominated in foreign currencies.

Another small island within the Eurozone has certain parallels with Ireland. Cyprus had developed a large banking centre as a safe haven for deposits in the Middle East. As political unrest increased in Lebanon, many depositors, particularly Russians, transferred their funds from Beirut to Cyprus. Given limited outlets for investment on the island, unwisely the local banks invested heavily in Greece, a country with which they had strong political links. As Greece experienced a financial crisis, it was inevitably transmitted to Cypriot banks through their large holdings of Greek bonds. A €2.5 billion loan from Russia in 2012 proved insufficient, when the rating agencies reduced Cypriot banks to junk status and the country was obliged to apply to the EU for a bailout.

After lengthy negotiations the Troika offered Cyprus a harsh €10 billion rescue package in 2013. Laiki Bank, also known as the Popular Bank, was closed down and its assets transferred to Bank of Cyprus. Because of the scale of the problem it was first proposed that all depositors would be levied. Eventually Bank of Cyprus was restructured and its uninsured depositors over €100,000 were subjected to a 40 per cent levy. The fifth Eurozone rescue package thus included a bail-in of large depositors.

The initial package imposed by the Troika as an alternative to disorderly bankruptcy was initially greeted with widespread protests. A year later the country started on the slow road to recovery, despite high unemployment and deflation, accompanying an economic slump. The Troika had accepted the principle of burning bondholders and large depositors, although they had refused such a course of action to Ireland just two years earlier. The new approach to a banking crisis was to penalise the shareholders first, then the creditors, including large depositors, and finally the public at large.

American Disasters

America had serious banking problems long before the emergence of subprime lending, addressed in Chapter 8.

A major debacle unfolded in the early 1980s in the Thrift or Savings and Loans Institutions, the US equivalent of building societies.[7] In an era of high interest rates the failure rate of these organisations increased dramatically. They sought to attract deposits by offering higher rates of interest, taking advantage of the federal guarantee available for small depositors. In the period of deregulation they were permitted to diversify away from traditional residential mortgages into wider real estate, and the often unsophisticated management became easy prey for smart Wall Street salesmen, offering various complex risky derivative instruments. In 1995 the cost of the industry bailout was estimated at $160 billion, of which the federal taxpayer was landed with over 80 per cent. Tighter and more independent regulation was belatedly introduced to prevent a recurrence. Eventually the cost reached about $300 billion.

The year 1984 saw the biggest rescue of a bank in US history, when Continental Illinois ran into trouble.[8] From 1976 to 1981 it had grown its loan book by 180 per cent, far more quickly than its peers, becoming the largest industrial and commercial domestic lender and the seventh largest US bank overall. It was very profitable, was highly regarded and its share price growth outperformed its competitors. Problems surfaced in 1981 following the failure of Penn Square Bank from speculative oil and gas loans, since Continental shared some loan participations with it. In 1984 the bank suffered a run on its deposits and the Federal Reserve felt obliged to intervene, since it considered Continental to be of systemic importance and feared that its failure would lead to contagion. It was described as being too big to fail. The Fed took control in a recapitalisation and removed the management, controversially removing the $100,000 cap to deposit insurance and guaranteeing all depositors. In the subsequent investigation into the management of the bank the regulatory authorities were criticised for their lack of effective intervention in its period of rapid growth and the period immediately prior to its failure.

In 1982 a problem burst on the US banks when Mexico's Minister of Finance informed the US authorities that the country would be unable to meet its debt obligations.[9] Following the second oil crisis in 1979 the banks had recycled the petrodollars by lending to third world countries, but when commodity prices fell the trouble started. Within a year many less developed countries followed suit, including 15 from Latin America of which the four largest were Mexico, Brazil, Venezuela and Argentina. These countries owed the largest eight US banks around $37 billion, considerably more than the combined capital and reserves of the banks. When the banks informed the countries of their difficulty in obtaining funding in future, the retort was that the US had a problem with the solvency of its banks. There followed a standoff.

The US authorities, in the face of the biggest international crisis since the 1930s, did not press the banks to make provisions on their restructured loans. To do so might have precipitated global banking failures. The result of this forbearance was that the banks could raise further capital and restore their balance sheets in the years which followed. In 1989 Citibank started the recognition of the inherent losses with a provision of over 30 per cent and the other banks followed shortly afterwards. Within two years the provisions amounted to 50 per cent.

One subsequent failure, LTCM, is worthy of special mention. Long Term Capital Management was a highly leveraged hedge fund set up in 1994 by John Meriwether, former head of bond trading at Salomon Brothers.[10] Its principals included two economists who were jointly awarded the Nobel Prize for their work on a new method in valuing derivatives, while working with LTCM. After some initial success, involving extremely complex and highly leveraged positions, it ran into trouble in the Russian financial crisis, as investors sought security in US Treasury bonds. LTCM was obliged to unwind its positions at an unfavourable time. Less than a year before its downfall it had returned $2.7 billion to its investors to enhance the return for others in what was a massive victory of greed over prudence. Given its enormous importance in Wall Street, the US Federal Reserve stepped in to organise a recapitalisation of $3.6 billion in 1998. It was considered to be too big to fail.

There were plenty of other debacles around the world during my banking career. Paul Erdman indulged in commodity speculation and brought down an obscure Swiss bank in 1970 before serving a prison sentence and later becoming a best selling author on financial matters. In 1974 Herstatt Bank in Germany collapsed due

41

to currency speculation, which created serious international ripples in the UK and the US. The Sindona affair shocked the world with irregularities at the Vatican bank, the strange involvement of freemasonry and the banker Roberto Calvi, known as 'God's banker', chairman of Banco Amrosiano, found hanging from Blackfriars Bridge in London in 1982. Johnson Matthey Bankers, part of a large UK gold bullion dealing group, had to be rescued by the Bank of England in 1984. In 1991 BCCI, a secretive Pakistani bank operating out of London, that had become one of the world's largest private banks, was closed in a welter of accusations of fraud and money laundering, which shook the regulatory system and led to an expensive law suit against the auditors. I will confine my comments to those failures or near failures which had some significant impact on and lessons for Ireland.

The Lessons Not Learnt or Forgotten

Just as local lessons were ignored in Ireland, so too were the large failures from abroad, although they were well publicised at the time. To some extent this is understandable, since the Northern Rock and Icelandic collapses broke out shortly before Ireland entered into crisis, while Cyprus followed much later. Nevertheless, their experiences can still help Ireland plot a safer course in future. The lessons from the US, on the other hand, provided very relevant and timely warnings for Ireland, but were still ignored, as their mistakes were repeated in Ireland.

From the UK we learn from Northern Rock that poorly thought out funding can lead to failure and even cause a run on a bank with a solid loan book, particularly if immediate corrective action is not taken once there is a major change in the marketplace. Barings showed not only that terminal damage can be caused in a faraway subsidiary by a rogue trader, if proper controls are not in place and carefully monitored, but also that large bonuses can lead to excessive risk taking. The UK fringe banks demonstrated how much damage can be done by ill-disciplined property lending and inadequate regulation. BCCI illustrated the dangers in aggressive bidding for deposits and the necessity for the regulator to check out the competence of the management.

Iceland confirmed the vulnerability of a large financial sector relative to the size of the economy and the perils of pursuing an international growth strategy without due attention to risk. It also manifested the difficulties in resolving the problems without imposing much hardship on its citizens. The Troika rescue plan for Cyprus established the principle that the interests of bondholders and large depositors were no longer deemed sacrosanct and could be 'bailed in' as part of a restructuring.

The US demonstrated the perils in allowing Savings and Loan Societies, financial institutions similar to building societies, to diversify their lending into speculative real estate. The failure of Continental Illinois highlighted the dangers in growing too rapidly and the problems resulting from being considered to be too big to fail, as was the LTCM hedge fund. The Latin American problems illustrated the inexact nature of loan provisioning and how the rules could be bent in a crisis, thereby deferring the recognition of losses in the interests of saving the banking system.

These errors were diverse and the causes of failure varied enormously, from reckless property lending or excessive growth of business to inadequate controls over key risks, becoming too large to fail and unwise funding, which could disappear in a crisis. Yet each of these issues had some kind of parallel in Ireland during the Celtic Tiger. If bankers were a typical animal species they could face extinction, due to their inability to learn from mistakes and adapt.

When it occurs, failure in banking is easy to recognise with its potentially devastating costs to employees, depositors, shareholders and taxpayers, as well as the reputations of the managers who are held responsible. Surprisingly, real success and prosperity is more difficult to recognise and evaluate. Many people would expect the success of a bank to be revealed in the annual accounts, which measure its financial performance. Accordingly, a careful reading and analysis of these accounts provides the usual starting point in assessing the level of its success.

PART TWO:

Identifying the Immediate Causes of Failure

CHAPTER 4

Alchemy and the Calculation of Bank Profits

The published annual accounts of most companies do not make for exciting bedtime reading. They are produced with a variety of audiences in mind. As well as shareholders, who read them to monitor their investment, they may be read by the tax and regulatory authorities, employees, competitors, customers and suppliers. The general public may be interested in financial and social aspects, so they may be perused by journalists too. In recent years they have become more extensive, at least partly to conform to ever increasing regulatory requirements. But whether or not they produce more valuable and useful information to their readers is a moot point. Indeed, whether these weighty tomes are studied in detail by many interested parties is doubtful.

The Issues in Financial Services

The accounts of financial institutions are more complex than most companies. The particular issue is that their business may have important impacts on third parties over a considerable period of time. For general insurance companies consideration needs to be given to policy holders. For mutual building societies and credit unions it may be their members, while for banks it is primarily their depositors. When problems arise, the interests of the various parties need to be protected in an appropriate manner. Failure can lead to loss of confidence with devastating repercussions around the industry. Regulators and governments have a strong vested interest to avoid failures. Managements wish to reassure their stakeholders of their solidity without providing useful information to their competitors.

General insurance companies have a particular problem in deciding the level of provisions which should be set aside for claims by policy holders. While, with sufficient time and information, sensible estimates may be made of reported claims, a greater problem arises in dealing with claims incurred, but not reported. The world famous self-regulated Lloyds of London teetered on the verge of collapse in the 1990s, when it was discovered that adequate provisions had not been made for such eventualities, despite the existence of a damning report on the subject. Yet it had a rule that accounts could not be closed until two years after the end of the accounting year. The timeframe possible may be very long indeed with certain 'long tail' claims, such as those relating to asbestosis. Ireland has experienced its share of disputes about the adequacy of general insurance provisions in recent years, whether in domestic or foreign-owned businesses.

Life assurance companies have a particular problem in recognising the profit on a policy designed to last over maybe forty years with a commission paid to the sales agent at the outset. The problem is that policies may be cancelled before maturity, so it will always be a matter of conjecture how long the average policy will be in existence. The likely life is difficult to estimate, so the task is usually left to actuaries, who may come up with a wide range of answers with different profit implications for the initial sale. When the issuers decide to guarantee certain surrender values at the outset, they are taking very brave, if not reckless, decisions. Equitable Life Assurance, the world's oldest mutual insurer, did that leading to large payouts by the UK Government to policy holders from 2010 onwards, since there was deemed to have been maladministration in its regulation.

In recent years there has been an increasing tendency for financial groups to provide a 'one stop shop' for their customers so that many banking groups contain insurance subsidiaries, making their consolidated accounts even more difficult to interpret. For example, Irish Life and Permanent, Bank of Ireland and AIB all had life assurance subsidiaries. Interpreting simple bank accounts should be easier, when there are no other different activities to disentangle.

A Banking Example

I shall take the example of a bank which focussed on traditional banking activities without an insurance involvement and had many admirers. It was awarded the Grand Prix by the prestigious *IR Magazine* first in 2003 and subsequently for the next five years. In 2006, Mercer Oliver Wyman, a leading consultancy firm, named it as the world's top-performing bank, based on its returns from 2001 to 2005. The following year, at the annual Davos meeting where world leaders meet, it named the bank as the best of the 170 banks worth over $10 billion surveyed, given its average growth rate of 35 per cent over ten years. In 2007, Standard & Poor's rated it 'A' long term and 'A-1' short term, both strong ratings. One must presume that the expert analysts perused its accounts carefully, calculated the relevant ratios and checked through the notes for any inherent weaknesses.

The 137 page report and accounts of the bank for the year ending September 2007 were released at the end of November that year. Its three main activities were business lending, treasury and wealth management. It had just delivered its 22nd year of uninterrupted earnings growth, which in terms of assets and profits had averaged 35 per cent over the past 20 years. Pre-tax profits had grown by 46 per cent to €1.2 billion, with a similar growth in deposits of 46 per cent, while assets amounted to almost €100 billion. The 'high quality' growth in customer lending of €18 billion showed an increase of 37 per cent. Overall the bank proclaimed an improvement in its cost income ratio, 30 per cent return on equity, earnings per share growth of 44 per cent and a 20 per cent dividend increase. The performance appeared strong in the aftermath of the US subprime crisis, which broke on the world that August.

The part of the accounts which receives most attention is usually the Chairman's Statement, which may comment on the past performance and the prospects for the year ahead. Shareholders were advised of its prudent credit policy, its strong capital position, its focused and disciplined business model, together with its stringent risk management. The bank boasted that impaired loans amounted to only €335 million, being 0.5 per cent of its customer loans of €67 billion, significantly less than that of its peers. The bank stated that it did not engage in speculative lending and the group risk management review completed in November showed that the bank was not experiencing any stress. The bank operated to the highest ethical standards and governance, aspiring to be a model corporate citizen. Looking ahead, the chairman expected further expansion in the UK and Ireland with earnings per share growth in excess of 15 per cent and confidently expected above market returns in subsequent years.

The accounts were those of Anglo Irish Bank, whose chairman was Sean Fitzpatrick, one of Ireland's best known bankers. But events were to unfold in a manner quite different to that anticipated by the chairman.[1]

Subsequent Events

In September 2008, after the collapse of Lehman Brothers, Anglo Irish experienced severe funding problems and was facing imminent collapse, initially attributed to liquidity issues rather than solvency. The Irish Government reacted by guaranteeing the main liabilities of all Irish banks, including Anglo Irish, which amounted to a massive €440 billion on 3o September, the date of Anglo Irish's year-end.

In December 2008 the bank announced its 2007/8 results with profits down by 37 per cent from 2006/7 to €784 million. The bank remained, however, confident in its business model and its stringent risk management, predicting profits for each of the next three years. However, that same month both Fitzpatrick and the CEO, David Drumm, resigned under a cloud. In January the Minister of Finance stated that the funding position of the bank had weakened and that 'unacceptable practices' had damaged the bank's reputation. The bank was then nationalised. Having been valued at more than €13 billion at its peak, it had become worthless.

It transpired that Fitzpatrick had undisclosed loans of €87 million from the bank, which had been temporarily warehoused with Irish Nationwide Building Society over the year-end, a practice which had occurred previously. Over €7 billion had also been placed with Anglo Irish over its year-end by another financial institution, which controversially was treated as a deposit, thereby enhancing its apparent liquidity. Finally, the bank had loaned €451 million to 10 major customers to purchase shares in the bank with personal recourse limited to a maximum 25 per cent of the borrowings, a serious exposure to the bank if the shares fell in value. In 2014, criminal charges against FizPatrick and two other directors came to court in connection with the €451 million loan. Fitzpatrick was acquitted, but the other two directors were found guilty of committing breaches of Section 60 of the Companies Act, which generally prohibits companies from making loans for the purchase of their own shares. Nevertheless, they were spared custodial sentences on the grounds that they were misled by the Financial Regulator.

Following nationalisation the bank's decline in fortune continued for all involved. The fraud squad and other regulatory authorities were called in. In what was the biggest such case in the history of the State, Fitzpatrick was declared bankrupt, while Drumm filed for bankruptcy in the US. NAMA, the Government's newly created 'bad bank', took over the large property loans of Anglo and five other banks at a large discount. Finally, the bank's efforts to provide a survival plan failed and its run down commenced with its deposit book being sold in 2011.

Not everyone would agree with the chairman in his statements contained in the 2006/7 and 2007/8 accounts during the years which followed nationalisation. As mentioned in Chapter 1, the report of the Central Bank Governor stated that Anglo Irish Bank was well on the road to insolvency at the time of the collapse of Lehman Brothers.

In 2010 the bank announced a loss of €12.7 billion with impairment charges of over €15 billion for the fifteen months to December 2009, a new Irish corporate record. It had also outstanding loans of €155 million to former directors, much of which is not expected to be repaid. A senior civil servant told the public accounts committee of the Dáil that senior bankers in Anglo were dishonest or disingenuous, at least in presenting its health in the crisis.[2] The new bank chief executive castigated the previous management over their governance, risk management and managerial processes.[3]

In 2011 it announced 2010 results which showed even greater losses, amounting to over €17 billion, requiring substantial further Government assistance. The bank which had boasted its low level of loan impairments on its €67 billion loan book three years earlier now seemed to be facing impairments of approximately €30 billion for the 2.25 years to December 2010. Indeed, by 2013 the total cost to the taxpayer of the failure of Anglo was generally estimated at around €30 billion.

The Department of Finance had commissioned PwC, a leading firm of accountants, to check the provisions of €4 billion at March 2009. They found the figure to be 'not unreasonable' based on a limited review of loans, though there would also be an €800 million charge for losses incurred, but not recognised, a term borrowed from the insurance industry.[4] It seems that PwC broadly concurred with the provisions set aside by Anglo Irish. Yet Anglo Irish transferred two tranches of loans to NAMA in 2010 with a value of €27.2 billion for a consideration of €13 billion, based on their estimated economic value, a discount of over 52 per cent. Given such a large write down, were the figures shown in the accounts previously overstated, or had such a massive deterioration occurred in just over a year? It is difficult for outsiders to pass judgement without knowing how provisions are made.

Interpreting Bank Accounts

Fundamental to evaluating the financial performance of any business, including banks, is an evaluation of the profits relative to the capital needed. One popular ratio is 'return on equity' which relates the profit in a given period to the capital provided by the shareholders, including the profits retained by the bank. If there is significant ambiguity around these figures the ratio can become virtually meaningless, so that comparisons with other institutions are problematic and insolvency is difficult to recognise. Examination of cashflow statements too has little relevance for banks, given that the nature of the business is receiving and distributing cash.

The key to understanding a bank's accounts is the adequacy of provisions for bad debts on its lending or 'loan impairments', as they are now termed. At one time banks in London were allowed to smooth their profits, putting profits to reserves in good times and withdrawing them when required. This practice was permitted to avoid a run on a bank in a bad year, but rendered the accounts virtually meaningless. A fundamental principle in preparing accounts traditionally was the concept of prudence. It was generally considered preferable to understate rather than overstate a profit. However, in an attempt to prevent directors from smoothing profits and avoiding some tax, this concept was increasingly cast aside.

My recollection of banking in the 1980s is that problem accounts were divided into four categories. If the loan was vulnerable to some adverse change, it was designated 'Watch' and monitored closely. More problematic loans were designated 'Substandard', which meant that with hindsight the bank would prefer not to have made them. Where a loss was probable they were deemed to be 'Doubtful', while 'Loss' was used to describe insolvent businesses. Only the last two categories required specific provisions. But the difference between 'Substandard' and 'Doubtful' was a fine line and a matter of personal judgement. Nowadays efforts have been made to standardise the approach, which is technical, complex and obscure, but nevertheless is fundamental to understanding bank accounts, given the potential size of the number.

Currently provisioning is governed by international financial reporting standards.[5] These standards are adopted by the EU and therefore Irish banks are obliged to follow them. The relevant rule stipulates that provision for impairment must be made on the basis of 'losses incurred'. The difficulty, of course, is determining when a loss has been incurred. General provisions for future losses are discouraged and do not constitute an allowable deduction for tax purposes. Instead, most provisions are made against specific loans or groups of similar loans, which become an allowable deduction for taxation.

Normally any impairment needs to be triggered by an event. If, for example, there is a rise in unemployment, it may be appropriate to increase the impairment charge on the mortgage book, since arrears in payments can be anticipated. The difficulty is that actions or inactions by the bank can impact the occurrence of such an event. Thus repossessing and selling houses may crystallise a fall in house prices, while inaction may postpone the problem. Similarly, where property developers are experiencing cashflow difficulties and are unable to meet repayment commitments, a restructuring of the loan by rolling up interest and deferring capital repayments means that the loan is no longer out of order.

Many accountants would prefer to provide on an expected loss basis, building up provisions over the life of the loan for expected future losses. If provisions were made, when the losses were anticipated, this would normally lead to their recognition earlier in time. But it is doubtful if either approach would deal satisfactorily with a sudden collapse in property prices, such as that experienced in 2007/8. Property valuation is an inexact science and there may be considerable uncertainty at a specific date. The appropriate impairment charge can be a matter of judgement and open to differing interpretations. In extreme cases banks have been officially permitted to defer recognition of problem loans. In effect, the US authorities did that in the 1980s, when they allowed US banks to defer providing for Latin American losses, as discussed in Chapter 3.

The review of the crisis produced by the UK Financial Services Authority supports this viewpoint, claiming that the current accounting policies are pro-cyclical, allowing banks to defer recognition of losses and thereby encouraging a policy of growth, while increasing management remuneration in a boom. It recommended that accounting bodies and regulatory authorities cooperate to resolve the problem. In the meantime it suggested that banks set an Economic Cycle Reserve in their published accounts to reduce profits in times of economic prosperity.[6]

In July 2014 the International Accounting Standards Board adopted International Financial Reporting Standard 9 (IFRS9). This standard, which should be applied in Ireland and more than 100 countries outside the US, is based on expected future losses and will require banks to recognise losses much earlier. However, it has not yet been endorsed by the EU and in any event will not become mandatory until 2018. Unfortunately, the US will adopt a different standard, while using the same basic principle, thus greatly adding to compliance costs for banks operating in different jurisdictions. In view of the continuing element of subjectivity it has not received universal support on its launch and it remains to be seen how it will be interpreted. When it is implemented, bank profits can be expected to be much more volatile than has been traditional. Meanwhile, considerable difficulty will remain in interpreting the financial performance of banks.

A second complication for some banks is the valuation of treasury instruments. Clearly, as discussed in Chapters 2 and 3, in the case of Barings in London and AIB in the US, treasury losses remained undetected for several years. The development of the derivatives industry has brought about complex valuation problems on an enormous scale. In preparing accounts banks need to ascertain the current value of these products. They are required to 'mark to market' these products, but often there is no obvious market price for many esoteric and incredibly mathematically complex products, some of which can be of enormous magnitude.

The other area which banks wish to present in a favourable light is liquidity. This they can do by window dressing, ensuring that the maximum amount of cash is available on the balance sheet date. Such activity should improve the apparent year end liquidity of the bank, even if it is removed shortly afterwards. There can be a fine line between what is acceptable and what is not. Whether or not the funds provided by Irish Life to Anglo Irish at its year end were properly accounted for may eventually be determined by the courts.

Given the amount of discretion and the scope for deferring losses which are possible, it is not surprising that many shareholders now view bank accounts with a high degree of suspicion. Most sets of accounts have becoming increasingly lengthy, as more disclosures are required. The 2013 AIB and Bank of Ireland accounts each run to well over 400 pages. Most shareholders lack the time and expertise to analyse a voluminous set of bank accounts, much of which is highly technical in nature and tend to rely on the 'experts' instead, hoping to pick up any problems through reports in the media.

The main independent 'experts' are rating agencies, stockbrokers and external auditors. Rating agencies earn their fees from the companies they rate, which calls into question their independence. They provide long- and short-term ratings, which should be adjusted in the light of the fortunes of the institutions covered. The three major service providers are American, all of which failed to identify problems in the subprime mortgage market there prior to 2007, as discussed in Chapter 8.

Not all Irish institutions were rated, so often the only independent 'experts' available were stockbrokers and the banks' external auditors. The evolution of stockbrokers and their relationships with investment banking are described in Chapter 9. Suffice it to say that their independence has been challenged on the same basis as the rating agencies and their ownership by banks can give rise to conflicts of interest. They have sometimes been reluctant to give a 'sell' rating to banks which may be a major source of business to them.

Most shareholders pay only cursory attention to the annual accounts, concentrating on the profit number, content when it shows an increase, but expressing concern when it falls. The financial press similarly will latch on to this figure when publishing their headlines. It must come as a surprise to many members of the public that there has been for years a technical loophole of a complex and esoteric nature which permitted banks to defer recognition of their losses. In the global financial crisis many banks failed or had to be rescued shortly after declaring substantial profits shocked the general public, while often obliterating the value of their investment. Even expert analysts were unable to identify the problem, let alone interpret the figures more cautiously. It is scant consolation that a new accounting standard is being introduced which should help address the problem some years into the future.

If asked to justify their faith in published accounts, typically shareholders would refer to the auditors, whose appointment and remuneration they approved annually at the Annual General Meeting. Should they have highlighted the uncertainties surrounding the figures?

The Nebulous Role of Audit

What of auditors and their responsibilities? While the ultimate responsibility for creating impairment charges lies with the directors, should the auditors not have a role in establishing the appropriate level of provisioning? What comfort can the reader of any set of bank accounts take from their reports? Certainly confidence in the statutory audit has been shaken, following the global financial crisis. None of the accounts of the Irish or UK banks contained any audit qualification, yet shortly afterwards they required substantial funds by way of a bailout. If any bank could not be considered a going concern, should this not have been disclosed or required an audit qualification?

Irish bank auditors are expected to be interviewed as part of the forthcoming Irish Oireachtas inquiry, so final evaluation of their role in the crisis is premature. Nevertheless, some information is already in the public domain. The Regling Report, mentioned in Chapter 1, stated that there is a need to probe whether auditors were sufficiently vigilant in some cases, but it took the matter no further. The subsequent Nyberg Report emphasised the limitations of audits. It pointed out that any qualification in audit reports would have damaging effects on confidence if they had referred to the excessive property lending or the reliance on wholesale lending. Since accounting standards based provisioning on 'incurred losses', auditors were restricted in insisting on earlier provisioning. The statutory audit has serious limitations, but these may not be appreciated by readers, so there is an 'Expectation Gap'.

The report stresses that bank auditors do have a wider obligation. Unlike the UK, Irish auditors have a duty to report specific matters, but has no right to report other matters. Their duties included copying the regulator with the audit findings and the management letter, which identified weaknesses in the system. The report states that there appears to have been no challenging dialogue about the business models and their growing property and funding exposures, which it considered to be 'unfortunate'.

In the late 1960s, when I trained as an auditor in London, statutory audit reports were very brief, a short paragraph stating that proper books had been kept and that the accounts showed a 'true and fair view'. If the auditor was unhappy with any aspect, this could lead to a qualification, which rarely happened in practice. The ultimate threat was resignation, which could provoke a major outcry from shareholders. More recently audit reports may extend to several pages, but whether or not they are more useful is open to question. Much of the report is spent on pinning the primary responsibility on the directors and setting out the scope of the audit. I doubt whether many readers of accounts read the report closely.

As a corporate lender, while working in banking in the 1980s, I would meet the external auditors to discuss any cases they were examining, but cannot recollect any difficult probing. Junior audit personnel seldom possess the expertise needed to challenge seriously an experienced lender, and in any case only cover a modest sample of cases. It is difficult for them to second guess provisions without a detailed knowledge of a loan and its future outcome. Auditors seek to ensure that accounts are adequately monitored, properly reported and the rules consistently applied.

A modern audit report, such as the PwC report on Bank of Ireland 2013 accounts, runs to five pages. It starts with the true and fair view statement before proceeding to outline the subject of the audit, what an audit involves and its scope. It goes on to specify the areas of focus and the work done in these areas, as well as addressing the issue of the going concern. It finishes with certain statutory matters on which it is obliged to report, the respective responsibilities of the directors and auditors and the name of the audit partner. However, while a fuller explanation of the audit work is helpful, the reassurance is limited, since it states that the impairment provisions are 'complex and subjective'.

Auditors have rarely been sued in Ireland, and when they have, the cases have been settled out of court beyond the public purview. As mentioned in Chapter 2, AIB did sue its auditors following the takeover of ICI. The case drifted on for years before it was eventually settled out of court. It did, however, provide grounds for the directors to remain in office, claiming that their resignations could prejudice the court case. More recently the administrators of Quinn Insurance have instigated a major claim against the auditors, as have the liquidators of IBRC, so the practice may be changing.

The auditors' independence often comes under scrutiny, not assisted by the reduction of the 'Big 8' firms, when I qualified, to the 'Big 4' today, which can generate conflicts of interest. For example, my old firm, KPMG, the auditor to INBS, had informed the Financial Regulator of many operational weaknesses in the bank's systems long before being appointed liquidator of IBRC, which had acquired INBS. Still, it was obliged to consider whether to sue itself, as the auditor to INBS. Although it received legal advice that it need not do so, attempts were made to join it as a party in the case by a defendant. Many businesses now are questioning the value of the statutory audit, which comes at considerable cost and may produce limited benefits.

Internal auditors with a close knowledge of the bank may be better placed to identify problem areas and bring them to the attention of the board audit committee. The main requirement is a strong sense of independence and professional conduct. Successive internal auditors did display such qualities in AIB before parting company with the bank. But internal audits can miss major weaknesses, as happened in the case of Barings Bank, where the internal auditors failed to spot breaches of trading limits and unauthorised proprietary option trading in their Singapore operations. Neither internal nor external auditors discovered the enormous losses by rogue traders in either Barings or AIB, even though they had continued over several years.

The Lure of Dividends

Many investors invested in bank shares because of their supposed safety and the high levels of dividends they paid out historically. 'Safe as the Bank of Ireland' was a phrase which entered the language. Bank shares were often recommended as a suitable investment for charities, pensioners and pension funds, which required a large fixed income for their members. In fact the bank shares comprised a large share of the Irish stock market for many years, being the mainstay of many portfolios.

The dividend tended to set a base level for bank shares. If investors expected say a 5 per cent return and paid out a dividend of €1, then the shares should be valued at €20. The underlying assumption, however, is that the dividend is sustainable, and will be paid in perpetuity. Banks traditionally have been aware of the income wishes of their shareholders and liked to keep a steady growth in the dividend per share. Above all, banks resisted cutting a dividend in a poor year, since this would disappoint their shareholders. Profit smoothing was not permissible, but dividend smoothing was perfectly acceptable.

In general the decision as to what level of dividends will be paid is a matter for the board of the company, subject to the availability of profits which can be legally paid out to shareholders. Prudent businesses will always ensure that there are sufficient reserves retained in the business to help fund its growth and any unforeseen eventualities. In general, dividends should be amply covered by available reserves. In these circumstances any statement about future payments received the closest attention, since it is a signal of the directors' confidence in the future.

In the summer of 2008 both Bank of Ireland and AIB intimated that they would be increasing their dividends. The CEO of AIB denied that the bank needed equity. Such statements gave considerable, if misguided, comfort to shareholders who had not studied the lengthy annual reports, but were anxious to maintain their income, at the very minimum. Only weeks later the bank guarantee was announced and the banks were fighting for their lives. The banks lost the confidence of their ordinary shareholders, who experienced a collapse in the value of their investments and have received no dividend since then. Yet few people could have foreseen the disaster by any analysis of the historic accounts and subsequent pronouncements by the banks.

There are clearly many uncertainties and difficulties in establishing the profits of a bank and interpreting their results. If the Governor of the Central Bank was correct in stating that Anglo was well on the road to insolvency in September 2008, then analysts must look beyond the latest annual accounts to discover its problems. The limitations of annual accounts also raise the issue of whether reported profits are a reliable measure of management performance and should form the basis of substantial bonuses paid to reward the senior managers.

CHAPTER 5

The Seven Deadly Sins –
The Route to Insolvency

In recent years, perhaps due to strong economic growth prior to the financial crisis, there has been little research on the causes of business failure. Much of the earlier work relates to failures of at least twenty years ago, particularly in the US and UK. Drawing on the common features of failure in this research,[1] an Irish academic researched nine publicised Irish corporate failures.[2] Four were rapidly growing 'adolescent' businesses, while the other five can be described as 'mature'. Many classical signs of failure were evident in both groups, although overtrading was generally absent in the mature group. Some of the signs overlapped and the academic's list of twenty signs has been condensed here to seven, which can be likened to the biblical seven deadly sins. They are based on my experiences evident in lending during the 1980s.[3] More recently Jim Collins, a US business consultant, has researched American business failures and identified five stages on the road to collapse, which have close parallels with the seven deadly sins.[4]

The Seven Deadly Sins of Business Failure[1]

'Pride' – Autocratic Management

Pride, as claimed biblically, does indeed come before a fall. A business rarely fails with the reputation of its management intact.

Often, an entrepreneur with drive but without the full range of management skills is reluctant to delegate responsibility. Autocratic managers rarely mend their ways. In 1971, UK government-appointed inspectors described Robert Maxwell, the well-known publisher and media proprietor, as: 'Not being a fit person who can be relied upon to exercise proper stewardship of a publicly quoted company.' Twenty-five years later he was raiding his company's pension scheme, while his sons as managing directors later protested in court that their father did not keep them informed about company business.

'Sloth' – Ignoring Change

Many businesses fail to spot changes arising from new competitors or technological innovations, often becoming complacent rather than being vigilant. If the company has no strategy or long-term plan, it is likely to experience unpleasant surprises in turbulent times. Without investment in technology, new products or people, survival is threatened. In a rapidly changing world paranoia may not be misplaced. Charles Darwin's adage that in nature it is not the strongest of the species that survives, nor the most intelligent, but the one that is most responsive to change, applies to business as well.

'Anger' – Lack of Control

In times of a recession or credit crunch control over cashflow is critical. Thoughtless or reckless expenditure must be curtailed with prudent financial management to the fore. This necessitates sound credit control, working capital management, rigorous budgeting, sound capital appraisal and timely management accounts. The tightening of trade credit, accompanied by the withdrawal of bank credit facilities, has made the control discipline imperative for survival.

'Gluttony' – Overtrading

After more than a decade of growth many businesses assumed that sales growth would continue indefinitely. The accompanying growth of overheads, spread over a wider base, all too often did not attract the attention it merited. With profits growing, banks obligingly financed the cash shortages so businesses were not forced to tackle inefficiencies and slim down their cost bases. Overtrading from unplanned and undisciplined expansion often went unpunished as a result, but is unlikely to be tolerated in a credit crunch.

'Covetousness' – Over-borrowing

The desire to have something belonging to others is the financial equivalent of high gearing or, to use American terminology, high leverage. High property valuations allowed businesses to increase their debt to equity ratios to levels which historically would not have been considered to be prudent. When borrowings are high, lenders can become nervous and demand repayment, thus precipitating the failure of businesses. Over-borrowing is particularly dangerous when the underlying business is subject to high volatility.

'Lust for power' – The Big Risk

The danger of big uninsured risks has always been a hazard that company boards are keen to avoid. Even risk-conscious businesses succumb periodically. Risks may be taken knowingly, when, for example, they are reliant on a single customer or supplier. But they can also arise when the complexities of products, such as financial derivatives, are not fully understood and the likelihood of problems severely underestimated. Frequently big risks are underestimated in takeovers. Sound risk management is critical for survival in the current challenging economic environment.

'Envy' – Creative Accounting

Imitating leading business competitors is understandable, but bending accounting policies to demonstrate financial success is not acceptable. The US accounting scandals of recent years have shown that, even in highly regulated markets, companies have resorted to dubious accounting policies and practices to bolster their reported performance. The purpose was often to enhance the income statement, by aggressive income recognition or under-statement of costs. Alternatively, they strive to enhance the balance sheet, either by overvaluing assets or understating liabilities. While international accounting standards, where they are adopted, have closed some loopholes, others remain to be exploited.

It may be interesting to investigate whether bank failures are fundamentally different from those in other industries. In particular, do failing banks commit the seven deadly sins? To address this question I shall examine three very different banks, whose difficulties attracted considerable international interest and also had a devastating impact on the banking systems of their respective countries: Lehman Brothers in the US, Anglo Irish Bank in Ireland and RBS in the UK.

Lehman Brothers

Lehman Brothers in 2008 was the fourth largest investment bank in Wall Street. During the 150 years of its illustrious history it was associated with advising many of the greatest businesses in America, such as F.W. Woolworth, Macy's, Campbell Soup and TWA. In the 1980s it changed its emphasis from traditional corporate finance advisory and fundraising to trading. In late 1983 there was an internal coup which resulted in the senior trader, Lew Glucksman, being appointed CEO of the banking partnership. After a period of infighting during difficult trading conditions the partnership, facing a crisis, was forced to seek extra capital. Eventually, after some trading losses it merged with Shearson American Express in April 1984 before being spun off in 1994 with Dick Fuld, a close associate of Lew Glucksman, as the chairman and CEO.[5]

The investment banking industry changed fundamentally in 1999 with the repeal of the Glass-Steagall Act of 1933, which had prevented investment banks from acquiring or operating commercial banks and gaining access to their substantial deposits. In the era which followed businesses developed on a global scale with financial innovation the order of the day.

In September 2008, however, with the spread of the subprime mortgage crisis, described in Chapter 8, the future of many venerable financial institutions was in doubt. Some institutions were considered to be too big to be allowed to fail and survived with varying degrees of Government support. Lehman Brothers, however, did fail and was forced to file for bankruptcy, generating catastrophic repercussions for the industry and causing major ripples worldwide.

Larry McDonald, a trader at Lehman Brothers, has written an insider's account of the collapse of the bank.[6] He portrays Dick Fuld, CEO since 1994, in a most unfavourable light, describing him as a poor listener, a recluse, greedy and a bully, who had never had a powerful deputy. The board was considered irrelevant, with only two of its ten members having banking experience, nine being retired and four aged over 75 years old. The executive committee was also accused of being unwilling to challenge Fuld.

Did the bank neglect the changes in the real estate market and consequently fail to anticipate the property bubble? The housing collapse had been foreseen by some traders in June 2005, some eighteen months before the collapse, when it was likened to an athlete taking steroids. These views were, however, ignored, despite the resignations of several senior executives, while the bank continued to create subprime securitisations, being caught in the end with a $2 billion property deal on its books.

Did the bank overtrade and over-borrow? From the first quarter of 2005, when revenues amounted to $7 billion, they expanded steadily every quarter until they reached over $13 billion in the last quarter of 2006. Gearing increased from 20 times net worth in 2004 to 32 times in 2006. By the end of 2007 it was reported to be 41 times, while early in 2008 a senior managing director protested that the multiple was estimated at 44 times net worth and had to be reduced.

What about controls and risk management? In response to the complaints about high gearing the company president was reported to have criticised the conservative attitude and affirmed that the aims of the company were growth, risk and major deals. The bank took on an enormous exposure to commercial mortgage-backed securities, estimated at €30 billion, which was considered to be a hedge against any weakness in the residential market. Real estate acquisitions continued. When the Treasury Secretary, Hank Paulson, urged Fuld to deleverage the bank and consider its sale, he apparently considered that the response demonstrated something between arrogance and disrespect.

Investors were critical of Lehman's accounting policies and questioned the value of its assets, even though it was still reporting profits. Concern was expressed over the exposure to derivatives in special purpose vehicles.

Another account by an outsider, a well-known financial journalist, broadly paints a similar picture.[7] Fuld's behaviour was variously described as confrontational, bullying, aggressive and hectoring. A senior colleague accused him of having a blind spot for weak people who were sycophants. It was suggested that in part he selected his deputy because he was not a threatening individual.

The board saw little wrong when, shortly before the end, an octogenarian member delivered a ringing endorsement of the executive: 'I want everyone in the room to know that I know that you guys have done a good job. This is just bad luck. We are a hundred per cent behind all of you.'

Fuld was reported to consider the bank as being too conservative. The Treasury Secretary was reported as regarding him as a reckless risk taker due to mistakes made in 1995 over exposure to the Mexican peso. Fuld was said to have little understanding or interest in the risks contained in complex derivatives. The risk officer's role was virtually nil and she was eventually removed from the executive committee. The bank had an enormous exposure to property and it was stated that it was turned into an all-in, unhedged play on the US real estate market.

Accounting practices were heavily criticised. Property assets were overvalued in the accounts, sometimes not being marked to market, so that write-downs could be deferred. Window dressing was employed at the end of the quarter to reduce the amount of gearing reported through the use of repurchase agreements ('Repo 105'), whereby assets were sold just before the period end, but repurchased shortly afterwards. The bankruptcy examiner was critical of these practices and indicated that there could be civil claims for filing misleading reports against certain members of management and the auditors.

Based on these two accounts, one by an insider and one by an outsider, it appears that Lehmans committed most, if not all, of the seven deadly sins: autocratic management, neglect of changes in the property market, overtrading, excessive borrowing, inadequate controls, enormous risk concentration and even dubious accounting practices. Perhaps the failure of the bank was best summed up in McDonald's book subtitle: The incredible inside story of the collapse of Lehman Brothers was 'a colossal failure of common sense', which is a devastating criticism on the management of the bank.

Anglo Irish Bank

In 1980 a young accountant, Sean Fitzpatrick was appointed general manager of Anglo Irish Bank, a small bank with assets of less than £500,000, which could be described as a mixture of a finance house and a merchant bank. In 1986 it merged with City of Dublin Bank and Fitzpatrick was appointed chief executive. For the next two decades it expanded rapidly growing organically and making occasional acquisitions.

The success of the bank began to challenge the two more staid market leaders, Allied Irish Bank and Bank of Ireland. Anglo rewarded performance and by 2001 Fitzpatrick, affectionately known as 'Seanie', was the highest paid banker in Ireland. A heavy emphasis was placed on knowing the customers, taking decisions quickly and usually obtaining personal guarantees. It had well established relationships with the leading property developers and provided finance for them not only in Ireland, but also in the UK and US. In 2005 Seanie stood down as chief executive, having run the bank for almost 25 years, but stayed on as chairman. The new CEO was a surprise appointment, David Drumm, who had run the US operations for several years. The rapid growth of lending continued.

The events surrounding the collapse of the bank have already been outlined in Chapter 4. In September 2008, after the collapse of Lehman Brothers, Anglo Irish experienced severe funding problems and was facing imminent collapse, initially attributed to liquidity issues, rather than solvency. The Irish Government reacted by guaranteeing the main liabilities of the Irish banks which amounted to a massive €440 billion on 30 September, the date of Anglo Irish's year end. On radio shortly afterwards Fitzpatrick attributed the problems to a systemic problem worldwide, denied recklessness and refused to apologise.

To what extent had Anglo Irish Bank committed the seven deadly sins?

Fitzpatrick was not a bully like Fuld in Lehman Brothers. One account describes him as a hard worker, a delegator, a fast decision maker and a virtuoso salesman.[8] Another calls him a quick-fix banker.[9] But a more recent account is less flattering: he is described by a former director as arrogant, a man who sought 'semi-yes-men' around him and did not want a board at all.[10] Fitzpatrick saw himself as neither technically a good lender, nor someone who involved himself in credit committees, but an entrepreneur and a businessman. He regretted his poor personal relationship with his CEO, Drumm, who disputed the amount of autonomy he was granted. However, for a long standing CEO, as Fitzpatrick had been, to become chairman does not constitute good corporate governance and his report in the 2007 accounts contained more than a hint of hubris.

Many of the details of the remaining sins can also be found in a book by two journalists to whom Fitzpatrick granted interviews, where he presented his side of the story.[11] Did Anglo neglect change in the property market? A decision was made around 2005/6 to stop development lending in Ireland, but the bank incredibly continued to support developers with a good track record, permitting them to gear up through equity release, a policy which Fitzpatrick believed led to the bank's collapse. So, if the bank did understand the property bubble, it failed to take the appropriate action.

Did the bank overtrade, over-borrow and lack proper controls? Average growth of 35 per cent over 20 years looks distinctly like overtrading. The Central Bank Governor, Professor Honohan, indicated that rapid growth in the balance sheet is a very simple warning sign for regulators. Despite the confident statement about the bank being adequately capitalised, the massive capital injections required by the State subsequently would indicate otherwise. The Nyberg Report, referred to in Chapter 1, indicated that there was a weakness in enforcement of controls.

Did the bank manage risk as well as it asserted? Fitzpatrick claimed that Anglo was a very 'solid bank, making very good profits, well diversified geographically, well diversified in terms of that (sic) our property lending was for investment property and some development'. The bank's rule of thumb was that loans to any one customer should be limited to 1 per cent of its loan book. It had, however, lent more than €1 billion to six customers, including an exposure of over €2 billion to the troubled Quinn group. By the end of 2008 fifteen customers each owed more than €500 million. The bank had a massive exposure to the Irish property sector in particular. Spreading into the risky UK and US property markets hardly constituted good geographic diversification. The bank also had another rule of thumb, limiting its exposure to development lending to 15 per cent of its loan book, but this figure rose to 25 per cent when in 2008 it reclassified a further 10 per cent as development loans.

Its claim that it adopted a prudent credit policy and stringent risk management is certainly open to question. As described in Chapter 7 most, if not all, banks had lowered their lending standards, but Anglo seemed to lead the way in this regard. An Irish developer claimed that obtaining loans from the bank was easy.[12] The credit committee comprised mainly associate directors, who headed up different lending teams, who liked to help each other. Nobody worried about the head of risk, because he was believed to have no power. An unnamed former Anglo lender in the US was reported as stating that credit checks could have been stronger,[13] while another commentator stated that Anglo was a deal shop with deal junkies and Dublin a rubber stamp.[14]

Was Anglo guilty of creative accounting? Until the various investigations mentioned above are completed, it is premature to pass judgement on this matter. However, Fitzpatrick has admitted that the warehousing of his loans, which he had considered to be perfectly legal, was inappropriate and unacceptable. There are plenty of loose ends remaining. The official assignee in bankruptcy is to examine a restructuring of Fitzpatrick's loans and those of his family in 2009. There is also the question, still not satisfactorily explained, as to why weeks before nationalisation at the time of the resignation of the chairman and CEO Anglo sold off its Austrian subsidiary, which contained €570 million in deposits and less than €35 million in lending, to a Swiss group for €141 million, even providing a loan to assist the purchaser, at a time when it was critically short of deposits. The bank, operating under strict Austrian secrecy laws, had sought business from a company that set up off-shore trusts, so the identity of the depositors remains unknown.[15]

In 2014 many investigations into Anglo continue, such as those of the Garda fraud squad, the Director of Public Prosecutions, the Director of Corporate Enforcement and Chartered Accountants Ireland, so judgement on creative accounting may be premature. Even if and when the results of these various investigations eventually become public, the saga of Anglo is likely to continue for many years. It announced losses of €17.7 billion for 2010, the worst financial results in Irish history, surpassing its own previous record. Over a two-year period it had accepted state assistance amounting to almost €30 billion. It is little wonder that in 2010 the *New York Times* posed the question: 'Can one bank bring down a country?' or that the subtitle of the *Fitzpatrick Tapes* is 'The rise and fall of one man, one bank and one country.' As in the case of Lehman Brothers, its fall could be ascribed to a lack of common sense.

RBS

Lehman Brothers and Anglo Irish Bank were not unique in lapsing into sin. Take the case of RBS, formerly Royal Bank of Scotland, a bank which briefly could boast to being the largest bank in the world before having to be bailed out by the UK Government, which eventually ended up with an 82 per cent shareholding, at a cost of £45 billion.

A recent account of its downfall identified many problems within the bank.[16] Its CEO, Fred Goodwin, was described by a senior executive as a classic bully. Most managers feared his sarcasm and rarely stood up to him. With its slogan of 'Make it Happen', the bank placed considerable emphasis on efficient execution of decisions, but much less on debating their underlying wisdom. Senior management failed to see the collapse of the property market. It had grown massively by acquisition ever since the small, conservative Royal Bank won the battle to take over National Westminster Bank, over twice its size, in 2000. It built a £350 million new head office, but lacked some basic controls. It took vast risks, particularly using derivatives in the US subprime market and commercial lending, not least through its Irish subsidiary, Ulster Bank. Finally, even though major problems were emerging in its business, it again doubled its size in October 2007 when it acquired ABN AMRO, its size then exceeding the UK national income. It had operated on the basis of avoiding excess capital, relying on short-term funding to an excessive extent.

A further more detailed account elaborates on the bank's shortcomings.[17] Goodwin's detractors variously described him as a tyrant, a 'sociopathic bully', even a sadist, running the bank as his own personal fiefdom with little control from the board and a 'semi-detached' chairman. His early bonus payment drew widespread criticism, as later did his final pension. After a dispute with the auditors, PwC, they were summarily dismissed and replaced by Deloitte.

The bank pursued the wrong type of growth. Organically, it chased increased market share, lending to 'anyone with a pulse' and taking on clients rejected by other banks. In Ireland the plan was for Ulster Bank to overtake both AIB and Bank of Ireland to become the largest bank, a policy which resulted in disastrous consequences for the quality of its loan book. Goodwin's management was conducted in a culture of fear with demanding targets imposed on managers to generate short-term profits, rather than developing profitable longer-term relationships. External growth was pursued through a strategy of unfocused acquisitions.

It might be expected that the man who had gained a fearsome reputation at Clydesdale Bank as 'Fred the Shred', a cost cutter, would insist on a high level of control. Indeed he did micromanage minute details of property management and interior decoration, but was far from frugal in other matters in which he took a close interest, such as the corporate jet and sports sponsorship. Most surprising of all the bank showed little interest in tightly controlling major areas of risk, such as derivatives.

As part of its acquisition strategy, RBS bought Greenwich Capital, a group of highly paid US traders who had earlier brought about the demise of Long Term Credit Bank of Japan through high risk trading. Backed by the financial strength of RBS they sought to establish a leading position in the subprime mortgage market, originating, distributing and trading securitised tranches of loans. As discussed in Chapter 8, derivatives are complex, high risk financial instruments. A report highly critical of the valuation model was presented to the heads of market risk, but was then suppressed. The US traders, who were to earn enormous bonuses, were granted a surprising degree of autonomy as they expanded the business at the top of the market. The UK management were to admit later that they had insufficient information about the business, just as Barings had done some years earlier. The bank also took on to its books a large tranche of securities, officially rated AAA, which turned out to be of very poor quality when the bubble burst.

The persistent deal making and acquisitions attracted much adverse media criticism. The bank was believed to be afflicted by 'the winner's curse', paying too high a price to justify the investment, particularly in the US. The share rating fell and for a period the bank desisted from further acquisitions. However, in 2007 Goodwin could not resist being drawn in to a hostile bid for ABN AMRO in competition with Barclays. RBS persisted with its consortium offer after the subprime crisis broke and the bid succeeded. But the due diligence investigation had been minimal and plenty of serious problems soon emerged. The bank was slow to realise the extent of its exposure to US subprime lending, which no amount of soothing spin could disguise indefinitely. Integration of the two groups proved much more difficult than had been the absorption of NatWest, with legal and cultural differences making rapid change particularly challenging.

Although over 94 per cent of shareholders endorsed the take-over of ABN AMRO, the bank had not arranged adequate long-term funding for the acquisition. The bank declared a £10 billion profit for 2007, followed by a loss of over £24 billion for 2008, when the global banking crisis emerged. A massive £12 billion rights issue in early 2008, the largest in UK corporate history, proved insufficient to stave off part nationalisation. The bank experienced a run on deposits and a collapse in the share price, as investors feared a serious lack of capital. The world's largest bank was forced to seek State aid to survive.

In the five years following the bailout the bank was to run up massive cumulative losses of £46 billion, a sum even greater than the Government's investment, as the chickens came home to roost. Its reputation was further badly damaged by its involvement in LIBOR and other market rigging scandals. Increasingly, it came under criticism from many quarters: disgruntled shareholders, especially those who had supported the rights issue; disaffected customers who complained about high costs for lower service, being sold unsuitable profits and not receiving normal bank credit; members of the wider public, who were shocked by the continuing high level of bonuses paid to senior management. The bank found itself under pressure to revert to a domestically-focused UK institution, serving the interests of its customers better, dramatically reducing its risk taking, radically tackling its cost base and rewarding its management more modestly. The goal of reprivatisation and recouping the taxpayers' investment still remains a distant ambition.

The two authors portray similar pictures of RBS. The CEO was a bully with enormous powers. The bank overtraded by pursuing a policy of relentless growth, both organically and by acquisition, driven by short-term profit targets. Changing market conditions in the property markets in the US and Europe were ignored. Key controls were absent and risk management was deficient, particularly regarding derivatives and acquisitions. The bank borrowed excessively to fund its acquisitions.

To sum up the reasons for failure after the rescue by the State the new CEO, Simon Hester, who succeeded Goodwin, explained that the bank had financed itself in an unstable way, it was too highly leveraged, the strategy was unfocussed, risk controls were poor, the management process was 'a bit dysfunctional' and the bank was driven too much by profit expansion. That encompasses most of the seven deadly sins.

Conclusions

Lehman Brothers, Anglo Irish Bank and RBS were very different kinds of banks with very dissimilar histories. Lehman Brothers was a classical US investment bank, developed from a traditional partnership. Anglo Irish Bank had a much shorter history as a major competitor in its particular market with a strong focus on property lending. RBS, the only one to survive, since it was considered too big to be allowed to fail, had evolved from a historically cautious, canny Scottish bank into a major global financial force through major acquisitions.

Yet it would seem that these very different banks had committed most, if not all, of the seven deadly sins. All boards seemed to have allowed considerable latitude to their CEOs, while both Fuld and Goodwin were described as bullies. All banks were ill prepared for a downturn in the property market, whether in the US subprime sector or the Irish and UK domestic markets. In focusing on growth they had all overtraded, expanding their balance sheets very rapidly and neglecting to put in place adequate controls. They all had adopted a strategy of high short-term borrowing, neglecting to raise equity or other longer-term funding in buoyant markets, while seeking to maximise their return on equity. Risk management was weak in all cases, especially in their dangerous exposure to the property sector, while both Lehman Brothers and RBS carried large risks in complex derivatives. Certain accounting and reporting practices have been questioned: repurchase agreements in Lehman Brothers, deposits in Anglo Irish and description of the overall financial situation in the RBS rights issue.

The fact that the sins were not recognised in the marketplace at the time is perhaps most surprising. Banks typically seek to identify such weaknesses in their customers, but failed to apply the same scrutiny to themselves, overruling any adverse comments and ignoring warnings from their own staff. They seemed content to report increased earnings, while remaining oblivious to the risks, ignoring in particular the potential impact of a severe economic downturn. Many 'experts' rated the banks highly and few security analysts predicted disaster. Admittedly, business failures were rare in times of strong economic growth and failures of major banks had not occurred for many years. Amazingly, too, for some time their respective share prices were slow to react to the warning signs. An analysis of the seven deadly sins may, however, explain the underlying reasons why banks ultimately fail more readily than a perusal of their annual financial statements, where these weaknesses may be hard to detect.

Businesses are most vulnerable in times of an economic downturn. It is not surprising that during a period of prolonged economic growth many managers discounted such a possibility, believing that politicians had conquered traditional business cycles. Despite their regular occurrence throughout history, bubbles can be difficult to detect, as they develop, while countries enjoy the fruits of rapid economic growth and politicians indulge in hubris, as they distribute the benefits. It is now time to examine economic cycles in general and the demise of the Celtic Tiger in particular.

CHAPTER 6

Riding the Celtic Tiger

The background to the birth of the Celtic Tiger formed the basis of Chapter 2. Its fate is described in this chapter. But to understand what happened, it needs explanation in the historic perspective of booms and busts.

Bubbles and Cycles over the Ages

There is nothing new in the concept of bubbles, which have occurred regularly over the ages. One history of bubbles described a series in the seventeenth and eighteenth centuries. The author described the infamous tulip bubble in seventeenth century Holland, where a single bulb reached a value of over 5,000 florins at the top of the cycle. The Mississippi Scheme was instigated by a Scottish gambler, John Law, who inveigled his way into the French Court and persuaded gullible investors to part with their money to make a fortune from the New World. A somewhat similar bubble developed in England, as investors were invited to make their fortune from the South Seas, which was thought to be the next El Dorado. All three bubbles gained a momentum of their own, driven by rumours and fuelled by greed.[1]

The cycle over time can be shown diagrammatically, as emotions change from rising markets to declines:[2]

Value

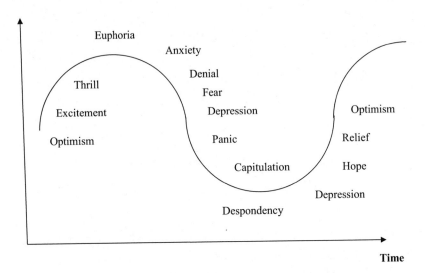

The cycle upturn commences with economic growth, inducing a mood of optimism, which, as it develops, evokes excitement in rising markets, the thrill of new found wealth and in due course a spirit of euphoria leading to its manic peak. When the bubble bursts, which may happen quite suddenly, euphoria gives way to anxiety, degenerating into denial and fear of losses, before collapsing into desperation, panic and capitulation, as the horror and distress of the downturn can no longer be ignored. This grim period, however, does not last indefinitely and the trough of despondency gives way to milder depression, followed by a wave of hope and relief, as real or imaginary green shoots of recovery are identified, until eventually the spirit of optimism returns, thus restarting the cycle, which inexorably leads again to what Alan Greenspan termed 'irrational exuberance'. Perhaps the most surprising feature of traditional cycles is the shortness of the collective public memory and loss of common sense, as the animal spirits of greed and fear overcome rational analysis.

The best known and most devastating of more recent crashes in the last century occurred in Wall Street in 1929.[3] The prosperity and excesses of the 'Roaring Twenties' had to end sometime. In the boom years borrowings increased with traders buying on margin and highly leveraged investment trusts being offered for sale. A leading economist stated that stocks had reached a permanent higher plateau. Sceptics were derided or ignored, while any proclaimed successful trader was treated as a guru.

The crash commenced in October 1929, but by 1932 Wall Street had lost almost 90 per cent of the value from its high point. No amount of repeated assurances that the fundamentals were sound or efforts at market support succeeded in stopping the slide. The euphoria which had accompanied the speculative orgy at the height of the boom had given way to denial, fear, anxiety, desperation and panic. As panic spread vast fortunes were lost, frauds were uncovered and some ruined investors resorted to suicide. While high leverage creates fortunes in a bull market, it can prove devastating in a bust.

The Great Crash finally gave way to capitulation and was followed by a deep depression, which was heralded by the failure of an Austrian bank, Kredit Anstalt, and only finally disappeared with the outbreak of the Second World War. Economists searched for remedies and a Briton, John Maynard Keynes, emerged as the leading thinker. He believed that countries should indulge in 'pump priming' and spend their way out of recession. In Britain this policy brought about some recovery, as did Roosevelt's New Deal in the US. Keynes himself was well aware of the influence of 'animal spirits' and the impact of psychological factors, but some of his followers believed that if central banks adopted sensible monetary policy and Governments kept to anti-cyclical fiscal policies, involving public spending and tax cuts, the crash of 1929 need never be repeated.

With economic growth taking off after the Second World War many believed that the new gurus were right. For over seventy years there was never a crash of similar magnitude. The first oil crisis in 1973/4 had led to a stock market collapse, but was followed by a sharp recovery the following year. There were some other sharp corrections. In October 1987 problems in the Asian markets led to 'Black Monday', after which world stock markets fell by over 20 per cent in a fortnight, causing serious job losses. Ten years later in October 1997 the Dow Jones dropped over 7 per cent in one day, bringing about the closure of the New York Stock Exchange, followed by a rapid rebound. The suddenness of the fall was accelerated by automatic computerised trading which resulted in selling orders once certain losses were triggered. But with minor regulatory changes life carried on and no recession ensued.

Another bubble of dotcom companies burst in 2000, when unhappy investors discovered that technology stocks had to be valued on some rational basis, rather than the hope of some new strange paradigm. A prominent economist, later to be awarded a Nobel Prize, writing at the height of the boom, questioned the sustainability of high stock prices, indicating that it was based on indifferent thinking, emotions and misguided perceptions of conventional wisdom. He described the mood as 'Irrational exuberance,' a term coined by the Chairman of the Fed, but his warning failed to burst the bubble.[4] Nevertheless, in less than two years the NASDAQ, where most of the stocks were listed, had crashed by 78 per cent before a gradual recovery. The only comparison with the Great Crash subsequently in terms of lasting effects was the meltdown following the subprime crisis in 2007/8.

Searching for Turning Points

Investors have always been interested in turning points in the cycle. If these critical junctures, either at the apex or nadir of the curve, can be accurately predicted, it should be possible to make great fortunes. Indeed, one hedge fund, correctly calling the subprime crisis in the US, did exactly that with the assistance of a battery of highly leveraged derivatives.[5] But for most people it is easier to spot turning points with the advantage of hindsight, since typically many people, some with strong vested interests, forecast no change, as the cycle develops. A few people may be lucky and sell out at the top of a boom, but not many can spot the elusive peak with a high degree of confidence.

Economists are seldom experts at predicting turning points in a cycle. When Queen Elizabeth, while visiting the London School of Economics in the aftermath of the global financial crisis of 2008, asked why it had not been foreseen by economists, no answer was readily forthcoming. In fact, historically, few academic economists, with rare exceptions such as the Irish born eighteenth century mercantilist Richard Cantillon and more recently John Maynard Keynes, have been successful speculators. In practice, economists rarely researched trade cycles during the era of prosperity. One US professor, Hyman Minsky, ignored by his peers during his lifetime and considered to be a maverick, did take an interest in the topic. He argued that financial systems were inherently volatile, moving in a pattern from stability to fragility, followed by a crisis. Since the recent financial crisis his work has gained in popularity and turning points have been named 'Minsky Moments'.

Minsky linked cycles to banking, since the expansion of credit was needed to fuel the boom and a contraction of credit invariably followed, as banks sought to restore order. He distinguished between three types of lending. 'Hedge' lending exists in a stable economy and sees borrowers able to pay interest and repay capital. 'Speculative' lending, on the other hand, does not allow for capital repayment, the assumption being that the asset prices will rise and so permit the loan to be rolled over. The riskiest form of lending is 'Ponzi' lending, named after an infamous Italian swindler, which does not allow for either the repayment of the loan or payment of interest until the asset is sold, when there may or may not be sufficient funds to repay the outstanding debt.[6]

Ponzi investment scams entail the age old trick of creating a bubble by puffing up performance, while using later subscriptions to pay off sellers – robbing Peter to pay Paul. It comes to an abrupt end when there are no new subscribers and the bubble bursts. The principle has been employed in schemes from the traditional chain letter to more complex frauds. Surprisingly, such schemes can continue undetected for long periods, particularly in rising markets accompanied by ample liquidity.

The most famous recent example was perpetrated by the US financier Bernard Madoff, uncovered in 2007. Some observers, incredulous of the strong consistent returns reported over many years and the absence of the usual financial footprints, reported their suspicions to the authorities. Nevertheless, it was only when his sons reported him that the massive $65 billion fraud was uncovered.[7] New funds had been supplied by feeder funds which had failed to check out the Madoff financial investment scheme with due diligence, perhaps sometimes mesmerised by the large commissions they earned. When markets fall sharply, there is often a dash for cash with the result that Ponzi investment scams, like Ponzi lending, can run suddenly into severe difficulties. On a smaller scale in Ireland, Breifni O'Brien was jailed in 2014 for running a private Ponzi scheme for friends and casual acquaintances.

A follower of Minsky was to apply his analysis of bubbles to the recent financial crisis. He endorsed the instability of financial markets, caused by the expansion and contraction of credit by the banks. The role of central banks should have included a willingness to prick property bubbles, but they had been reluctant to do so, protesting that they could not outguess the markets. Accordingly, they unwisely relied on the efficiency of markets, which were expected to reflect the real value of property and only intervened once the downturn arrived. If stability is to return to the system, it is vital that central banks recognise and contain them by constantly monitoring credit available in the economy.[8]

It is now time to consider how cycles and bubbles apply to the Irish case and how lenders contributed to the crisis, especially since Minsky firmly places credit creation at centre stage.

The Tiger Bounds Forward

The birth, growth and eventual demise of the Celtic Tiger have been well recorded.[9] Timing its birth in the year 1994, when the term was first used, in a booming world economy Ireland had eventually started to achieve rapid economic growth. Over the next seven years it averaged nearly 8 per cent per annum. Over 500,000 jobs were created and unemployment fell from 16 per cent to just over 4 per cent. Every broad indicator appeared strong: consumption and investment boomed, while Government borrowing declined as deficits turned into surpluses and exports surged.

There was no shortage of parties seeking to claim responsibility for this massive turnaround. Politicians praised their economic management and ability to make the most of EU membership.

Business and trade union leaders pointed to industrial peace as a consequence of wise national understandings over pay increases. Teachers boasted of the well-educated labour force which attracted overseas investment in new industries. It would seem churlish to point out that economic policy was overly expansive, that generous wage increases would lead to loss of competitiveness or that foreign industrialists found an inadequate supply of scientists and information technology specialists. The country found a new self-confidence, frequently being extolled as a great success story and a role model for small open economies which wanted to attract global businesses.

Indeed, much of the economic growth must be attributed to the success of the IDA in attracting foreign multinationals, particularly from the US, to set up manufacturing plants in Ireland, which could provide generous tax allowances, a low rate of corporate tax at 12.5 per cent and copious grants for the creation of employment. Ireland did not have a long industrial history with adversarial industrial relations, which was an advantage to new incoming industries in sectors such as technology, pharmaceuticals and medical devices. It did have a supply of English speaking graduates and was well placed to serve the European market.

A further part of the explanation must be that Ireland was catching up with the rest of the EU and was bound to benefit from its membership and access to new markets. It also had a favourable population structure with a large number of young people of employment age, reversing years of a high dependency ratio. In particular, Irish women were entering the labour force in large numbers, enabling it to grow quickly. In any case it made it more difficult to justify special claims for Ireland to act the poor mouth and claim special grants from the EU, once the Irish GDP per head exceeded the EU average and the country enjoyed low levels of unemployment.

As part of this economic growth there was a need to build new factories, as well as houses for an increasing number of immigrants. Naturally, the building and construction sector thrived in the face of increased demand. House prices rose strongly, while parents complained of the difficulty of placing their children on the housing ladder. Perhaps they should have realised in this game, as well as ladders, leading to the top, there can be snakes, returning to the bottom of the board.

The Tiger Stumbles

The impressive growth in house prices paused in 2001. In part this was a reflection of changes in the world economy. The burst of energy required to tackle the millennium had evaporated, the dotcom bubble in Silicon Valley had exploded, while the attack on the World Trade Centre had sapped American confidence. Domestically an outbreak of foot-and-mouth disease in the UK badly affected Irish agriculture. Competitiveness had also been reduced in the high growth era. Residential property prices fell and the Government feared that it was battling a slowdown. It did not wish to end the property boom and introduced measures to restore confidence by increasing interest relief for investors and reducing stamp duty, thereby adding fuel to the fire.

Many cheerleaders voiced their general approval, as they enjoyed the fruits of their new found wealth. Politicians of most parties were to the fore, preferring to act out the role of Santa Claus than the miserly Scrooge, when facing the electorate. A minister for finance was reputed to have stated in 2002 that when he had the money, he would spend it and when he did not have it, he would not. The Taoiseach later led the way, proclaiming that 'the boom was getting boomier' and advising moaners to commit suicide.[10]

Most economists, especially those employed in the private financial sector, endorsed the broad lines of Government policy, predicting at worst a 'soft landing' for the property market. The media with strong advertising revenue and estate agents with rising commissions had a strong vested interest in keeping the party going. There were a few siren voices which warned of trouble, but they were lost in the general excitement and treated as mavericks by the banks.

One economist, who had warned of its dangers at the time, has since explained the background.[11] Ireland in the 1990s experienced enormous economic growth, based on improved competitiveness in the heyday of the Celtic Tiger. However, from 2000 onward growth continued solely based on a boom in construction. Ireland went from deriving a normal 4–6 per cent of its national income from house-building in the 1990s to 15 per cent in 2006-7, with a further 6 per cent coming from other construction. Bank lending to the non-financial private sector rose from a modest 60 per cent of GNP in 1997 to 200 per cent in 2008 (or around 270 per cent if securitised mortgages are included), while deposits only amounted to 125 per cent. Irish banks were more exposed to commercial real estate in 2007 than Japanese banks were in 1989 at the height of their property boom.

Ireland went from completing around 30,000 housing units in 1995 to more than 60,000 units in 2007. Traditional mortgage finance rose from up to three times the main family income to 10 times for a new house in 2006 or 17 times for a second-hand house. Traditionally, building societies advanced 65–75 per cent of the cost of a new house, but in 2006 only 24 per cent of first-time buyers had loan-to-value ratios of less than 80 per cent, while 64 per cent exceeded 90 per cent, including 30 per cent which had 100 per cent. The term of mortgages increased from a traditional 25 years to 35 or even 40 years in some cases. Clearly the banks had enormously increased the riskiness of their housing loans and would experience big problems with negative equity, when house prices had fallen by over 50 per cent, as they often had by as early as 2011. The problems were exacerbated by the fact that the banks had offered a large volume of unmatched 'tracker' mortgages, which they were obliged to fund at a significant loss, as soon as their funding costs exceeded the low rates offered on such mortgages.

An important aspect of the boom was the funding of the banks. In 1999 under the European Monetary Union the Irish pound's rate of exchange was irrevocably fixed to the euro. Irish interest rates had converged with German interest rates, precluding the Government from increasing interest rates to curb inflation. When the new notes and coins were introduced in 2002 Ireland became an increasingly attractive destination for Eurozone banks which wished to participate in the success of the Celtic Tiger. It was not necessary to open up bank branches, but instead funds could be borrowed on the interbank market without any exchange risk. When Irish banks could not satisfy their funding domestically, they could resort to German banking sources to finance their needs.

The Tiger Falls

From March 2007 in the light of the international property slow-down house prices in Ireland started to fall. To finance their enormous growth banks increasingly came to rely on overseas sources through the interbank market and bond issues. When these markets dried up in the international financial crisis following the subprime collapse in the US, Irish Banks suffered severe liquidity problems. The lending problems were compounded by the banks' poor funding of their own growth, failing to raise equity when stock markets were firm, over-reliance on the short-term interbank market and a reluctance to tackle their inflated cost base. The Celtic Tiger was badly wounded, finding its life blood cut off.

Eighteen months later, in the aftermath of the fall of Lehman Brothers in the US, international confidence collapsed. The threat of bank failure was imminent and the Government, as mentioned in Chapter 1, took the decision to save the banks by an enormous guarantee of depositors and bondholders. For most observers, ultimately, this marked what was to be the final demise of the tiger.

The Casualties

Fatally wounded tigers can still inflict enormous pain on those unwise enough to cross their paths. The first casualty was the property owner who was to see values halve, which meant insolvency for some who had borrowed heavily and prolonged hardship for many others who found themselves trapped in negative equity.

The next casualty was the banking system. With the recapitalisations in the spring of 2011 the enormous cost of the banking bailout became clearer. As already outlined in Chapter 1, the capital required to recapitalise the six Irish banks amounted to approximately €64 billion, and the total losses including the overseas banks exceeded €100 billion, making it one of the most expensive crises in history. All six Irish banks fell under varying degrees of state ownership with two of them being wound down, a third merged and the bond ratings of the remainder severely reduced by Moody's.

Suffering spread quickly to business and the wider public, as the country entered the 'Great Recession'. One consequence of the banking crisis was that the banks were short of capital and therefore were unable to lend. The inevitable result was the credit crunch. Businesses with perfectly acceptable business plans were refused credit and consequently faced failure. Irish industry was starved of working capital and many viable businesses were forced into insolvency. It was a national disaster, which ultimately caused massive unemployment and a rapid rise in emigration.

The Government's fiscal policy became a further casualty. While initially the ratio of Government debt to GDP was low, this quickly changed with enormous deficits. Excessive reliance on property-related taxes meant that revenue streams diminished swiftly, while social protection costs increased with rising unemployment. Risks to the banks' funding position and risks to sovereign financial health remain, as an IMF report elegantly stated, were 'elevated and highly correlated'.

Another serious casualty was the independence of the State. Two years after the granting of the guarantee, the Government found itself unable to carry on its business, as it was running out of funding. Irish borrowing costs rose markedly and effectively decoupled from those of Germany and other strong euro members. Spin doctors might deny the problem, but ultimately Ireland could not resist the power of the bond markets, which eventually ceased to provide finance to Ireland so that the country was obliged to seek emergency funding from the European Central Bank. Despite many protestations to the contrary, it was forced to ask for assistance from the Troika: The EU, The ECB and the IMF. Ireland had now forfeited its economic sovereignty and was obliged to rely on the kindness of strangers, in turn unburdening some of its problems onto the struggling euro.

The final casualty was the faith of the public in the overall system, especially from the perspective of equity. As householders struggled to meet their mortgage payments, it seemed that rich and powerful developers were able to enjoy a much higher life-style, whether or not they had been technically declared bank-rupt. When NAMA was set up, the public was told that develop-ers would be pursued to repay their debts in full. While there was little available information available, due to the opaque nature of NAMA, suspicions abounded that developers were not treated as harshly as ordinary members of the public were when they dealt with their banks. As the liquidator of IBRC sold off large chunks of its loan portfolio, the possibility arose for developers to reach deals to obtain write-offs, while generating a quick profit for the new holders of the loans. It appeared that at the end of the day the greatest transfer of wealth since the foundation of the State had taken place at the expense of the taxpayer.

Who Killed the Tiger?

The Celtic Tiger had wrought considerable damage in its demise, but who should carry the blame for slaying this animal, which had mesmerised the country and many others around the world? The search was on for the killer and those scavengers which fed off the carcass of the wounded beast. Many commentators placed much of the blame on the politicians and the Financial Regulator.[12,13,14] A former property practitioner exposed the spin of economists and estate agents in predicting a 'soft landing'.[15] A prominent journal-ist and independent politician[16] identified many parties collabo-rating to inflate the bubble: banks, developers, stockbrokers, es-tate agents, government and media. The Central Bank Governor pinned the primary responsibility on the door of brokers, auditors and accountants, as well as the Regulator and the bank manage-ment. But no party is totally innocent. The Central Bank itself had repeatedly reassured the public that the Irish banks were well capitalised.

Yet, if Minsky's analysis is accepted, the real culprits in the dra-ma were the banks and the poisonous weapon employed for the death was bank credit, enabling developers to expand in a reckless manner and create the bubble. The other players were merely ex-tras in the drama who benefited from the success of the tiger and stood idly by or even encouraged the villains to spread their deadly venom.

In view of the enormous economic distress caused by the property crash, avoidance of future bubbles must be a priority of the Central Bank. In this case the Central Bank should monitor bank credit closely and ensure that no bank has an excessive exposure to the property and construction sector in general and the speculative building sector in particular. This would require an examination of current definitions of property lending to ensure that all loans for the purchase of buildings by, for example, professional firms, are appropriately designated. No bank should be permitted ever again to build up an exposure such as that reached by Anglo Irish Bank, nor should the banking system have such a concentration of risk to the sector.

Kathleen Ní Houlihan, as Ireland has been romantically described, has been dangerously mauled by the Celtic Tiger, is now severely ill and her children face a prolonged fall in their living standards or in some cases destitution. Her freedom of action is seriously constrained, given that independent monetary policy has been removed and fiscal policy is set by her creditors. When she left the bailout in late 2013, there remained plenty of creditors peering nervously over her shoulder, proffering their advice. The challenges facing the country and policy alternatives are reviewed in Chapter 16.

The banks have much to answer for over the conduct of their business during the Celtic Tiger era. Could their traditionally prudent lending have degenerated into speculative and then Ponzi lending over a few short years and, if so, why did that happen? If the primary responsibility for the debacle does indeed reside with directors and senior management of the banks, it is time to assess how well they conducted their core business – the lending of money.

CHAPTER 7

The Fundamental Rules of Lending

I started in corporate lending with no formal training. As an accountant with an MBA and some corporate finance experience, I was expected to be able to read a set of accounts and assess a business proposition. Reading files of different loans it soon became clear what was expected in any application. The same questions needed to be asked and satisfactory explanations given, if the credit was to be approved.

The Traditional Lending Fundamentals

The fundamental questions should be obvious to both lenders and borrowers:

- Who exactly is the borrower?
- How much capital is required?
- How long is it needed for?
- How will it be repaid?
- What happens if things go wrong?

Retail bankers sometimes spoke of the '4 Cs'. These were: Character, Capital, Capacity to repay and Collateral. Under 'Character' they would examine the trustworthiness of the borrower. For 'Capital' they would check the respective contributions of the applicant and the bank to the total amount required. In respect of

'Capacity to repay' they needed to assess the cashflow projections and the time period needed. Finally, 'Collateral' demanded an evaluation of the available security, if for any reason the loan ever had to be called in.

The overall evaluation rarely required rocket science. More often it was sound common sense and an ability to say 'No' when any aspect could not be satisfied adequately. If, for instance, the borrower was deemed untrustworthy it was best to decline the business. I recall one branch manager telling me that a certain local businessman was not to be trusted and he duly advised his successor not to let him into the bank, even if he wanted to open a deposit account! The advice was disregarded and the new manager lived to rue the day when the individual caused the bank a serious loss.

The purpose of the credit had to be clear. Bridging loans with no definite exit were frowned upon, as were working capital facilities which should be funded by retained profits. If there was any taint of illegality, there could be immense problems, particularly where it breached Section 60 of the 1963 Companies Act, which prohibited lending money to a company to buy its own shares, whether directly or indirectly, except for a bank in the normal course of its business.

Common sense set a reasonable limit to the amount any individual should be able to borrow. People now toss around the phrase 'a billion euro', as though it were an insignificant sum which might be lent to an individual, but a billion – a thousand million – is an enormous number. A billion minutes ago from today would lead back to the year 111AD, almost to the time of Christ. Margins had to take account of the risks involved. Security needed to be completed before the drawdown of the loan, since it was notoriously difficult to get the borrower's attention once the funds had been advanced.

I started to formulate principles when training corporate auditors during my time in banking. Later I was struck by how many mistakes were commonly made by large banks. One particular instance was the Goodman meat group, whose imminent failure in 1990, following Iraq's invasion of Kuwait, led to the introduction of the Irish examinership legislation, since it was considered by the Government too important a business for Irish farming to be allowed to fail. Its troubles were widely reported and so there was sufficient information in the public domain to use it as a case study.[1]

There were a total of 33 banks providing financing of £683 million on an uncoordinated bilateral, rather than a syndicated, basis. There was a disturbing amount of talk of irregularities concerning the conduct of the business in the press. Many bankers had never met Larry Goodman or seen his accounts. The company was unlimited, but Goodman himself was not personally liable, since the shares were held through an offshore trust. Mostly the banks thought they were lending short-term funding to cover the purchase of cattle, but Goodman was building up large shareholdings in two UK food companies, Unigate and Beresford. Doing business in Iraq had traditionally entailed an extremely high level of risk and much publicity was given to the withdrawal of export credit guarantees by the Government. They lent to different companies within the group and had conflicting interests when failure threatened. Apparently, many banks were attracted by what were high margins, compared to what was normal in London, but they failed to understand properly the risks they were taking. The larger the borrowing requirement, the easier it was for sophisticated international banks to ignore lending fundamentals.

The Dubious Side of Building and Construction

The construction industry was always a complex industry for lenders. Tax problems were such that the State introduced legislation to enable taxation to be deducted at source from subcontractors, who formerly received 'lump' payments. Structural problems could arise in buildings where buyers were rash enough to buy properties off the plans. Local authorities insisted on bonds, which obliged developers to complete estates after the houses had been sold. Planning permissions were sometimes improperly obtained, as the jailing of a prominent lobbyist revealed. The image portrayed by the tribunals or the Galway race tent suggest that undesirable practices have not been totally eliminated.

While the risks overall were high, they varied depending on the particular element of the building chain selected. Developing the services on sites with planning permission and selling them on was relatively low risk. Building houses on a speculative basis was deemed riskier, since sales were notoriously difficult to predict. Buying land without planning permission and hoping to obtain high density planning permission was the riskiest of all. Flats or apartments were riskier than housing, since they usually needed to be built all at the same time.

With offices and shopping centres large profits were possible, since the valuation was based on a multiple of the rent achieved. The risk was greatly reduced if a prime tenant were signed up or, in the case of a shopping centre, if a supermarket chain were obtained as an anchor tenant. The rent should never reduce, since leases were over 21 or 35 years, usually with upward only rent reviews every three or five years and no break clauses for the tenant. They were also drawn up on a full repairing basis, so that the tenant bore that risk too.

The 20 'C's of Credit

Derived from the Goodman case study, I developed a rather more extensive list of 20 'C's, providing four for each of the following five fundamental questions:[2]

- Who is the borrower?

- What kind of business?

- How much?

- Repayment?

- Terms & Conditions?

The principles would not have been considered very controversial by bankers 25 years ago, with most banks applying them in a sensible and consistent fashion. A checklist of questions to be considered in any loan application is set out in the appendix. The model has been successfully employed by bankers overseas, but was not used in Ireland, where the banks had their own expertise and systems. Training in credit was considered a core competence best conducted by line management. In the following example the 20 'C's are applied to financing building and property development in an Irish context.

Who is the Borrower?

1. Character or Culture

Banks traditionally examined carefully the 'character' of the borrower. The old adage was, if the borrower could not be trusted, the loan should not be made. In larger organisations the culture of the business would be similarly important. In an industry like property development, over the years, there have been matters which would suggest a cautious approach to lending in a high-risk industry. Historically it has been a cyclical business, where large fortunes were often made and lost as high spending developers moved from boom to bust, without always adopting best practices, too often taking legal and fiscal shortcuts. Developers tend to run their businesses personally and privately. They can be driven by ego, collecting trophy assets, such as homes, helicopters and jets. They are tough, entrepreneurial and willing to take large risks, providing they can obtain the funding.[3]

2. Competence

The skill of being a successful developer is more than the skill of constructing and selling houses, flats or offices. The developer, either alone or with the help of a small group of professional employees, must buy the property in the right location at a reasonable price, obtain the appropriate planning permission and manage the risk that sales might be slower than expected. The developer must be able to deal with the inevitable cyclical downturn and avoid being left with large illiquid work-in-progress, which may have been purchased as part of a land bank for future developments. The existence of unsold estates in remote rural locations suggests that not all developers had this competence.

3. Continuity of Management

Banks lending to SMEs have usually concerned themselves about succession in 'one man bands'. The question is asked: What would happen if he (it is normally 'he' in the male-dominated construction industry) walked under a bus? Where there is no management succession it would be normal to limit the bank's exposure with a conservative cap. Judging by the enormous scale of the lending to small organisations, centred on a single entrepreneur, not all banks concerned themselves with this risk.

4. Corporate Constitution

Many building groups are complex legal entities, often comprising a myriad of associated companies. It is quite common for each development to be undertaken by a different company, not necessarily legally connected to a holding company. The failure of any one development will thus not necessarily collapse the entire group. Cash, of course, can be quickly moved among the companies as required. It would be a foolish banker who does not obtain a full picture of the legal structure of the group.

What Kind of Business?

5. Customers and Competitors

All businesses should understand the needs of their customers: for the speculative builder this implies the market for houses and offices in Ireland. It seems incredible that anybody could believe that there was a sustainable demand for 70,000 housing units per year. Even more questionable was construction in markets outside of Ireland where the Irish builder was competing with locals who were better positioned to understand the limitations and complexities of the market. There is more to successful competition than having the largest cheque book and acquiring poor sites at exorbitant prices.

6. *Controls over Cash and Costs*

Building booms have often been accompanied by rising costs of labour and materials. The availability of skilled tradesmen from Eastern Europe and elsewhere may have limited labour cost increases, but excessive competition between banks and low interest rates led to massive increases in site costs. In boom times, when high margins were available on sales, many developers disregarded cost control in an attempt to complete construction as quickly as possible. The wise developer also would not have focused on building for tax breaks and would have sold on sites when cashflow tightened.

7. *Capacity to Contract*

Those developers with a successful record and a portfolio of investment properties clearly are well placed to meet the downturn by reducing their borrowing exposure. Evaluating the quality and spread of investment properties is critically important. Developers may differ on valuations, and be reluctant to incur losses, but so long as any market exists, there may be a way to trade out of a property crash with surplus assets, if they have both the capacity and will to contract.

8. *Credibility of Financial Statements*

The reliability of their audited accounts is a key feature in assessing the record of property developers. Builders' accounts are often not easy to interpret due to the presence of a large amount of work-in-progress. The absence of consolidated accounts or poor quality information from operations outside the Irish jurisdiction may also present problems. Where there have been unexplained cash drawings or distancing of assets, tax issues can arise.

How Much Should be Advanced?

9. *Cause or Purpose and Term of the Loan*

Some property loans are inherently riskier than others. A loan to a builder to construct houses for a local authority is relatively low risk. A loan to a developer to buy a site for which no planning permission exists and repayment is dependent on obtaining higher density than is available under zoning regulations is extremely speculative, particularly if building finance must be arranged subsequently. Schemes which are focused on tax breaks must be commercially justified. The buy to let market also is very vulnerable to a downturn in demand. The term of the loan should be consistent with its purpose, so when the purpose is highly speculative a short-term loan may be inappropriate, if lengthy planning delays are anticipated.

10. Capital Needed in Total

Estimating building costs realistically is something of an art practised by quantity surveyors. Development of the site and provision of services may run into unforeseen problems, while material or labour prices may increase unexpectedly. Prudence may dictate that the lender should assess the total capital required for all of the group developments, where cash can be transferred between group companies and work undertaken from elsewhere in the group. A conservative limit should be set to what any one developer should borrow in total.

11. Capital Contribution of the Borrower

The loan that any bank is willing to advance will be governed by what it wishes to lend to the sector, the maximum it will advance to any single developer and the amount put up by the developer himself. The Irish banking sector as a whole massively over-lent to the construction sector, advancing a greater percentage of total credit to the sector than even the Japanese banks achieved at the height of their bubble. Prudent limits to individual borrowers seem to have been overlooked on occasions and an ever increasing loan to value advanced.

12. Concentration of Risk

Traditionally, when borrowers sought facilities in excess of the prudent maximum level for a single bank to grant, the facility could be provided on a syndicated basis. The lead bank would arrange the terms and monitor the loan on behalf of the members of the syndicate and also coordinate the creditors. In this way it was possible to avoid overly exuberant competition between banks and a race to the bottom in terms of credit standards. To judge from recent banking results this means of reducing risk was not widely enough employed.

When Repaid?

13. Commitments

Obtaining a complete list of repayments for a single developer may prove no easy task. With multiple banks, multiple companies and multiple projects in different jurisdictions the complexities can grow. Yet, without a clear overall picture, the lender is unlikely to be able to assess realistically the prospects of repayment. In addition to building loans there may be substantial other financial commitments connected to the primary home, holiday homes or personal loans for anything from helicopters to yachts or racehorses.

14. Contingencies

The building industry seems to have its share of legal disputes, to judge by the number of cases appearing in the Irish courts. Some relate to the quality of building, such as the cracking of foundations or flaws in compliance with safety regulations; others seem to relate to the terms of the loan or involve disputes over payments due to suppliers or the Revenue. Naturally, the repayment schedule should cover all eventualities, including the crystallisation of contingent liabilities.

15. Comprehensive Cashflow Projections

To ascertain whether the borrower can honour all repayment commitments and contingent liabilities, a master cashflow projection is required. The difficulty is likely to centre on the timing and prices of sales, where conservative assumptions are required. In any event there needs to a considerable cushion should the expected sales fail to materialise. Where the forecasts were naively optimistic, adherence to the original term becomes improbable. In these cases the bank may have to follow its money to minimise losses. Traditionally, neither the roll-up of interest nor the granting of non-repayable or 'evergreen' loans was commonly permitted.

16. Current Trading

If proper controls are to be maintained over the loans, current trading needs to be monitored through the regular production of good quality management accounts. If this takes place the bankers should be well positioned to take swift action when the inevitable downturn occurs. If the banks place a greater priority on growing their loan books than in monitoring performance, loan impairment and losses can be anticipated. Monitoring problematic loans in many cases appears to have been far too limited.

What Terms and Conditions?

17. Conditions of Drawdown

There were two effective ways of limiting losses through sensible restrictions on the 'drawdown' or availability of loans. The first was that security was to be completed before funds were advanced. Suitable solicitors' undertakings to complete security were sometimes permitted, but only for a short period. The relaxation of this standard has led to serious losses with multiple commitments improperly given over single properties. The other safeguard was the use of revolving credit facilities with suitable security cover, together with independent verification of the work completed. If sales were slow, developers were not able to obtain further finance and were obliged to cease building.

18. Continuing Covenants

As well as restrictions on drawdown, borrowers were obliged to satisfy covenants on issues such as profitability, gearing and liquidity on a continuing basis. The initial reluctance of some banks to realise security would suggest either that loans were advanced on a 'covenant lite' basis or that bankers were slow to react to the down-turn, which would be consistent with their dubious reassurances about the adequacy of their stress tests and expectations of a soft landing.

19. Collateral or Security

Few bankers relish realising security, which is usually the consequence of poor lending in the first instance. Where the security is illiquid property realistic valuations and ample cover are vital. Sadly, the failure to take adequate security has led to massive loan impairments. The provision of non-recourse loans, where the developer is not personally liable, seems to be particularly unwise, since the borrower may elect to walk away from a problematic situation.

20. Contribution to Profits or Margin

Traditionally, loans to builders have always attracted higher interest charges than less risky industries. However, no commercial rate can compensate for a poor quality loan book. Where banks take an equity position in a development, the contribution is more difficult to evaluate, while a potentially serious conflict of interest exists if the project experiences difficulties. The ultimate question to be answered is whether the lender's margin is adequate in light of the risks inherent in the proposal?

The Problems with Unreliable Financial Statements

During my lending days there was often a problem with the reliability of the annual accounts of smaller businesses. Despite the fact that they were audited, owner managers produced them mainly to satisfy the requirements of the tax authorities and profits could be materially understated. Bankers could learn from experience which auditors could be relied upon. I recall one sole trader showing me his accounts for the first time and seeing concern in my face asked me to explain the problem. I told him that his balance sheet showed an excess of liabilities over assets and that he was bust. He assured me that he had an extra £250,000 of stock excluded from the accounts.

The difficulty with unreliable accounts was that it was difficult to satisfy the reader on any of the 20 'C's. Not only was the trustworthiness of the borrower in question, but also his competence, since the track record was unclear. The financial strength was difficult to assess and there was always the possibility that a large tax liability could emerge, making it difficult to evaluate the repayment prospects. In such circumstances it was prudent to limit any exposure and ensure that ample direct security was available before any credit was granted, backed up by a personal guarantee.

While some developers produced reliable accounts, this was not always the case. Even though the absolute figures in the accounts were large, they often resembled those of a smaller owner-managed business. A high lifestyle could be supported by undisclosed cash drawings. Interpreting the accounts of even the best performers was difficult, because of the large figure for work in progress, which could sharply decline in value when problems emerged in the course of the development.

The Collapse in Standards

During the property boom there can be no doubt that lending standards in Irish banks had collapsed and there were serious deficiencies in lending. It is difficult to name any of the 20 principles listed above which had not been breached by banks. The failings, as described in Chapter 1, were devastating and the criticisms originated from well positioned authorities. Both the Chairman and the CEO of NAMA outlined appalling weaknesses, while the Governor of the Central Bank outlined major deficiencies in five loans from five different banks. For the Chairman to accuse the banks of 'reckless abandonment of the basic principles of credit risk and prudent lending' leaves the public in no doubt of the gravity of the decline and constitutes a truly shocking indictment on the management of Irish banks.

It seemed therefore that the problems were not limited to any one bank. The fact that NAMA took on large loans, based on economic value, at a discount of almost 50 per cent indicates the depth of the catastrophe. Many such loans could reasonably be described as Ponzi loans, where repayment of interest and capital from the outset should have been considered doubtful, if traditional credit control standards had been observed. It appears that cashflow analysis for repayment prospects had given way to simplistic calculations of loan-to-value exposure and a naive faith in the value of personal guarantees. Loans seem to have been poorly structured and inadequately monitored, while the policy of equity release compounded the problems and massively increased the overall risks.

Conclusions

The problems could and should have been avoided. Property bubbles are not new, but formerly they did not imperil the banking system. When the Gallagher property empire collapsed in 1982, this did indeed severely damage confidence and Irish property prices, but banks had adhered to their traditional values, thus limiting the aftershock. Loans to individual developers, together with any connected parties, were capped at prudent levels, while reasonable loan-to-value limits were observed. Risks were spread and exposure to property limited. Security was usually ample and put in place strictly prior to credit availability with only occasionally reliance on solicitors' undertakings for short periods. Above all, further drawdowns of the loans were prevented until certain sales targets were achieved. Accordingly, when markets tightened, funding under revolving credits was withdrawn, so that both banks and borrowers stayed out of trouble.

The source of my error in believing that the UK property crash would never be repeated here is now clear. I had believed wrongly that the traditional values around credit were deeply embedded in Irish banking. Lending in the 1980s was what Minsky termed 'hedge' lending, where the borrower is expected to pay interest and repay capital without relying on increasing property prices.

What is still unclear is why Irish bankers degenerated into Ponzi lenders. Values do not normally change overnight in any organisation, and prudent risk management was one such basic value in banking. To find out what changed it is necessary to examine the culture within banking and the nature of the competition between banks. But, before addressing these issues in Part 3, it may be helpful to understand how risks are spread within the system.

CHAPTER 8

How Contagion Spreads Risk

The world has long known about runs on banks which can lead to failure. Once confidence is lost and depositors panic by withdrawing their funds, then the bank can no longer continue to trade, even if its underlying lending business is sound. While many developed economies had not experienced a run on a major bank for years, this does not mean that it can never recur. To try to prevent a run caused by mismanagement banks are obliged to hold certain volumes of liquid assets, which can be converted into cash should an emergency arise. In addition they are obliged to maintain a certain amount of capital relative to their assets as a shield against insolvency.

Bank runs endanger the banking system, but in former times they would normally stop at national boundaries. But contagion too is not a new feature of finance. Governments had experienced it in the Asian crisis of 1997. In the era of globalisation, financial innovation and hedge funds the speed at which a problem can spread increases significantly in both small and large banking systems.

The Icelandic Case

Iceland provides a good example of how this can happen. As described in Chapter 3, Icelandic banks had expanded aggressively, financing large deals, particularly in the UK. By 2006 the assets of the banks had grown to 800 per cent of GDP. They had managed to avoid subprime lending, but nevertheless experienced funding difficulties, first in 2006, which they overcame, and again subsequently after the subprime crisis broke.

The biggest and strongest Icelandic bank was Kaupthing, which had been awarded an AAA rating by Moody's in January 2007, shortly before the international banking crisis. The CEO of the London subsidiary explained how it failed.[1] In 2005 credit default swaps were written on the bank, which in effect is an insurance policy against the failure of the bank. This was a financial innovation introduced by J.P. Morgan ten years earlier. For Kaupthing the cost was initially a modest 0.2 per cent of the exposure. After a few unfavourable credit reports the cost rose to 1.00 per cent in what was known as the Geyser crisis, indicating a much higher default risk, as speculators lost confidence in the krona. The bank improved its liquidity by issuing bonds in different markets and the crisis passed. Nevertheless, with a balance sheet which equated to 2.5 times Iceland's GDP some investors thought the bank was too big to save by the Government, if a crisis were to recur.

When the global liquidity crisis broke in July 2007, it seemed that the bank was in relatively good shape. It had slowed its growth, enjoyed a strong capital base, held a reasonably high quality mortgage loan book with an exposure of less than 60 per cent loan-to-value and had been given a AAA rating. Corporate Icelandic loans had security cover of 200 per cent, though this would decline quickly when the investment companies found themselves in large illiquid deals. But the market realised that it was heavily dependent on wholesale funding, with the result that the cost of credit default swaps rose to 5 per cent at the start of 2008 and within months reached 10 per cent, as rumours spread and hedge funds speculated on the bank's failure. The bank reacted quickly, selling off assets and entering the internet banking market, offering depositors attractive interest rates, particularly in the UK and Holland.

After the collapse of Lehman Brothers in September, the two other main Icelandic banks fell into severe difficulties and had to be nationalised. One of the rating agencies, Fitch, reduced Kaupthing's rating to BBB, almost sub-investment grade. Deposits fled, interbank funding almost vanished and the entire Icelandic banking system came under threat. Efforts to find a major new investor failed and a mooted Russian loan to Iceland foundered. The final straw came when the UK Government failed to get assurances from Iceland to guarantee UK depositors. It passed emergency legislation to confiscate the bank assets in London and Kaupthing's London subsidiary was forced into administration, not quite a month after the failure of Lehman Brothers, as the banking system collapsed. The Icelandic banks had become too big to rescue.

The Cataclysmic Global Meltdown

When the news broke in August 2007 that serious problems in the US subprime lending were emerging, the bubble burst and trouble quickly spread in Wall Street.[2] In September the surprise failure in the UK of Northern Rock, a mortgage provider, reliant on securitisation to fund its growth, did nothing to boost market confidence. In March 2008 the brokerage house Bear Stearns had a bad debt exposure of $220 billion and was forced into a takeover by J.P. Morgan with the backing of the US Government. In September the Government agreed to bail out AIG, the insurance giant, which had a large position in derivatives, with a loan of $85 billion. At the same time in London HBOS was rescued by Lloyds in a $12 billion bid. A month later Lloyds itself was in trouble, facing part nationalisation. Even the giant Federal-sponsored mortgage issuers, Fannie Mae and Freddie Mac, were nationalised.

The crisis had lurched towards meltdown when the attempted rescue of Lehman Brothers aborted. The assets of Washington Mutual were seized by the Federal Government and sold to J.P. Morgan, making this the biggest American bank rescue in history. In London Bradford & Bingley, a subprime-focused bank, was in trouble, along with Lloyds TSB and Royal Bank of Scotland. On the European front the Dutch-Belgian Fortis experienced difficulty, while in Germany Hypo Real Estate had to be rescued by the Government. It was a meltdown of unprecedented magnitude, making some people wonder if Karl Marx's prediction that capitalism was destined to collapse from internal contradictions had some substance.

Comparisons with the Great Crash of 1929 were inevitably made. The US reacted by introducing TARP, the Troubled Asset Relief Program, a $700 billion rescue plan, but this proved controversial with many believing that the public should not bail out the private sector and was initially rejected by Congress. The authorities also brokered a shotgun wedding between Citigroup and the ailing Wachovia, while providing a $12 billion stake for the taxpayer. In the UK the Government announced that it would invest £25 billion in seven major banks, while also underwriting bank loans totalling £400 billion. It ended up owning 60 per cent of RBS and 40 per cent of Lloyds/HBOS. The troubles had now spread globally. Yamato Life went bust in Japan. The search for rescuers extended to the Middle East, when Barclays became one-third owned by the Bank of Qatar and Abu Dhabi. Credit Suisse sold a substantial shareholding to Middle East investors, while UBS followed suit and was part nationalised, as was ING in Holland and Citicorp in the US.

One way to measure the scale of the destruction left in the wake of the financial tsunami was to compare stock market capitalisations before and after the crash. In October 2007, at the peak of the market, the 54 main world stock exchanges were capitalised at $63 trillion, but 13 months later they had dropped to $31 trillion, a fall of over 50 per cent. Put another way, in late 2007 RBS bought Dutch ABN Amro for nearly $100 billion. A year later that sum would have bought six banks – Citibank ($22 billion), Goldman Sachs ($21 billion), Merrill Lynch ($12 billion), Morgan Stanley ($11 billion), Deutsche Bank ($13 billion) and Barclays ($13 billion) – with cash to spare.

Another way to measure risk was the extra amount a bank has to pay over the cost of US Treasuries, known as the 'Ted Spread'. Traditionally, this was around 0.3 per cent, but in the crisis it rose to over 3 per cent, before reaching 4.64 per cent in October 2008, if and where funds were available. This market verdict indicated that the banks had become highly risky and would inevitably lead to a credit freeze and widespread insolvencies. Yet it all led back to the subprime lending crisis and the fact that nobody knew where the losses, totalling maybe over \$1 trillion, lay. So what was the subprime crisis and how did it arise?

The Horrors of the Subprime Crisis[3]

Banks in the US lent aggressively to the American subprime mortgage market in the early 2000s. By definition, subprime borrowers, receiving 100 per cent mortgages with initial 'teaser' rates of interest of 1 per cent, would be likely to experience repayment difficulties when rates were reset, particularly if property prices were to fall. 'NINJA' loans were made to borrowers with 'No Income, No Jobs and No Assets'. 'Liar' or self-certified loans were made to people who were asked to fill in their own financial details, which were not checked by the lender. Documentation was limited and 'no doc' loans became accepted. Unfortunately, independent checks by internal or external auditors, and regulatory authorities, either failed to highlight effectively the dangers and risks involved or else were ignored.

How could such foolish lending happen in the staid world of banking? One factor was the insatiable demand from investors in securitised loans seeking higher returns, while not appreciating the risks involved. They could easily be persuaded by smart salesmen, often motivated by commissions and unconcerned whether their products were suited to the customers' needs.

Essentially, however, it happened because of the way that bankers were rewarded and the fact that the bank making the loan did not intend to retain it, but pass it on to a third party (who was a greater fool than the bank itself) through the process of securitisation. If the bank disposed of all its loans to investors, it carried no risk of incurring future losses however poor the underlying credits. Mortgage brokers could offer finance on terms that no bank would accept if the loans were to be retained on the bank's books. When the rating agencies provided the packages, known as CDOs, or collateralised debt obligations, with a strong and unjustified AAA rating, all parties appeared happy and were well rewarded in the short run. The loans themselves were administered by a third party for a modest fee. The banks made enormous profits and paid out large bonuses to their staff, usually in cash.

There existed, therefore, every incentive to advance high risk loans which could be packaged together with many other such loans, in bundles that few people could understand due to the complex slicing and dicing. These complex packages turned into deadly toxins, spreading their poison widely throughout the financial system whenever they changed hands. The system of paying large cash bonuses to individuals who originated the loans actually encouraged the spread of the practice, creating an unsavoury culture of greed which exacerbated the property bubble and ultimately led to the global credit crunch.

The Tipping Point

It may be further instructive to see how such greed and recklessness can become an epidemic which has threatened the global economy. The spread of social epidemics was set out some time ago in a popular American book entitled *The Tipping Point* by Malcolm Gladwell.[4] It has been used to explain the spread of sexual diseases, consumer fashions and even the start of the American Revolution. Only a few parties need be involved, but if the message is 'sticky' or easy to pass on, and the context favourable, the disease may tip into an epidemic.

There were few key parties involved in the spread of the subprime crisis, although the amounts of the loans involved were large. First, there were the banks, which originated, packaged and distributed the loans. They acted as 'persuaders'. Occasionally, they held on to a portion of the loans in incestuously related hedge funds, termed 'conduits' or 'structured investment vehicles', which were not consolidated in the banks' accounts, were off balance sheet and out of sight. These acted as 'connectors'. The other parties that facilitated the transactions were the rating agencies which provided a stamp of quality to the loan, certain insurers which underwrote some of the debt and the brokers who assisted in the distribution. All parties benefited from the boom, since their fees, conveniently paid by the banks, grew correspondingly. These parties acted as 'evaluators', because their involvement was likely to influence other parties.

Loans were 'sticky'. Innovations from securitisation had transformed the traditional relationships between borrowers and lenders. Banks wanted to pass on the loans, rather than raise extra capital and hold them. Investment funds wanted to hold bonds, which they considered to be low risk. The fees involved encouraged the transmission between the various parties. Doubtless too the momentum was reinforced by the tendency of banks to adopt a herd mentality, encapsulated by Chuck Prince, CEO of Citicorp, who remarked at the height of the boom in July 2007: 'As long as the music is playing, you've got to get up and dance. We're still dancing.' With only a few major financial centres, and modern electronic technology, it was easy to transfer loans around the market without being stopped at national boundaries.

The context was supportive in an opaque world with low levels of disclosure, high financial gearing and often little regulation.[5] The siren voices warning of the regulatory flaws in the system were ignored.[6] Wall Street vested interests were strong enough and sufficiently well connected to whichever political party was in power to see off its critics. Nationally, the goal of universal home ownership was lauded, so there was little political will to curb the boom.

The policy of light touch regulation discouraged intervention. The regulator believed in the invisible hand of competition, almost as an article of faith. Market forces would inhibit banks from taking undue risks, because the share price would suffer if they did. The complex technical risks inherent in derivatives often were not well understood by those responsible for managing the system. Indeed, Alan Greenspan, the doyen of regulators, advocated a policy of laissez-faire, relying on competition between the banks and a general expectation that bankers would act in the best interests of their shareholders.[7] Restrictions would be strongly opposed by the banks on the grounds that it would put America at a competitive disadvantage in what had become a global industry.

Many believed the economic policy of 'the Great Moderation' with low inflation, high growth and mild recessions had brought an end to economic volatility, thus permitting higher levels of risk taking. The authorities, adopting a hands-off approach, had been lulled into a false sense of security and were ill prepared to tackle a financial pandemic. Small wonder then that the deadly toxins could eventually be transformed into viral weapons of mass destruction, contaminating all who come into contact with them.

It was only a small step then, when it became known how badly affected various financial funds and institutions were, that confidence in the entire financial system evaporated and several long established banks themselves collapsed. The rating agencies belatedly downgraded securities and lenders demanded enhanced security, bringing down many highly leveraged funds and banks. In the ensuing crisis, blame was laid at many doors: the rating agencies, the hedge funds, the regulators and those who serviced the loans. However, the problem could not have started without the banks and the way in which they remunerated themselves and managed their organisations. Where bonuses were paid in cash or shares which can be sold immediately the incentive to disregard longer-term problems was exacerbated.

The Sinister Role of Derivatives

Financial innovation in the form of derivatives played a central role in the subprime crisis and subsequent global meltdown.[8] Derivatives are any financial instruments whose value is derived from and dependent on the value of one or more assets or events. The size of the derivatives markets had grown rapidly from the 1990s onwards, particularly in the era of low interest rates. By 2008 the world derivatives market was estimated to be in excess of $600 trillion. In due course derivatives with strange sounding acronyms were created for such dubious purposes as enabling US citizens to avoid capital gains tax, Mexican banks to bypass exchange control regulations and Japanese banks to defer recognition of trading losses, all the while generating massive fees for the investment banks which devised them.

Many people have questioned the usefulness of derivatives or emphasised their inherent risks. Paul Volcker, a former Federal Reserve chairman, had stated in 2009 that the most important financial innovation in the preceding 20 years was the Automatic Teller Machine (ATM), which dispensed cash to customers, rather than the development of derivatives to transfer risk. Warren Buffett, one of the world's most consistently successful investors, denounced them as 'financial weapons of mass destruction'.

The opaque marketplace where these instruments were traded is difficult to penetrate. The inventors were often highly numerate mathematicians known as 'quants'. But the risks were meant to be measured by VAR or value-at-risk, a statistical tool, based on 95 per cent probability and a normal distribution of risks, a model which did not stand up when many events, individually considered unlikely, occurred together. Various explanations have been offered from 'fat tail' distributions to chaos theory. Whether the model broke down because the variables were insufficiently independent or because of some dubious assumptions buried deep within the models matters little. The result was that enormous sums of money were managed without adequate risk controls. One former trader has gone further and questioned whether random events could be predicted with mathematical probabilities in the uncertain world of 'unknown unknowns', which, if accepted, would totally undermine the VAR model.[9]

The hedge funds managed by these mathematicians tended to be highly leveraged by borrowings or other means, so that successful trading multiplies the gains, but mistakes also multiply the losses. Ultimately, the mismanagement of derivative risks jeopardised the entire financial system. Even the brightest could misjudge the risks and underestimate the possibility of market failure, as demonstrated by the collapse of LTCM in 1998, whose principals included two eminent winners of the Nobel Prize in Economics, following the liquidity crisis when the Russian economy ran into problems. The models of the 'quants', for all their mathematical sophistication, could not deal with a new reality and were to fail again in 2007/9, as their funds collapsed in value.[10]

One popular derivative was the interest rate swap, whereby borrowers could agree to pay a fixed rate of interest instead of a more uncertain variable rate. However, the swaps often contained a nasty risk element. While the initial interest rate was usually very attractive, the rate could rise dramatically under certain circumstances. Corporate treasures were all too readily persuaded to take on these risky contracts by smooth talking Wall Street salesmen, who earned enormous fees and ultimately bonuses from these lucrative contracts. As time went on and more banks entered the business, derivatives became increasingly complex and the real risks harder to evaluate. In many cases there was no ready market value when traders operated in the over-the-counter market, so that reliance had to be made on obscure computer models. Banks seemed unconcerned by the fact that they were selling products which could cause their customers to 'blow up'. Over time for many banks the amounts earned from derivatives trading became the major contributor to their profits. The casino had largely taken over the investment bank.

Perhaps the most pernicious of derivative instruments was the credit default swap, or CDS. Initially they were designed as an insurance product for banks and investment funds seeking to reduce the risk of credit failure in a financial institution on which they depended. However, they were widely used by hedge funds, which had no insurable interest in the institution, other than hoping it would fail and, in so doing, generate massive profits for them. Most people would be uncomfortable if they discovered that mafia elements were taking out insurance policies on their homes or lives, since the mafia could influence events. So could the hedge funds by spreading rumours, which might not be true. The Icelandic Government was critical of hedge funds taking bets on the failure of their banks, as had been many Asian Governments ten years earlier and as Anglo Irish would also in the meltdown.

Another important feature was the presence of hedge funds in the shadow banking world, which largely escaped regulation. The success of these funds centred on the ability of the managers to outperform markets, thereby justifying the large fees paid by their customers. They had very substantial funds at their disposal and were prepared to make very large bets based on their judgements. Their defenders state that they are risk managers for professional investors, needing no bailouts when they fail, so there is no need for regulation.[11] Many others believe that they indulge in insider trading and market manipulation, amplifying risk in a crisis. Given their scale and leverage, their actions dangerously destabilised the entire system, as evidenced by the need to rescue LTCM in 1998.

George Soros, the speculator, who originally accumulated enormous wealth by anticipating the devaluation of sterling in 1992, believes that they should be banned. In his book written years before the subprime crisis, he propounded a theory of reflexivity, whereby he questioned the economists' presumption of the existence of an equilibrium and instead predicted that fluctuations would be the norm. He explained that the participants could influence outcomes, which in turn would influence their behaviour. He predicted a major collapse of the financial system.[12]

Over 20 years later he wrote to explain the current financial crisis, which he described as a super bubble imposed on top of the credit bubble created by the banks. The credit bubble gave rise to moral hazard for the banks if they were to believe that they would always be rescued. The globalisation of markets spread the problem internationally. Financial innovation and the absence of proper regulation allowed the bubble to further develop. Given the strength of these forces, a new equilibrium was unlikely to emerge in a period of prolonged financial instability.[13] He went on to describe credit default swaps as a licence to kill and recommended that they be banned. The problem of controlling or banning derivatives is, however, far from straight forward, since it would require agreement from global regulatory authorities. This still remains unfinished business and would face strong opposition from the banks.[14]

Securitisation was also a force which could lead to instability. While I was in banking Irish banks were beginning to dabble in the field. The divorce of the creation of the credit and its management always struck me as dangerous, since it blurred the responsibility for its monitoring. I could see how such loans might be administered for a small fee in good times, but where problems arose there would need to be a significant investment of time and money to recover the loans. Given the increased interconnectedness and high complexity of the large markets, the financial systems became unstable through the growth of securitisation and derivatives.

The Tragic Irish Experience

In Ireland there is no dispute as to when the damage from the banks' problems spread more widely. It occurred on 30 September 2008, when the Government took the decision to guarantee the liabilities of the Irish banks, thereby socialising them by shifting a private sector liability onto the State. But what led to that fateful decision? The events of the preceding months have been well recorded.[15]

After the subprime crisis broke the share prices of the Irish banks, in common with their peers globally, fell sharply. However, when their 2007 results were released they remained relatively upbeat and there was no case of dividend cuts. After the fall of Bear Stearns in March there was renewed selling leading to the 'St Patrick's Day Massacre', as Irish bank shares were dumped on the London market on the national holiday. Short selling accelerated the falls in their share prices and was in due course banned.

By September matters had deteriorated further. Rumours began circulating about the future of INBS. They were denied, but the rating agency Fitch downgraded the institution. The collapse of Lehman Brothers added to the panic which was spreading across the globe. Anglo Irish Bank proposed to the Government a merger with INBS to be backed by the State, but this was declined. The Minister for Finance rebuked the national broadcasting authority for stoking up fear in small savers, as the nervousness spread internationally. The State guarantee for small savers was increased from €20,000 to €100,000. AIB and Bank of Ireland sought an emergency meeting with the Government, to be attended by the Chairmen and CEOs of the two banks, together with the relevant public servants. Clearly Anglo Irish was suffering an alarming run on its deposits and the banks feared that this could spread. It was not so much small savers as larger institutions which were withdrawing their cash.

The extent of the bank guarantee, which covered all deposits, interbank loans and most bonds at €440 billion, was enormous. It could have been larger, if the two UK banks with large Irish property exposures had sought guarantee coverage for their Irish subsidiaries, Ulster Bank and Bank of Scotland (Ireland). Fortunately they refrained from requesting a similar guarantee, so whether the Government would have been obliged to cover them in the interests of fair competition was never tested. The UK's guarantees and liquidity provisions to their banks totalled £400 billion, while the US TARP rescue amounted to $700 billion, so Ireland's solution was vastly bigger in relation to the size of its population. Judging by the Minister's remarks about the cheapness of the bailout, the real magnitude of the risk seemed not to have been appreciated. A large call on the guarantee, while legally possible, was somewhat naively considered to be unlikely in the light of what was then known about the banks' solvency.

The scale of the guarantee was driven by two key factors. The first was that all major banks were to be covered, including both Anglo Irish Bank and INBS, which were deemed to be of systemic importance. In a grandiose gesture, rightly or wrongly, it was felt that no Irish bank should be allowed to fail because of the damage to confidence in the system. The other factor was that bondholders were included along with depositors. It was believed that it would be difficult to discriminate against bondholders, since they were ordinary creditors in a winding up, just like depositors. In any event, the ECB did not favour any burning of the bondholders. Under the latest EU rules, bondholders and depositors over €100,000 can now be bailed in to any rescue scheme, before the general public.

The forthcoming banking inquiry and future historians will doubtless debate whether a cheaper solution could have been found. Professor Honohan and other commentators, such as Donal Donovan and Antoin Murphy, referred to in Chapter 6, considered it the least bad option. The decision was clearly made under considerable time pressure and the misguided belief that the solvency of the Irish banks was not in question. With more time and better information a more cost effective solution might have emerged. The decision was also made unilaterally without consulting the EU in advance. Allowing Anglo Irish Bank and INBS to fail would have created havoc and displeased the EU authorities. But, if these banks were of systemic importance, since their rescue was to the benefit of the European financial system, in all fairness should not the burden have been spread more widely, as many members of the Irish public hoped when the gravity of the situation became apparent?

Irish bankers cannot reasonably blame the global financial crisis for their predicament. Ireland was not the victim of massive derivative trading by hedge funds. The financial system suffered a run on deposits, which caused serious liquidity problems, but the withdrawal of cash occurred because some shrewd depositors genuinely feared for the solvency of the institutions. The ultimate reason for the crisis was that the banks had mismanaged their risks during the property bubble, however much they might choose to deny it. Accordingly, it is to the banks' attitude to risk and to their culture that I next turn.

PART THREE:

Culture, Competition and Culpability – Revealing the Root Causes

CHAPTER 9

Retail and Investment Banks – Two Conflicting Cultures

Most people working in banks get to understand the culture of the organisation fairly quickly. They learn the kind of behaviour which is acceptable and that which is not. They discover the basic rules which must not be breached. These values are fundamental to the reputation of the business, so much so that serious breaches, such as minor acts of dishonesty, can lead to dismissal. Sometimes they are set down in mission statements, but often they are behaviours which are carefully explained to new recruits and jealously protected by senior management.

The release of the Anglo tapes in June 2013 shocked and horrified many people, not only in Ireland but throughout the world. The tape recordings of conversations between senior management of the bank revealed language and behaviour totally unacceptable to the vast majority of people anywhere. The coarseness of the language and use of vulgar slang with ruthless determination to get their own way was bad enough, as was the contemptuous attitude towards the regulatory authorities, but what was worse was the bank seeking a €7 billion loan from the State to give it some 'skin in the game', although the bank did not expect to be in a position to repay the loan right from the outset. But, if the State was on the hook, it could be expected to follow its money. For good measure they then went on to insult Germany, a major creditor of Ireland.

117

Was this the kind of behaviour the public expected from the senior management of the banks?

Traditional Retail Banking Culture

Most Irish people in bygone years regarded their bank managers as staid, respectable and conservative individuals. Along with the priest, the doctor, the teacher and the solicitor, they were considered to be the pillars of the local community. Parents would encourage their children to get a job with the bank straight from school, because it was permanent and pensionable, even if it did not offer an attractive long-term salary. In the early days of the State it was considered to offer good career prospects and was an alternative to the civil service, the ESB or Guinness' brewery. The vast majority of the employees in retail banking did not have university degrees, but did their banking exams, which provided them with their professional training and were required for promotion.

The conservative nature of the banks naturally led to friction with growing businesses seeking loans. They were not permitted the same levels of gearing or borrowing as could be found in some other countries and, when told to invest more equity, stated that none was available, whether from friends, family or institutional sources. The banks retorted that it was not their duty to take business risks, since their basic role was to protect depositors' funds. So the argument continued over the years.

In the early days pay was modest and good performance was likely to be rewarded by nothing other than a word of thanks, rather than a bonus. It was a paternalistic, male-dominated world. People working with me could recall times where the employees needed to seek permission to get married, lest they found themselves in financial difficulties which could lead them to stray. Women were expected to resign once they got married to look after their families.

The traditional ways were to change in no small measure due to the activities of the IBOA, the Irish Bank Officials Association, which improved the lot of their members and provided pay scales often better than those of their UK counterparts. Bank clerks were designated as 'bank officials' with a higher status. Most managers initially joined the IBOA and benefited accordingly, particularly after the first two bank strikes in the 1970s. They also retained an invaluable perk in that they were entitled to become insurance agents and so could personally earn useful commissions from the policies taken out by their customers. This perk was eventually bought out by the banks. The other important perk available to most employees was a cheap house loan, carrying an interest rate of only 3 per cent, when the commercial rate could be in double figures.

The influence of the IBOA diminished after the third bank strike in 1976. The banks were able to maintain a reduced service, partly through advances in technology and partly due to the fact that many senior managers were no longer IBOA members. The strike left a bitter legacy in some cases with resentment towards those who had stayed working. Nevertheless, bank employees were by then reasonably well remunerated, enjoying security of employment and a decent pension. This comfortable way of life could be endangered by dishonesty, leading to dismissal.

Retail banks continued to prosper. Their inherent strength was their deposit base which was accessed by the banks through their branch network. Deposits tended to stay with the local branch even though more competitive rates might be obtained elsewhere. I recall my father introducing me to his local bank manager in Dublin in 1963 as I started out as an undergraduate, just as his father had done for him a generation earlier. I still retain the account. Thus the branch had three generations of family accounts which to the best of my knowledge never gave them any cause for concern.

The benefit of retaining good customers' accounts was enormous to the banks, even if it were not always recognised as such. Many customers kept large credit balances on their current accounts, on which no interest was paid, thus providing the banks with free funds. There was also the endowment effect of old accounts of dead customers, which remained unclaimed, providing a permanent source of free or very cheap finance. With a strong retail deposit base any bank was well positioned to face any downturn in business.

The Wholesale Banking Culture

When the banks spread their activities into wholesale banking they recruited from a different pool, seeking in the main graduates and professionally qualified people, especially accountants, usually male. These recruits expected reasonable salaries, pensions and perks, such as a company car, over and above what was available in retail banking. There was no union involved and people were expected to work long hours, when required. They had to source funding from the interbank market for which competitive interest rates had to be paid. They might also receive bigger deposits from the branch network, which could be lost if a competitive rate were not available at the branch. They certainly had no endowment effect of free or cheap deposits. They claimed to survive on their wits, in contrast to the retail banks, which survived on their deposits.

The culture within these banks was essentially that of the merchant banks in London with which they retained close links. These banks, which varied in size from very small to large, powerful, well capitalised houses, comprised the members of the Accepting Houses Committee. This small elite club comprised the only banks traditionally permitted to guarantee commercial short-term debt issued by companies. Naturally, by putting their names to these debts they were able to charge a suitable fee. Their other main sources of income were fees for fund management and corporate finance advice associated with mergers and acquisitions, or the flotation of companies on the stock exchange. Originally set up as partnerships, they lacked the capital base to engage seriously in corporate lending. To succeed they needed to be entrepreneurial and carefully protect their reputations on which their business with their clients, as they called their customers, depended.

Big Bang and the Financial Revolution of 1986

The year 1986 heralded changes in the City of London which were to revolutionise the way banking operated there and elsewhere.[1] Change centred around three main elements. First there was the ending of the division in share dealing whereby brokers dealt with

120

the public and jobbers made the market for brokers with entities now being permitted to become market makers. As had happened in the US in 1975, the fixed rate of commission on brokerage charges was abolished and the market was opened up to full competition. Finally, banks were permitted to take shareholdings in stockbrokers' firms.

The changes had been well flagged in advance and preparations had been made over the three previous years. The result was that many partners in firms of stockbrokers made their fortunes accepting offers for their businesses from the banks, which were seeking to extend the scope of their offerings. One estimate of the total payments amounted to over £1.5 billion, which provided a vast bonanza for old and young alike.[2] Golden handcuffs were provided to encourage partners to remain on and maintain their connections, while key managers were offered enormous salaries, compared to what was normal for professional people. The old world of well-maintained relationships and old school tie networks was to disappear and inefficient businesses were destined for failure.

The ensuing revolution had long lasting consequences.[3] Fundamental was the 'disintermediation' of the banks in the role of providing funding to businesses. Bonds and short-term paper money could be issued by companies and distributed by investment bankers, thus bypassing the traditional banks offering loans. A world of brash young traders moved centre stage, pushing aside the smooth syndicate lenders in the banks. Fortunes could be made in the deregulated world with unpredictable exchange rates, high interest rates and huge trade imbalances needing to be funded.

As deregulation and liberal capitalism spread the business became truly global, operating from the three major centres of New York, London and Tokyo, together with smaller centres, such as Frankfurt and Paris in Europe, Hong Kong, Singapore and Sydney in the Far East, together with the Gulf States and Cyprus in the Middle East. With all time zones covered, around the clock trading became a reality.

Initially competition was expected from both the Japanese and the Americans, but with the fall and then stagnation of the Tokyo market, followed by increased problems in its zombie banks, the

Japanese threat receded. The Americanisation of the City of London accelerated rapidly. The US banks had first invaded London in numbers during the 1960s, as they sought to enter the lucrative eurodollar market, a large fund of dollars based outside of America, which had its base there, due to exchange and interest rate regulations in the US. From 1979 onwards, when UK foreign exchange restrictions were lifted, many UK fund managers wanted to diversify their portfolios to include American shares and US brokerage houses benefited accordingly. They could now use their financial muscle and compete head on with the UK firms, particularly if they could obtain the client lists of the existing UK establishment. They were also to change the prevailing culture of the City with their enormous remuneration packages and high fees.

The other side of the revolution was the enhancement of consumer protection. The Securities and Investment Board (SIB) was given overall responsibility for regulating financial services and set up a series of Self Regulating Organisations (SROs) to manage different parts of the industry. They were intended to raise standards and were empowered to fine offenders. Essentially, however, it was a system of self-regulation, rather than central control.

Before long it became clear that there were indeed ethical problems in the industry. In 1988 Drexel Burnham Lambert, the US junk bond specialists, admitted to various counts of fraud, paid a large fine and went bust a year later. Its driving force, Michael Miliken, was jailed, as was the well-known broker Ivan Boesky, who was found guilty of insider trading. In London, scandal erupted in the Guinness takeover of Distillers and several high profile investors were jailed for participating in an illegal share support operation.

The Rise of Investment Banking

The US investment banks were to make big inroads into the London market and subsequently to spread their influence globally. Since 1933, with the passing of the Glass-Steagall Act in the US, investment banks had been kept separate from commercial banks. The Wall Street investment banks had been deemed to have some responsibility for the Great Crash of 1929 and 'bangsters' had gained a bad reputation. Congress decided to separate the two activities. Mainstream commercial banking was the mainstay of the economy and a limited federal guarantee was available to its depositors. Investment banking, broadly similar to UK merchant banking, was not offered the guarantee and was thus more limited in its capital raising. Wall Street firms served the richer members of society and, if they wished to speculate, they were obliged to raise their own funds.

Investment banks were powerful lobbyists, major contributors to political parties and had friends in high places. From 1987 the Federal Reserve started to relax this separation of functions, with a consequence that by 1996 trading had reached 25 per cent of turnover. In 1999 the Act was finally repealed, along with a number of other steps increasing the deregulation of financial services. Blurring the boundaries between two very different types of banks gave the investment banks access to the vast balance sheets and resources of the commercial banks.

In the decade following the 'Big Bang', investment banks' power and influence expanded quickly. The American banks brought to London their large pay packages, generous expenses and much higher fees, gained by pitching aggressively for business with high powered salesmanship. Advances in information technology, which provided assistance to speed up the transfer of money and the growth of the foreign exchange markets, presented them with new opportunities. Fortunes were made from privatisations of public bodies, which arose in the Thatcher/Reagan era. But most important of all was the growth of the global derivatives markets, driven by deregulation and advances in technology. In the ensuing war with the traditional banks the powerful US investment banks were to emerge victorious in a relatively short period of time. With their large cheque books they were able to recruit the best talent available.

But there were also some disquieting features surrounding the rise of investment banking. There was the dotcom bubble, where many small investors took their advice and lost fortunes. Accounting scandals were revealed in the accounts of major corporations, such as Enron, WorldCom, Tyco and Global Crossings, important investment clients. The banks were accused of having conflicts of interests, where they acted on both the buy and sell side, particularly for dotcom stocks. They were accused of placing internet stocks, which could appreciate in value enormously on the first day's trading, with favoured clients who were expected to respond by giving business back through vast trading commissions. Traditional relationship banking, where the banks advised on strategy, seemed to be losing out to transactional banking, where the only consideration was completion of the deal. Some of them appeared more to resemble casinos than traditional banks, as they took bets on various positions or events. What were the core values espoused by these organisations?

The Seedy Side of Investment Banking

It is not easy to get a handle on the culture of these powerful banks. Normally, departing executives are bound by strict non-disclosure agreements, preventing them from revealing any of the bank's secrets or doing anything detrimental to its reputation. The image most familiar to Americans was the fictional bond salesman in Tom Wolfe's popular novel and subsequent film, *Bonfire of the Vanities*, which portrayed the arrogant banker as a self-styled 'Master of the Universe'. However, from time to time former employees are prepared to write and provide insights into this arcane world.

One such widely read description of the investment banking ethos came from a junior bond salesman working at Salomon Brothers, the leading bond dealer, exposing much of the culture in such places.[4] It was a jungle devoted to Mammon, where aggressive, brash, foul-mouthed, sharp, quick thinking young male traders held sway, making their enormous bets as would be customary in a casino. There seemed at times to be little supervision or position limits, particularly in the rapidly growing mortgage trading department, where they made vast profits exploiting market inefficiencies. Even trainees had an elevated view of their own net worth with large salaries, lavish expenses and enormous bonuses available to those who made the most profit. Loyalty to the bank was limited and star performers could be lured away with large remuneration packages.

In such a world proprietary trading – trading on behalf of the bank itself, rather than its customers – thrived. Salomon Brothers could place large bets on its own behalf, a dangerous practice in what was a zero sum game, where the winnings by one party were matched by the losses of another. Smooth talking salesmen, however, were not averse to passing on losses to their customers, who were then 'blown up' when the occasion demanded. They even allowed customers to leverage up their positions by lending to them funds on the security of the instruments purchased. The problems existed right to the top of the bank and a year after the book was published the bank was found guilty of rigging the US Treasury bond market, leading to a large fine, the jailing of a senior banker, the resignation of the CEO and the eventual takeover of the bank by Citigroup.

Such reprehensible behaviour was not unique to Salomon dealers and traders. A decade later a banker who created derivative products at Morgan Stanley explained the behaviour of salesmen there.[5] They too would sell instruments to customers with enormous hidden risks before 'ripping off their faces', leaving them with serious losses. Yet this was an offshoot of the bank famous for J.P. Morgan's dictum: 'First class business in a first class way'. It seemed as though standards had changed in the way investment bankers treated their customers.

The US authorities reacted to the many scandals by bringing in the controversial, bureaucratic Sarbanes–Oxley Act in 2002, requiring much tighter governance rules on business and auditing, together with a special section for investment banks. But prior to the financial crisis of 2007 many commentators felt that this alone would not bring the scandals to an end. Besides insider dealing and market manipulation, there were issues around independence, misrepresentation, unauthorised trading, favouritism and kickbacks. Investment banks had successfully resisted outside regulation in their industry.

One senior banker, a former Group Managing Director of Shroders, the London merchant bank, believed the fault lay in the structure of investment banks, leading to inevitable conflicts of interest which could not be contained by imaginary 'Chinese Walls' between departments.[6] In a severe indictment on the industry he considered the large US investment banks to be in many respects a cartel, or at least a complex oligopoly, making it difficult for newcomers to gain entry at the top level, while generating enormous profits and paying massive compensation as a result.

It seems that dubious ethical behaviour was not limited to the bond markets. Before 2007 a Trinity graduate wrote of his experience in corporate finance, the home of smooth, white-shoed bankers, in Goldman Sachs, which had once held the high ground, refusing to take on many clients on ethical grounds.[7] This was no longer the case and valuations could be stretched, if necessary, to achieve this end. Later, at Morgan Stanley, he deplored the decline in standards, particularly regarding the quality and independence of research during the dotcom bubble. This view from an investment banker, who had risen to senior positions quickly, provides a serious indictment on the industry.

During the meltdown following the subprime banking crisis evidence of further excesses during the boom years began to surface as various participants published their experiences. A young derivatives analyst in a small London-based bank painted a picture of lavish entertainment with fine wines, gambling and even upmarket prostitution employed to gain business in a world driven by bonuses.[8] His own debauchery and the equivalent financial debauchery or massive risk taking of the bank led both to his own downfall and that of the bank, contributing to the credit crunch, while leaving him comparatively wealthy.

Another trader in a firm of London stockbrokers wrote in a similar vein.[9] He reported of traders' addiction to cocaine, gambling and alcohol. Traders, dealers, brokers, market makers, hedge fund managers – none of them were portrayed in a favourable light. The whole culture was male, macho and homophobic, where bullying was commonplace. Portfolios could be churned to generate commission, short-term speculative success could be booked to personal accounts, while insider dealing was claimed to be rife and compliance regulations often ignored. Brokers could profit by 'front running', whereby they placed personal orders for themselves or their firm ahead of either a big institutional order or the release of favourable research with a strong buy recommendation.

A popular journalist, who had worked as a share analyst in a firm of London stockbrokers, depicted a similar seedy scene.[10] It too revealed a squalid world of cocaine, sex clubs, extravagant expense accounts and gambling, but included also insider trading and share price manipulation by rumour mongering. It seemed that any behaviour was acceptable in pursuit of profits and bonuses. The flow of information was uneven, since friendly analysts could be favoured with early news releases. Financial models could be distorted to produce 'Buy' recommendations in markets which were far from being efficient. It was quickly heralded as an accurate portrayal of life in the City.

Probably the most notorious account of the dark side of the prevailing culture was outlined in a memoir by the celebrated founder and CEO of a large, prominent Wall Street brokerage, which was to become an international bestseller and later a popular film.[11] *The Wolf of Wall Street* depicted a sordid and depraved life of excess in terms of lavish entertainment, drug addiction, alcohol abuse, prostitution, physical violence and boundless greed. Rapid wealth accumulation was the aim and the route to riches was based on generating sales, irrespective of the best interests of the customers. Personal relationships were founded on the exercise of power, duplicity, enormous financial rewards or threats and unquestioning loyalty. Legal requirements and ethical considerations were generally ignored in the relentless pursuit and worship of Mammon. Instead business was conducted, not by skilled financial analysis, but by high powered personal selling and massive stock price manipulation, centred on new share issues allocated to favoured insiders before prices were artificially inflated.

The author ended up serving a prison sentence after being indicted for securities fraud and money laundering before, surprisingly in view of his dubious pedigree, starting to make a further fortune after his release as a motivational speaker, charging substantial fees to those willing to hear his advice on how to become rich. But the widespread publicity engendered by the book and the film did little to enhance the already tarnished image of Wall Street amongst the wider public. The discovery that behaviour and business practices more normally associated with criminal gangs or share hustlers in unregulated bucket shops could exist in a leading Wall Street brokerage was profoundly disquieting. Although such malpractices may not have been universal, to judge from this memoir and other accounts of life in the fast lane of high finance, there were too many people in different institutions who behaved dishonestly, while trying to ensure that their improprieties stayed undetected by the regulatory authorities.

The Impact of the Changes on Irish Banking

Ireland could not remain immune to the changes in business practices occurring in world markets, particularly those in neighbouring Britain. Staid old Irish stockbroker businesses found themselves objects of renewed interest and the major firms were purchased by the banks, though this process was eventually reversed with management buyouts and trade sales. The investment banks eventually were absorbed by the retailing banking groups, thus spreading their new ways more widely to retail bankers, who had traditionally adopted a more cautious approach in dealing with their customers.

On the wider front British bankers were to learn of the large remuneration offered to investment bankers in the major global centres. As US investment banks had recruited UK nationals to their London businesses, the money culture from Wall Street infected the traditionally staid world of the City. Enormous financial rewards became a source of envy and had to be replicated by competitors, if they wished to attract and retain the brightest employees. Inevitably, word spread to Dublin, where several of them operated subsidiaries, and also to its job market where bankers were not slow to demand greater rewards. But before looking at remuneration it is necessary to understand something of the culture of Irish banks and how they competed with each other.

CHAPTER 10

Competition in Ireland's Unique Banking Culture

The Irish banking sector is tiny by world standards, as Dublin has lived for long in the shadow of London, the undoubted centre of many financial markets. Yet the fall from grace for Irish banking occurred remarkably quickly, along with its lending standards. Most banks have a series of safeguards to prevent overly exuberant, imprudent growth which could imperil their future. The question must be asked: what were these checks and how did they fail in the property bubble? In particular, why did these dogs not bark when danger loomed or, if they did, why was the appropriate action not taken?

The Triple Lock that Failed

The first line of safeguards is obviously the bank's own procedures and standards regarding lending. Traditionally, lenders examining any proposal would be reluctant to recommend a loan proposition which was likely to be turned down by their superiors. Thus many proposals were refused at the screening stage, if repayment prospects were insufficiently clear or the security offered was deemed inadequate for the risk entailed.

Larger loans were required to be sanctioned by a credit committee, comprised of experienced bankers who would assess the risks in the proposed credit. They would frequently send back the proposal, seeking further information on certain aspects. Some of these requests arose from poor presentation of the information, particularly where branch managers lacked basic writing and communication skills. On other occasions it could be that certain important aspects had been overlooked. Regrettably, it was sometimes simply bureaucratic indecision, which would particularly irritate both the loan officers and the customers. Well-functioning credit committees would frequently improve the quality of the credit by attaching suitable preconditions for the drawdown of the loan and continuing restrictive covenants. If, however, the bank has a policy of expanding its loan book aggressively, the credit committee is likely to reflect this policy in its attitude to loan approvals.

Credit committees do not always err on the side of caution and the avoidance of high risks. I recall being asked to look after a major commercial exposure of the bank. I quickly became concerned that the business was exhibiting many of the classical signs of business failure and predicted that it would fail within twelve months. I was particularly concerned with the quality of the information provided, especially the annual accounts which were audited by a small, one-man firm. I persuaded my boss, the CEO of the investment bank, to back the appointment of independent accountants to establish the true situation, but we were overruled by the wider credit committee. As the situation deteriorated I reported again with the same recommendation and had lined up accountants to commence work the following day. Again, I was unable to convince the credit committee, which did not wish to offend a valued customer. The business collapsed in a welter of adverse publicity almost to the day I predicted a year earlier, and the bank was left with a much larger loss than would have been the case had my recommendation been accepted.

As well as credit committees banks usually have a high level risk management committee, which should examine the major risks facing the institution. One would expect major concentrations of risk in terms of business sectors, such as property, and individual borrowers to receive close scrutiny. If this did happen, it appears that either the risks were underestimated or the requisite corrective action never took place. On a wider front, the committee would examine the distribution of the total assets and liabilities of the bank and ensure that adequate funding was available. There seem to have been deficiencies in some or all banks in this regard.

The other major internal check is that of the internal audit, which would check not only the lending of the branch network, but also the central commercial and corporate lending. A reduction in lending standards should have been brought to the attention of the board audit committee, if and when it was uncovered. If, however, the loans were in line with management policy there was little internal audit could do. The key to its success was the degree of independence granted to it, so that it was not afraid to criticise the actions of senior management.

One person who is singularly well positioned to understanding the reasons for the failure of the banks in the UK is a former Chancellor of the Exchequer, Alistair Darling, since he had dealings with the senior management of the major banks at the time. Writing after the crisis, he concluded that bankers did not understand what they were doing, the risks they were taking on and often the products they were selling. Coming from a knowledgeable source the criticism constitutes a devastating indictment on the underlying competence of bank leaders. Driven by a relentless pursuit of growth and misguided by excessive optimism, they had made catastrophic errors of judgement. Based on the failures of Northern Rock, outlined in Chapter 2, RBS in Chapter 5 and HBOS described below, he had plenty of examples of their risk management to support his views.[1]

Do Irish bankers fare any better in their management of risk? They were spared the necessity of evaluating complex derivatives, but competed aggressively with the British banks, not only in Ireland but also in the UK where they won significant business from their British peers. Their competition in retail lending, corporate banking and deposits is described below. Their management of traditional property risks was disastrously weak, as was evident in the massive discount at which the loans were transferred to NAMA and their enormous dependence on State support. Their explanations after the crisis indicated that even then they did not understand how they had mismanaged key risks, both in lending and funding. The first line of safeguards failed both in the UK and Ireland.

The second line of safeguards is outside scrutiny from the external auditors and regulators. As mentioned in Chapter 5, the auditors tended to concentrate on the systems in place to deal with the sanctioning of loans initially and the monitoring of problematical loans. They rarely possessed the requisite skills and experience to second guess the decisions taken by senior management. Much criticism contained in the official reports to date has centred on the role and effectiveness of the Financial Regulator. Clearly major weaknesses have been highlighted. The judge in the criminal proceedings against the Directors of Anglo Irish Bank was trenchant in his criticisms of the conduct of the office over the scheme to finance the purchase of the bank's own shares. I do not wish to underestimate the importance of these deficiencies, but, as explained at the outset, this is not the focus of this book.

The third line of safeguards must be the board of the bank itself, which should play a major role in the management of risk. The board is uniquely positioned to address difficulties. The CEO reports to the board and is normally a director, as may be other senior members of the management team, including the Finance Director. The internal and external auditors will generally submit reports to the board audit committee, drawing its attention to any weaknesses in the systems. The individual directors typically can draw on a wide range of business experience and are usually well rewarded for the performance of their duties. They have responsibility for the overall conduct of the business and should have access to the relevant reports from the management team and auditors. Yet they singularly failed to restrain the management team's expansion of credit during the property bubble. Either they failed to identify the existence of the problem and its serious potential implications or, if they did, responded inadequately to protect the future of the business. Why did this third critical element in the overall system behave in such a dysfunctional manner?

Irish Bank Boards – The Sound of Silence

Bank boards are normally made up of one or more executives and a considerable number of non-executive directors, drawn from prominent figures in business and the professions. Amongst their duties they hire and fire the chief executive, determine the remuneration packages of senior management, report to shareholders who elect them and ensure that good governance is observed. But at least as important is their duty to question the overall strategy proposed by management and to evaluate the risks. Perhaps some clues to their failure lies in the choice of board members and the ways in which they operated.

'Crony capitalism' is a term first used to describe the ways business was conducted in Asia. It was felt that favouritism was applied to many appointments and indeed to the allocation of loans. Since the financial crisis of 2007 the allegation has been levelled against a much wider group of countries. Irish journalists have often complained that a golden circle exists, where board additions are likely to be carefully chosen friends of existing directors, who on occasions can in turn reciprocate by offering directorships to those who appointed them. Certainly it is difficult to get a director elected who does not have the backing of the board or even to stay on sometimes after criticising policy. The EBS board successfully ousted a director in 2007 after she had disagreed with them. Naturally, senior business figures strongly resent any accusations of crony capitalism and maintain that in a small country it is inevitable that they should know the likely candidates.

Appointments of directors are normally investigated in detail by a nominations subcommittee of the board and their recommendations are then sent to the full board for approval. An interview given by Lawrence Crowley, a respected former Governor of the Bank of Ireland,[2] the strongest of the surviving banks, throws some light on how candidates are selected. He stated that boards were reluctant to appoint directors they did not know for fear they might endanger the cohesiveness of the board. Whatever else this policy might achieve, it is not a strong basis for challenging the status quo.

Once elected bank directors rarely resign, even after some disaster, as was evidenced by the aftermath of the AIB takeover of ICI. Nevertheless, in light of the enormous losses incurred it is perhaps surprising that more changes were not made in the senior echelons of the Irish banks. Certainly the chairmen and chief executives of the five banks participating in NAMA were replaced. But many of the directors and senior managers remained in situ some three years after their liabilities were guaranteed. Niall FitzGerald, formerly CEO of Unilever, posed a challenge to them: 'If you knew what was going on, were you complicit? If not, were you competent?' No answer was forthcoming, except to urge the public to move on, though many of them ignored this advice in relation to their own positions. Professor Honohan, speaking in Washington, stated that keeping in place the management that had made poor decisions had prolonged the tendency to remain in denial about the problems.[3]

Another aspect of board procedures is the apparent reluctance to address contentious issues, which a former CEO of the Bank of Ireland terms 'the culture of silent dissent'.[4] In Ireland there has been a longstanding distaste for whistleblowers and informers. Pressure can be brought to bear on directors holding unpopular views not to express them publicly lest they damage confidence or the share price. If directors and dissenting managers can be 'persuaded' to remain silent, proper discussion of relevant problems can be suppressed and difficult decisions avoided.

When directors are selected on the basis that they are already known and debate is stifled, it is unsurprising that the result is groupthink, as I had pointed out in 2009, long before the Nyberg Report identified the weakness. There is a long history of banks staying with the herd, avoiding an isolated position which, if proved wrong, could lead to censure. So the warnings about a property bubble, as published in *The Economist* magazine and occasionally voiced by academic economists or commentators, were conveniently ignored. Instead, reliance was placed on in-house forecasts and the promises of a 'soft landing'. When boards could have challenged the gung-ho policies of senior management, they failed to do so effectively. Thus, the third critical safeguard failed to operate when it was vitally required.

Retail Lending Competition – From 3-6-3 Banking to Tracker Trash

In the 1970s lending was dominated by the four retail banking groups with their branch networks, the two state-owned ACC, serving the farmers, and ICC, serving small and medium-sized businesses, and three American banks which cherry picked some of the prime corporate business. The main newcomer was the Belgian IIB, later to become KBC, with a competitive tax-based lending product. The best known of the smaller banks was Anglo Irish Bank, growing rapidly both organically and by acquisition. For the most part banks could retain customers, unless there was some serious dispute.

Competition in these circumstances was limited. Banks tended to move their interest rates practically in unison, which caused them to be denounced in the press as a cartel. It was occasionally referred to as 3-6-3 banking, a phrase borrowed from the sleepy American thrift banks. Pay 3 per cent for deposits, lend them at 6 per cent and ... be on the golf course at 3.00 pm!

EU membership brought in new banks trying to obtain a share of the lucrative market, a trend which was to increase in the Celtic Tiger era of the 1990s and culminate with the introduction of the euro as a common currency in 2002. There was now a very changed competitive framework: Anglo Irish Bank had grown to be a major threat to the dominance of AIB and BoI, the large Dutch Rabobank had acquired ACC and Bank of Scotland had acquired ICC.

For much of the period interest focussed on the Irish domestic mortgage market, which enjoyed margins which were the envy of foreign banks. The building societies had historically dominated the sector, but the field was to change, when BoI acquired Irish Civil Service Building Society in 1985, when Irish Permanent was floated in 1994 and finally when First Active was floated in 1998. Most of the building societies in turn subsequently spread their attention to financing developers with disastrous consequences.

Bank of Scotland provided an unexpected impact to competition on the Irish market. Sometimes described as the best bank in Britain, it was highly regarded as a conservatively managed bank with a low cost base and prudent financing, which sought to stay with its customers in times of difficulty. When Bank of Scotland merged with the Halifax Building Society to form HBOS in 2001, the new management was dominated by the 'Haliban', a group of sales-focused managers, which struck fear in the much admired, if somewhat dour, organisation. Abandoning the canny, conservative tradition of Scottish banking and the staid growth of the UK's largest building society, HBOS embarked on an aggressive strategy of high borrowings and rapid growth of lending; the personal touch of bank managers with a close understanding of their customers gave way to more remote relationship managers. Corporate banking chased big high risk deals and took large equity stakes.[5]

The main thrust of competition in Ireland lay in the housing market. In retail banking risky new products, such as 125 per cent mortgages and self-certified loans, were launched as part of a new sales-based culture. Top management were generously rewarded, while ambitious targets were introduced for staff, generating large bonuses, to drive performance forward. The Irish mortgage market was targeted both for selling down corporate loans and developing its mortgage base. In due course in 2008, with serious problems emerging, HBOS was taken over by the more conservative Lloyds TSB, but eventually that bank had to be bailed out by the Government.

The initial change to the status quo came with the advent of Bank of Scotland to the market when it offered interest rates of less than 4 per cent, over 1 per cent cheaper than the competitors, in 1999. The other players quickly followed suit and a full-scale mortgage war broke out. Profit margins quickly fell from 2.4 per cent to 0.5 per cent. During this war loans were increased from 2.5 or 3 times borrowers' income to 4 times income. Loan terms were increased from 20/25 years to 30 or even 40 years. Finally, in 2005, First Active offered the first 100 per cent mortgage, rapidly followed by its competitors. The sales-based culture of HBOS had a profound impact on the Irish market in which it operated, as imitators sought to replicate its apparent success. Standards had dropped to a dangerous level in a macho world of wild and aggressive competition.

But perhaps the most reckless development was the introduction of tracker mortgages. First introduced in 1999, the interest rates tracked the equivalent rate at the European Central Bank. When the cost of funding for the banks rose significantly above this rate the paper thin margins were totally eradicated and the banks and building societies found themselves carrying a large part of their loan books with negative margins. They had broken a fundamental funding rule to base their loan rates at a margin over the cost of funding.

Competition in Corporate Lending – A Race to the Bottom

Margins in corporate lending in Ireland had traditionally been good in comparison with those available in Britain. The range in my time in banking was between 1 per cent and 4 per cent, depending on the assessment of the risk, but usually exceeding 2 per cent. Provision was made for increasing the rate if any extra cost was imposed on the bank due to Central Bank liquidity requirements. Only State organisations, backed by a State guarantee, could command margins less than 1 per cent. Yet in London major corporate customers could receive loans on margins of considerably less than 1 per cent. We had to learn a new language of 'basis points', where a hundred basis points equalled 1 per cent. Lending at such fine margins seemed to rely on the absence of bad debts and could barely cover the administrative costs involved.

When banks are determined to grow their loan books quickly, the simplest way is to do it in large chunks. This is difficult in most industries, particularly where Ireland was becoming increasingly uncompetitive after 2000. If large industrial corporations do not undertake substantial capital investments, their demand for additional funding must be limited. Many overseas banks had an unhappy experience lending to the Goodman group, so Irish industrialists were not the prime target. Builders and developers, on the other hand, are always willing to borrow, if they wish to undertake large construction projects and any project could require funding to the tune of hundreds of millions of euros.

There were plenty of willing lenders in this field of activity. There were still the four traditional retail groups, but as well there was Rabobank and Bank of Scotland, together with all the major traditional building societies, including Irish Nationwide, but excluding Irish Permanent. Above all, there was Anglo Irish Bank, which had enjoyed a period of sustained high growth which was the envy of its competitors.

Competition sometimes was not only on margin, but also on other terms and conditions for the loan and the speed with which a decision could be made. There were signs that banks were prepared to lend on easier conditions when I was in banking during the 1980s. I recollect offering funding to a house builder, but failing to gain the business. On enquiry I discovered that another bank had offered funding at the same interest rate, but had not limited the exposure to the number of unsold houses at any time, which was a prudent term to include in this type of lending. Naturally, the builder chose the facility which provided him with the greatest freedom.

The major banks took the growth of Anglo Irish Bank as a serious challenge. It had established strong relationships with most or all of the major developers. In 2004 AIB set up a 'win-back' team, while BoI decided to increase its property exposure. Bank of Scotland and Ulster Bank were also aggressive competitors in the field, together with Danske Bank and Rabobank, so developers could shop around.

Anglo Irish was renowned for its speed of response, often making funds available before all security had been put in place, relying on the guarantee of the builder and undertakings from solicitors to complete security in due course, while charging a substantial arrangement fee and profit margin. To judge by the discounts on the portfolios of loans being sold to NAMA by the Irish banks and the published losses of the overseas banks, lending standards must have dropped in a determined effort to gain or recover business, at least from 2004 onwards.

Competition for Deposits – Defrauding the Taxpayer

As well as competing for lending Irish banks had to compete for deposits in an era of high personal taxes and inflation. One bank's efforts in this regard became notorious when it became public knowledge in 1997, as a result of litigation in a private company.[6] As was well known in banking circles, Guinness Mahon, the long established traditional merchant bank, had set up a subsidiary in the Cayman Isles, renowned for its secrecy and confidentiality for depositors. For over 20 years wealthy businessmen would give funds to the CEO, Des Traynor, who would transfer the funds to the Cayman subsidiary, later to be named Ansbacher (Cayman) Bank, where they could earn market interest rates. Funds were withdrawn by bank draft or cash and only numbered accounts appeared in the bank's records with the identity of the owners kept in a secret memorandum account.

After a tribunal revealed and then investigated the matter, high court inspectors were appointed to obtain the details. The Central Bank was castigated for its failure to address the problem over the years. Eventually, the names became public and included many prominent figures in Irish life, including the Taoiseach, Charles Haughey. The unauthorised personal banking business was run by Des Traynor from the headquarters of CRH, Ireland's largest industrial company, of which he was the chairman. By 2006 over €50 million in tax had been collected from 108 account holders.

A year after the Ansbacher scandal broke, another tax scandal in NIB was publicised on the state television early in 1998. Based on leaked bank documents, it was revealed that an insurance product with Clerical Medical Insurance (CMI), based in the Isle of Man, was being marketed to bank depositors. Since it was located offshore it was apparently a safe haven for undeclared hot money. In many cases the funds were recycled back to Ireland and could be withdrawn through anonymous numbered accounts. The bank charged a very large commission of up to 9 per cent for the product, which had been marketed since 1991. It was soon dubbed 'the poor man's Ansbacher', since it was targeted at middle class businessmen.

A civil servant's report indicated that the sums passing through the scheme were huge, amounting to over £50 million. High Court inspectors were appointed in 1998 and after six years reported back with damning findings.[7] They concluded that between 1986 and 1998 bogus non-resident accounts were widespread in the Irish branch network. The bank had encouraged tax evasion by taking in hot money, and further by allowing the interest to go untaxed. In addition, there was widespread overcharging of customers by loading interest rates, fees and charges onto current accounts. By the end of 2005, 306 investors in the CMI scheme had been forced to pay over €56 million in tax. The Director of Corporate Enforcement issued disqualification proceedings against various senior managers in NIB, and nine of them were duly disqualified from acting as company directors in 2005. The bank's reputation was ruined and in 2004 it had been sold to Danske Bank.

It was widely known that there existed in Ireland widespread tax evasion on deposit interest in accounts held in building societies and banks. To counter this problem, in 1986 the Government introduced the Deposit Interest Retention Tax, abbreviated to DIRT, whereby banks were obliged to deduct tax at source and remit it to the tax authorities. In an attempt to encourage emigrants to remit funds home, this tax did not apply to non-residents, once they completed the relevant 'Form F'. Many Irish citizens completed the form with bogus UK addresses, which were accepted by bank branches without questioning, as they sought to increase their deposits.

The problem was uncovered by AIB internal audit in 1991 and passed on to senior executives, since there could be a tax liability to the bank as high as £100 million – an estimate which was ridiculed by the senior management. Some years later the contents of the report were leaked to the press and the scandal broke in 1998. The matter was investigated by the Public Accounts Committee of the Dáil and it was revealed that the banks had been involved in supporting tax evasion for years. All banks, including those owned by the State, were complicit. The tax authorities were able to collect €225 million from 25 financial institutions, including €90 million from AIB. The Revenue Commissioners then set about collecting tax from the individuals concerned. By 2006 it had collected €386 million from 8,500 individuals. Further taxation trusts for Irish residents lodged funds in the branches of Irish banks in offshore havens such as Jersey and the Isle of Man, creating further scandals and tax liabilities. Eventually, by the early 2000s the State would receive over €1 billion from all these sources. The whole saga badly damaged the reputation of Irish banks.[8]

The Irish banking system had been badly tainted by its unrestrained competition, its low lending standards and its cavalier attitude to the Revenue Commissioners. The banks have primarily themselves to blame for their misfortunes. By permitting high gearing, both by developers and householders, they took enormous risks at fine margins in a sector which was traditionally cyclical and to which they were severely overexposed. To what extent had they been infected by the global investment banking culture? Some clues could lie in the remuneration systems and how they incentivised senior managers.

CHAPTER 11

Shareholders or Management First?

Alan Greenspan, the Chairman of the US Federal Reserve Board and doyen of the financial industry, testifying to Congress in 2008, admitted he was in a shocked state of disbelief and that he had made a mistake in believing that the banks would do what was necessary to protect their shareholders and institutions. There was a flaw in his ideological model that defines how he perceived the world.[1]

Perhaps he should not have been so shocked. Dissident shareholders, acting as 'greenmailers', often threatened to sack the board and make a better return for the shareholders unless they were bought off at the expense of the shareholders at large. Where boards submitted to this pressure were they not placing the interests of directors ahead of the general body of shareholders? He could also have pondered the growth of leveraged buy outs (LBOs), where managers seek to find new ways of enhancing businesses when they become owners, which they could not discover when working for shareholders. These LBOs either made fortunes for the managers or sometimes caused the collapse of the business with losses for employees and creditors.[2] Also, many critics of investment banking had complained that the senior bankers put their interests ahead of customers and shareholders when awarding themselves with excessive remuneration, rather than paying out larger dividends.

The Broken Model

The implications of Greenspan's flaw in the system are far-reaching. The policy of light touch regulation discouraged intervention. The regulator believed in the invisible hand of competition, originally propounded by Adam Smith, and assumed that the banks would always act in the best interest of their shareholders, which included managing the risks effectively and abiding by the rules of prudent banking. Market forces would inhibit banks from taking undue risks, because the share price would suffer if they did. Alan Greenspan advocated a policy of laissez-faire, relying on competition between the banks.[3] Any restrictions would, of course, be strongly opposed by the banks on the grounds that it would put America at a competitive disadvantage in what had become a global industry.

Many economists and commentators believed the economic policy of 'the Great Moderation', with low inflation, high growth and mild recessions, had brought an end to economic volatility, thus permitting higher levels of risk taking. This concept had been a fundamental tenet of American capitalism during the boom years. The era of free market capitalism heralded by Margaret Thatcher in the UK and President Ronald Reagan in the US had spread widely around the world. The intellectual roots of this thinking lie with the pre-war antipathy to the spread of socialism, typified by the 'Austrian School' of economists and, in particular, Friedrich Hayek.[4] The modern management of public finances was based on this mode of thinking, epitomised by neoliberal economists, such as Milton Friedman since the 1980s.[5] It followed a 'Washington Consensus', with Government intervention in the markets being avoided at all costs. So the realisation that such a policy was based on faulty premises had indeed devastating implications for economic management.

An alternative view existed, which regarded the 2007 problem as nothing new in the history of economic downturns, since the usual signs of a financial crisis were evident in the US some time before the crash. House prices were rising rapidly, household borrowings had accelerated at an alarming rate, and output was slowing. Above all, the twin deficits on the current account and trade balances had resulted in large international borrowing. The authors of this alternative view, whose research went back to 1800, identified recent parallels in the UK, Spain and Ireland.[6]

Yet many people in decision making positions deluded themselves that this time it was different. They believed in the superiority of the US financial and regulatory systems, the deep understanding of monetary policy, the vast sophisticated capital markets, and that the impact of globalisation and new technology heralded a new dawn. Rapidly increasing developing countries needed a secure place to invest their funds. Above all, securitisation and other financial innovations had enabled risks to be widely spread and higher levels of debt were therefore deemed acceptable.

Banking crises historically were often preceded by large capital inflows and resulted in a variety of other crises such as inflation, devaluation, and domestic and sovereign defaults. Severe banking crises were likely to cause prolonged recessions, steep falls in property and equity prices, rising unemployment, a reduction in economic growth and an explosion of Government debt. The Washington Consensus provided a false sense of confidence, which postponed corrective action and in turn deepened the crisis. Alan Greenspan's model, based on this analysis, was deeply flawed.

The Tyranny of 'Short-termism'

In trying to explain financial management to non-financial mangers, I often pose them with a problem at the outset of a discussion. If they were asked to take a one-year contract with no prospects of an extension, and were to be rewarded with a bonus equal to 20 per cent of the profits, what changes would they make to the business, if they were to act selfishly? Managers quickly identified costs to cut, especially capital investment and discretionary spending on items such as research and development, marketing and training.

This should boost short-term profits and therefore the bonus, but would hardly constitute sound financial management. Indeed, if continued over a prolonged period, it could lead to the collapse of the business.

If the above actions still did not achieve any profit, what might they then be tempted to do? The answer given is to take major risks with short-term investments, such as gambling business funds on a horse or purchasing some high risk financial derivative. If managers are unconcerned about the future of the business, it could be in their own personal interest to do so. But it does not constitute prudent financial management, which is concerned with creating long-term value for shareholders. This means, as well as maximising profitability, that it is necessary to manage risks and cashflows. The stock market should punish anti-social behaviour for personal gain by reducing the share price.

Yet one of the most common criticisms of the current system is excessive 'short-termism'. Managers hate to see a fall in earnings and may take decisions, damaging to the future, in order to avert any fall. Venture capital investors, who typically have a five-year time horizon, may veto sound capital investment proposals in the later stages of this period, since any drop in short-term profits could adversely affect their exit price. In the US, where results are published quarterly, there is even greater pressure to avoid a setback. The short-term reaction to a fall in reported profits is often a fall in the share price, since investors fear it may be part of a longer-term trend. Retiring CEOs or Chairmen too may wish to leave with the graph of profits ever rising and so fail to invest in their final years.

It is not difficult to understand why managers are often driven by short-term profitability. Shareholders usually want to see growth of the business, accompanied by rising profits and dividends, when it is the policy to distribute profits. They compare performance with peer group companies. In the case of Irish banks, this has often put undue pressure on bank boards to imitate their much vaunted competitors. Undoubtedly, Bank of Ireland's unwise expansion into the US with the purchase of First New Hampshire Bank was an effort to emulate AIB's successful acquisition of First Maryland. Similarly, Anglo Irish's spectacular growth rate put pressure on both BoI and AIB. Shareholders, with the support of the press, were demanding 20–25 per cent growth, even though this target is unreasonable when the economy is growing in single figures. Spectacular growth rates are normally accompanied by high risk taking, although this may be hard to spot.

Owner-managers have an advantage when it comes to running their businesses. They should be able to take good longer-term decisions without being driven by the tyranny of short-termism. But large companies tend not to be 'owner-manger' businesses, since shareholders are usually happy to delegate the management function to professionals. This managerial revolution evolved over the last century and was publicised 70 years ago.[7] The problem, known as the agency issue, has been well known in finance for years: How can business managers be persuaded to act in the best interests of their principals, the shareholders?

Elusive Market Efficiency

A key factor in light touch regulation is a belief in the efficiency of the markets. If markets are efficient they will absorb fresh information more or less instantaneously and the share price will adjust accordingly. Portfolio investment managers are familiar with the concept and the difficulty in discovering underpriced shares. The evidence is that the vast majority of active investment managers underperform the markets, as reflected in the market indices, after account is taken of their own substantial fees. Accordingly, many investors have moved into passive funds, designed to reflect the indices exactly, with much lower fee levels.

But do stock markets behave efficiently for all shares and do all investors have equal information? In the crash following the financial crisis many banks were in reality insolvent, but the share prices took considerable time to adjust accordingly. Large, well informed investors, in particular hedge funds, were able to take advantage of the situation and accumulate fortunes by short selling shares they did not own in the expectation of buying them back later at a lower price. It would seem that in the short run stock markets may not be efficient.

Increasingly academics are questioning the basic assumption that shareholders are rational beings. They make decisions to buy or sell very quickly without analysing the relevant financial data. Often they operate by using rules of thumb to assist them, but can be influenced by their emotions, such as refusing to recognise a loss and consequently hold shares which can be expected to decline further. A whole new area of behavioural finance has opened up to understand better seemingly irrational behaviour by investors.

Markets themselves may not always be independent judges of value. They can be manipulated by spreading rumours (which may or may not be true) with the purpose of moving shares in a certain direction. Companies may issue press releases during market falls seeking to reassure investors and sometimes denying the seriousness of their financial situations, preferring to blame the fall in their share prices on speculators. Nor is all advice necessarily independent. Stockbrokers and investment banks may earn fees from their client companies who are unlikely to be happy to have the company rated as a 'sell'. Certainly 'buy' ratings tend to be more common than 'sell' ratings, particularly for companies which are clients of these institutions.

While accepting that it is difficult for investors to outguess the market without inside information in the short run, it is difficult to believe that the overall level is somehow efficient. Clearly markets can rise or fall in ways which cannot be explained by interest rate movements or earnings prospects, resulting in considerable fluctuations in share prices. What is true of the stock market applies equally to the market for real estate, which tends to be much more illiquid. Much of the value attaching to houses relates to the site value, which can fluctuate wildly with market sentiment and available credit. In such circumstances it is difficult to accept that markets price property efficiently and that laissez-faire is the appropriate response from Governments and regulators, especially since property downturns can entail enormous social costs.

Striving to Create Shareholder Value

Companies have long struggled with the problem of how to ensure that management run the business in the best long-term interests of the shareholders. Frequently opinions have been voiced that management do not obtain the best return for their shareholders and are excessively rewarded for poor performance. Too often, however, they are well protected by carefully drafted service contracts which make it very expensive to dismiss them. In any event they can normally rely on institutional shareholder support to see off any revolt by dissident shareholders. So what is the best way to track the performance of management from a financial perspective?

Stockbrokers tend to examine earnings per share, which relates the after-tax profits to the number of shares issued. By relating the figure to the share price it can be seen whether the share is cheap or dear. Companies with a good track record and good prospects will merit a higher rating than their less successful peers. It is, of course, purely a profit metric and ignores any balance sheet considerations. Also, over the years the figure was manipulated to exclude losses, deemed to be 'extraordinary', and excluded from the calculation, while including once-off profits, which were deemed to be 'exceptional'. The UK Midland Bank tried at one stage to deem its Latin American bad debts as extraordinary, though banks always experience loan losses.

A preferred calculation was Return on Investment (ROI) or a slight variant, Return on Capital Employed (ROCE). This compared the operating profit, or profit before interest and tax, with the capital employed as found in the balance sheet. The return could be compared with the cost of financing the investment, usually considered to be the relevant rate of interest. But this calculation too had its limitations. Economists have long argued that accounting rates of return place no cost on equity capital, and that the true rate to apply should be an average of the cost of debt, as measured by interest rates, and equity, a more complex calculation. It is not necessary for managers who lack financial training to understand the complex statistical background to this calculation.

Suffice it to say that it is considerably higher than the cost of debt and therefore the average cost of capital must be higher than the cost of loan capital.[8]

In the 1980s and subsequently many management consultancy organisations offered to adjust companies' accounts to establish if they were truly creating shareholder value, or economic value added, as it was sometimes termed. Typically, they would try to establish the 'free cashflow', rather than the accounting profit, which could be manipulated by the judicious choice of accounting policies available to them. They would then compare the actual return on capital with the average cost of capital, including equity. While the consultants argued the merits of their own particular approach, they tended to be broadly similar.[9] The conclusion was that many traditional, capital intensive companies, such as auto manufacturers and steel producers, were in fact destroying value, when the higher cost of capital was employed, yet they were declaring an accounting profit every year. On the other hand, many new high tech companies, which required little financial capital, were generating very high returns.

While the approach was followed by many leading industrial corporations, initially in the US but later in the UK and to a lesser extent on continental Europe, it was particularly difficult to apply to banks. One fundamental issue was establishing free cashflow in a business dealing in cash. Another was the complexity of many financial service groups, containing retail, wholesale and life assurance businesses which were very dissimilar in their financial structure. Above all, it required an assessment of the quality of the loan book, which was difficult to assess externally. Nevertheless, one leading firm of consultants set out an approach designed to apply the model to the banking industry.[10]

Banking, by its nature, can be a particularly complex business, given the difficulties of identifying and controlling risks. Trying to measure performance by a simple metric has its dangers since it may be manipulated. Banks would do well to remember a law originated by Charles Goodhart, Emeritus Professor at the London School of Economics and advisor to the Bank of England. He stated that when a measure becomes a target, it ceases to become a good measure. He may have based his law on macroeconomic targets, but it could also be applied to industry in general and banking in particular.

While few European banks tried to apply the concept, it found enthusiastic support from Lloyds Bank, where the longstanding CEO, the much respected and conservative Sir Brian Pitman, was a keen advocate of it. Lloyds Bank for many years was the most successful of the UK retail banks and avoided diversification into stockbroking or investment banking. He believed that the focus should be on the longer-term creation of value for shareholders and in aligning the remuneration of senior management to their success in this regard.

Incentivising Management

The spread of the shareholder value approach to business management was closely linked to its implementation through the rewards systems. In the US the comparative pay of top management was much higher than in Europe. To justify large remuneration packages they needed to demonstrate that they were doing a good job for their shareholders. The time involved in making onerous changes to the accounting information was substantial, and the fees charged by consultants were high. A key selling point was the introduction of rewards for those who created value for shareholders.

The principles of incentivising senior management were set out by consultants. One such firm explained the basics in a book, endorsed by Brian Pitman of Lloyds.[11] Senior management in particular should have their compensation set with regard to their success in achieving their strategy of creating value for shareholders. The time scale should be that of the strategic plan and payouts made as milestones are achieved. Even if the overall targets are not met, those managers who achieved their targets should be rewarded for doing so. Managers should be able to take their bonuses in cash, if they so desired.

In general, compensation should be set by benchmarking the total package with that of a peer group. Typically they suggested that basic pay should be set at about 80 per cent of the peer group average, and the upper limit set at, say, 160 per cent for CEOs, so that the bonus might range from 0 to 100 per cent, which was not unusual for the US. There seemed to be no special exceptions made for different industries, although the implicit assumption was that the relevant profit figure measuring performance could be accurately measured.

Spreading the Gospel

The ideas underlying shareholder value were widely promulgated by business schools worldwide. Two Insead finance professors in a book for executives set out further guiding principles regarding compensation.[12] Bonuses should be based on the success in creating economic value added, and conversely poor performance should be penalised. It should be calculated over a period of years, typically three to five. The reward should not be capped and should represent a relatively large proportion of a manager's total remuneration. The bonuses should not be restricted to senior management, but spread down through the organisation.

The ideas underlying rewarding management for creating shareholder value were well received by successful companies. Good performance could attract large bonuses payable in cash. The message was particularly well received in the banking world, which recruited heavily from business schools, where many young MBAs had been taught the concept.

Even where no formal shareholder value model had been adopted the ethos could affect remuneration. Most boards have remuneration committees, which would usually compare the pay of their senior management with that of peer groups, either directly themselves or through the services of specialist remuneration consultants. Increases in one company could therefore spread quickly through the market, as others sought to emulate the pay levels for their own management, if they considered them to be equally meritorious. It gave perhaps some justification to the famous line in the film *Wall Street*, where Gordon Gekko pronounced the immortal words 'Greed is good', which reflected the distorted and perverse values of the age.

It is also easy to see how a pay spiral might develop. Where several businesses are competing for top place in an industry, they would want to retain their top performers and therefore ensure top place in the remuneration league table. If all businesses offer above-average compensation, who is left to pay below-average pay? A game of pay leapfrog can quickly develop with competitors upping the levels once their competitors' remuneration levels are published.

On a wider front the high levels of remuneration available in the US can influence pay in the UK and continental Europe. In view of the globalisation of the industry, and the importance of London as a financial centre, one industry which could not ignore these developments was banking. Bankers were particularly mobile and could be poached by rivals seeking the skills of those deemed to be experts in their field. Multi-million dollar packages could become available even to young people in their twenties with guaranteed bonuses and 'golden handcuffs', even if this was not quite what shareholder value experts might recommend.

The next question to be addressed obviously is: How might this impact the compensation of Irish bankers and the way they might manage their banks? Also, could it be that managers in Irish banking would not act in the best long-term interests of their shareholders in the way that surprised Alan Greenspan in the US?

CHAPTER 12

The Rewards System and the Insidious Bonus Culture

A theme running through this book has been the influence of bonuses on the behaviour of bankers. My own experience of bonuses is limited. In my banking days employees periodically received a small bonus, representing a maximum of 10 per cent of salary. As I recollect, it was more a team- than individual-based reward, which I accepted as a gesture of thanks from the parent company for a job well done.

At the IMI I would also receive a modest, though slightly larger, cash bonus in good years. Since the IMI was a not-for-loss as well as a not-for-profit organisation, it encouraged the specialists to run extra courses and seek out new customers so that respectable remuneration could be paid for the long hours involved. The annual bonus did lead to some friction, since measuring financial contribution was bound to create anomalies for people who were exploring new products or markets. Nevertheless, with its mixture of group and individual bonuses the system worked reasonably well in a collegiate atmosphere, where everyone worked for the common good.

Bonuses in Banking – Greed is Not Good

The logic behind bonus payments is obvious, especially in a cyclical industry. Salaries are a fixed cost and therefore difficult to reduce in troubled times. Bonuses, on the other hand, are variable and when related to profits can automatically be reduced in a downturn. If employees are optimistic about the future they may be induced to stay, anticipating larger payouts in future years. In an industry with high labour mobility, retaining key staff is an important key to success. It may be possible to set a relatively low basic salary, but offer an equal amount by way of bonus if the profits justify it.

Bonuses in banking seemed to operate in a different manner, not least because of the scale of funds involved. A senior UK merchant banker described the system as a kind of joint venture between the bank and the employees.[1] Revenues would be split roughly evenly between employees and shareholders, leaving the shareholders with whatever profits remained after the deduction of expenses. The consequence was that the enormous bonus pool in successful years allowed bankers to receive a bonus of up to ten times their salary. Thus a banker on a relatively modest $100,000 salary could receive a bonus of $1 million. Multimillion dollar bonuses for senior bankers were not unusual. In the world of large bonuses and a culture of fear and greed, it should not be surprising that reckless decisions could ensue in pursuit of higher bonuses.

Such a division of the spoils between shareholders and management is highly questionable for several reasons. It may not be known or agreed by the shareholders, many of whom might find it wholly inequitable and an unnecessarily generous incentive for management to perform their functions effectively. The justification for the split presumes that the profits are predominantly the outcome of the skills of management, rather than the strength of the brand or pure good fortune, particularly in times of rising markets. Dangerously, it is based on a calculation of profits, which may prove illusory in the longer term when provision must be made for impairment of loans. Also, the scale of the bonus pool can result in the bank retaining inadequate reserves to fund growth and provide for unforeseen contingencies. Above all, management have a conflict of interest in conducting their business, since they are incentivised to pursue short-term profits at the expense of prudent risk taking.

Clearly, with the potential for large payouts there was much to play for at bonus time. According to one British investment banker, describing the scene at the start of this century, a considerable amount of time in the last quarter of the year was customarily spent setting the appropriate levels for individual bankers, based on formalised reporting or personal lobbying.[2] A feeding frenzy developed with all employees boasting their worth to the bank, and claiming involvement in any lucrative deal which had taken place or advancing spurious personal reasons for special treatment. The accepted practice was never to appear to be satisfied with any bonus, however large. Those who were unhappy could threaten to leave, taking their clients with them, if they could. It was not long before the concept of the guaranteed bonus emerged to retain staff or to attract key bankers to join from a rival institution. In these cases golden handcuffs removed the uncertainty and reliance on profits. Bonuses were simply seen as an entitlement.

It is not clear how or why bankers considered themselves to be entitled to be rewarded on a level much higher than other industries. They may consider that they possess rare skills and work long hours under stressful conditions with job insecurity, but so do senior people in other professions. Often there is an aura or mystique about what they actually do, covered by an attitude of arrogance which discourages serious questioning. When pressed to explain why they are paid so much, the answer is likely to be a smug, 'Because we are worth it'. In their own eyes bankers may well feel entitled to high rewards.

Treasury Bonuses and Rogue Trading

Nowhere can this have been more obvious than in the treasury departments of banks, where traders are in daily contact with their peers in other banks. Treasury departments, which manage the cash resources and funding requirements of the bank, tend to have their own particular culture with a strong emphasis on short-term profits which are readily measured in the simpler products. Since individual traders' profitability can be calculated, they are well aware of their contribution to banking profits and tend not to be slow in demanding their share. One anonymous female trader, who had overcome the numerous obstacles facing her sex and appeared to lead a less degenerate life than many of her male counterparts, detailed her experiences as a proprietary trader in London.[3] In it she disclosed that traders could expect to receive 40 per cent of the profits they generated for the bank, while being insulated from their losses, other than the threat of termination of employment.

Large bonuses can clearly lead to temptation. Nick Leeson of Barings Bank initially became a rogue trader to cover up mistakes made by his staff. When this proved successful, however, he resorted to hiding losses again without any such excuse. His bonus for 1993 was £135,000 and he expected £450,000 for 1994. He appeared to be making all the bank's profits and yet several directors were to receive bonuses of £1 million. Leeson claimed that the senior management wanted to believe in his profits and did not properly scrutinise them, ignoring various warning signs.

An independent source provides further insights as to how the bonus system operated in Barings.[4] When the Bank of England attempted to mount a rescue in February 1995, there was concern over the mounting losses which had been revised upwards to £650 million. Included in the losses was an amount for bonuses for 1994 totalling £105 million to be paid on the following day. Many of the bankers accepted the proposition, since otherwise key staff could be expected to leave. The figure was based on unaudited profits of £204 million. The real group profit before the Singapore losses turned out to be under £20 million, while Leeson's losses amounted to over £860 million. The Dutch bank ING, which acquired Barings, in due course paid out bonuses of over £90 million. The bondholders fared less well with an offer of 5 pence on the pound with a vague promise of a possible further 20 pence. The employees of a badly managed bank, on the other hand, had been well rewarded.

The cases of other rogue traders, such as John Rusnak in First Maryland and Jerome Kerviel of the French bank SocGen, are also instructive. Rusnak was undertaking proprietary trading involving the use of options. Originally he feared that if he lost $1 million his position would be closed down. His bonus was based on a formula of 30 per cent of profits in excess of five times his salary. In 1998 his salary was $104,000 and his bonus amounted to $128,102 based on trading profits of over $1 million. In fact, his hidden losses were over $41 million at the time.[5] Almost a decade later Kerviel was to incur far greater losses from taking enormously risky trading positions after he had received a bonus of €300,000.

Do Bonuses Tempt Bankers into Sin?

It has long been recognised that poorly designed rewards systems can lead to unwelcome and unexpected consequences.[6] The surprising fact is how often such situations exist. If traders can earn bonuses equivalent to five times their salary, or even more, there is a logical reason to take risky bets for their personal enrichment. If the bets go wrong the likely downside is the loss of employment, and imprisonment only if some fraud is involved.

Traditional retail banking had little emphasis on bonuses. They were, however, much more commonplace in other areas of financial services, such as life assurance, which were driven by sales growth, and stockbroking, which was based on fee income in a cyclical industry. Both AIB and BoI had morphed into 'Financial Service Groups', encouraging the cross-selling of their financial products. In this new environment the bonus culture was to spread throughout the organisations. The conflict between the traditional conservatism of old style lenders and the new growth orientation of product salesmen led to a new hybrid culture with inevitable ethical conflicts.

The bonus culture can spread down an organisation through targets and budgets. If top management's rewards are based on a certain profit performance, it is natural that these profits are assigned to managers further down the chain. In a properly functioning budgetary system such targets should be set by negotiation. In a less well run organisation targets may be imposed. Where unreasonable targets exist, and failure to achieve them is likely to lead to some form of chastisement, mangers may be tempted to transgress.

High Court inspectors, examining the affairs of NIB in connection with selling a flawed insurance policy and overcharging on customer accounts in 2004 concluded:[7]

> The operational environment in the Bank at the time has also to be taken into account and the behaviour of individual branch managers and staff must be viewed in this context. The branch network was target driven – there were, amongst others, targets for fee income and deposits, but limited support by way of systems or training to enable achievement of these targets. Managers felt under pressure to meet these targets, in the setting of which they had negligible participation and which many considered unreasonable; they feared criticism and possible humiliation before their fellow managers if they did not meet the targets set.

Liberal bonuses originating in one department of the bank can quickly spread elsewhere. Treasury departments were making a large contribution to bank profits and were playing a role of an ever increasing importance in obtaining funding beyond the normal deposits within the system, particularly in Ireland, as the Celtic Tiger needed large amounts of cash to satisfy its appetite. However, other people, whose profit contributions were more difficult to measure, on the basis of equity naturally wished to claim their share of the bonus pool. The easiest answer, though not necessarily the wisest, was to provide generous bonuses throughout the organisation. As a minimum, it is likely that the top management will seek bonuses at least as big as top traders. Once growth takes over as the supreme goal it is easy for prudence and risk management to be overlooked.

The temptation to act recklessly is not restricted to traders. It has been seen that the directors of Lehman Brothers allowed enormous levels of gearing or financial risk taking in their quest for growth in profits and therefore future bonuses. In effect, they bet the bank and lost, bringing down the long established bank and spreading financial turmoil globally. Similarly, the management of Northern Rock were castigated for following a high risk funding strategy in pursuit of growth, which ultimately proved fatal. Banks which relied excessively on the interbank market for funding are open to the same criticism. In the words of one astute traditional Irish banker, depending on the interbank market for funding was akin to relying on one single large depositor who might suddenly withdraw his funds at any time. Similar charges could be laid on managers who unwisely concentrated the bank's lending on a small group of property developers. The question arises: Did managers act recklessly of their own accord or were they encouraged to do so by the rewards offered to them?

In the UK the Turner Review by the Financial Services Authority believed that inappropriate rewards had a role during the crisis in providing incentives to take excessive risks. Remuneration systems were belatedly being examined by regulatory authorities globally. Where Governments had provided widespread financial support, they had a legitimate interest in management remuneration. The review sought to defer a majority share of future bonuses above a certain level over a period of years with the payment of deferred bonuses dependent on subsequent financial performance.

Subsequently, the FSA proposed that bonuses should not be paid until banks had achieved a certain risk-adjusted return on capital, and that any surplus should be divided between management and shareholders on an agreed formula. An element of the bonus should be deferred to encourage sound risk management. Otherwise, management might be encouraged to avoid conservative valuations and ignore concentration of risk.[8]

However, some British banks seem reluctant to accept such an approach. In 2014 Barclays caused a furore when bonuses increased by 10 per cent, while their reported profits fell by over 30 per cent. Just a year after shareholders had invested £5.8 billion, £2.4 billion was to be paid out in bonuses, almost three times the amount of the dividends. Commentators questioned whether the bank was being run in the interests of the management or the shareholders, while many institutional shareholders actively opposed the payments. Eventually, the UK Government intervened to curb bonus payments. A similar outcry greeted RBS shortly afterwards, when they announced losses in excess of £8 billion after paying bonuses of over £500 million. The CEO of both Barclays and the part-nationalised Lloyds Banking Group both paid sub-stantially more than a hundred times the average pay of workers to their CEOs, raising further calls to curb such payments.

Secret Rewards in Irish Banking and Their Justification

None of the official reports into the Irish banking crisis addressed in any depth the issue of bankers' remuneration and its possible impact on the way banks behaved. They could not do so readily, since no such mention of it was included in their terms of reference. Yet the conclusion was that the management of the banks must bear the primary responsibility for the crisis. It would seem an obvious next step to see what their overall objectives were and how the management was incentivised to achieve these objectives.

For an outsider to attempt to do this is almost impossible. Information is limited to what is available in published accounts. Documents such as the minutes of the remuneration committee are not available. It would be fascinating to know what bonuses were awarded and why, but little detail is known beyond what was the actual remuneration of the directors. So any conclusions must necessarily be somewhat tentative.

Over the years the pay of certain chief executives, when disclosed, has attracted considerable adverse criticism, but otherwise information is limited. One interesting insight concerning the pay of senior management at one bank, AIB, did emerge with the Faldor scandal in 2004.[9]

The bank, still recovering from a scandal centred on overcharging their customers in foreign exchange transactions, released the story. It revealed that some senior executives had benefited from Faldor, a company based in the British Virgin Islands, the Caribbean tax haven. The consequence was that they had breached tax laws and had significant liabilities to the Irish tax authorities. In addition, they benefited from 'unacceptable deal allocation practices', whereby they received profits at the expense of AIB clients in the early 1990s. Many of those involved professed not to be aware of the details and were critical of the practices. Nevertheless. it was shocking that such improper arrangements should have been put in place at the bank to provide financial rewards for their very senior management.

The pay and benefits of senior Irish bankers prior to the outbreak of the financial crisis has received widespread publicity, when compared to rewards available elsewhere in Ireland.[10] David Drumm of Anglo led the pack with a package of over €4.6 million, including a €2 million bonus, bringing his four-year total to over €12 million. Brian Goggin's package at Bank of Ireland in 2007 peaked at €4 million, dropping to €2.9 million in 2008. He received little sympathy when he stated that it would fall to under €2 million the following year. In 2006, for his first year as CEO of AIB, Eugene Sheehy received €2.4 million, including a bonus of €1.3 million. In fact, these remuneration packages compared favourably with UK peers, where bonuses were often deferred, rather than being paid in cash, as was normal in Ireland. Goggin was paid more than the CEO of either HBOS or Lloyds, both substantially larger than Bank of Ireland. Termination payments for many early departures in the industry seemed equally generous, while the chairmen of Irish banks were well rewarded also. Outside the UK, remuneration packages for bankers in continental Europe seemed generally more modest.

In defending the pay of senior executives at Bank of Ireland, the Governor, Richard Burrows, explained that remuneration levels were set to attract and retain the best people, so pay rates were compared with bankers outside Ireland. The argument is difficult to sustain. Virtually all senior appointments were made internally, so attracting people for the top job was not too complex a task. Few top Irish bankers had been poached abroad over the years, although some had been transferred around large groups such as National Westminster Bank in the UK, and others had successfully made careers in London by working their way up through the ranks. There were occasional exceptions, such as Don Carroll briefly heading up Lloyds in the 1970s, and Peter Sutherland becoming chairman of Goldman Sachs, but he had far wider credentials than being a former chairman of AIB. Yet the remuneration levels of bankers available in London were known in Dublin and inevitably influenced thinking at senior levels in the same way as

American pay had influenced British pay levels in the aftermath of 'Big Bang'.

It is not difficult to see how remuneration committees in the leading banks could grant generous packages. Once one bank gave a substantial increase to its top management, comparisons would inevitably be made by others and a game of leapfrog could ensue, when bank policy was to pay salaries higher than the industry average or in the top quartile. Yet they all managed banks which before long were to destroy all or virtually all of their shareholders' wealth. Certainly the Government was to disagree, and in 2009 recommended cuts in the pay of top bankers of up to 64 per cent. But however questionable the rewards in the large banks might be, they were outshone by the generosity of a much smaller competitor – the Irish Nationwide Building Society – where all of the owners' wealth was eventually destroyed.

A Case of Grubby Fingers

One individual who has attracted much public odium is the former CEO of Irish Nationwide, Michael Fingleton, popularly known as 'Fingers'. Originally, the building society was notorious for its heavy penalty charges on customers in arrears, but it was rather more generous in providing mortgages to journalists and politicians. Subsequently the society had turned to funding developers. It morphed into a mixture of a subprime lender, a property bank, an investment house, an equity house and a property developer. Two journalists were to reveal fascinating and alarming insights into the business.[11] Their views were broadly endorsed by a national television programme.[12]

Reports by the auditors, KPMG, commissioned by the Central Bank in 2000 and 2005 highlighted serious deficiencies. Internal audit and treasury were both weak. Documentation was poor and too much reliance was placed on assurances from management. There was not even a documented policy for establishing loan provisions. Commercial property loans were advanced with insufficient checks and monitoring was inadequate. Risk management, reporting systems and corporate governance were all censured.

The bank even failed to check the profits of its joint ventures. The chairman rejected the criticisms in the second KPMG report and even denied that joint ventures with developers could lead to conflicts of interest.

Michael Fingleton, who ran the business as CEO for 37 years, had built up strong business and political networks. He was described by several people as running the bank as a sole proprietor and a bully. He kept a low cost income ratio by economising on recruitment of middle management, while several senior people found that they could not work with him.

A further later report by Ernst and Young disclosed fundamental problems of corporate governance in INBS. The board had granted Fingleton extraordinary powers originally in 1981, but reinforced them in 1994 and 1997. He was empowered to set, vary or alter interest rates and fees and to make individual arrangements with members without consulting the board or anyone else. He was, in short, all powerful.

However dangerous such powers were in offering domestic mortgages, they were to prove disastrous in speculative commercial lending, conducted both in Dublin and London, which was to grow to 80 per cent of the loan book. Lending files were poorly documented and loans were poorly structured, often without recourse to the principals. Loans were granted before credit committee approval, or for amounts different from those approved, and advanced without preconditions being satisfied or to different companies. Independent property valuations were not always obtained for large loans. Large fees were paid for services of unclear value. There was no proper arrears management system and some loans were not regularly reviewed, while the reporting pack on the management of credit risk was discontinued in 2007.

In these circumstances it is not surprising that INBS had more than its share of 'Ponzi' loans. Its €8.9 billion of loans transferred to NAMA attracted a 64 per cent discount, described as 'worst in class'. Irish Nationwide showed many of the classical symptoms of business failure, described in Chapter 5, especially after it moved into commercial lending. Its management centred around one controversial individual. It failed to anticipate the change in the property market. It overtraded and its controls were weak. Its funding was stretched and its loan book was excessively concentrated around a small number of property developers. In the end, it was nationalised and its loan book wound down. The question arises from the debacle as to how the CEO was rewarded and incentivised.

Some information was available on Fingleton's pay in the early 1990s. In 1992 he received pay and benefits amounting to £201,000, which increased to £249,000 the following year, a very large figure compared to his building society peers. Thereafter another executive was appointed to the board and it was not possible to separate out Fingleton's remuneration. Towards the end of his tenure the figures were again made public. In 2007 he received a 10 per cent salary increase to €893,000 and a bonus of €1.4 million. His pay for 2008 was to be at least matched at €2.4 million, as an inducement to remain with INBS, making him better paid than the CEO of AIB, a much larger bank.

In addition to his generous pay, Fingleton was to receive a large pension package. In 1995 a separate pension fund was set up for him, and in 1997 in an incredibly generous gesture the board agreed that his final salary for pension purposes was to include the average bonus of his last three years. The cost of this gesture was an extra €12 million, together with an additional €2 million for his wife, whose widow's pension was upped to 100 per cent, if she outlived him, bringing his pension pot up to €27.6 million. Astonishingly, the society only needed to find €4.3 million with the balance coming from the gains in the fund, managed by Fingleton himself. This new arrangement gave him a strong incentive to grow the bank in the expectation of an increased bonus and pension.

In the outcry which followed the emergence of the very serious problems at INBS, the Minister for Finance asked him to repay his 2008 bonus. Despite initially agreeing he later refused, claiming that it was his entitlement and not dependent on performance. He similarly declined to return the expensive watch presented to him on his retirement, or many of the personal expenses for which he had been reimbursed, including some arising after his departure from office. He protested too that the society had only made pension contributions on his behalf of less than €3 million. More light may be thrown on some of these issues in a review by the Central Bank, announced in 2014.

Fingleton's considerable personal wealth subsequently suffered from forays into property development on his own account at home and abroad. The members of INBS never received their bonanza from the expected sale of the organisation, and the Irish taxpayer was to pick up the bill of over €5 billion for the excesses in financing Irish and overseas property oligarchs. The bonuses and rewards granted did little to promote an orderly conduct of the business. Of course, whether or not the directors broke the law is a matter for the courts, if and when they consider it.

Seeking a Return to the Payments of Bonuses

In 2014, AIB sought permission to restore the payment of bonuses to retain key staff. The request was promptly turned down by the Minister for Finance, who considered it to be premature until the Government had disposed of its shareholding. There has been no detailed examination of the role of bonuses in the risk taking by Irish banks, but there was much public disquiet about the level of remuneration paid, and the risks taken, by Irish banks during the property bubble. To judge by UK research by the FSA, there is at least a case to answer and it is a legitimate area for concern by the regulatory authorities globally, but especially for banks in receipt of public support.

It is difficult to justify the return to bonuses in the short term before a sustained return to profitability. If bonuses are to be paid in future, in view of the difficulty in measuring short-term profits, it would be preferable to pay them in restricted shares, rather than cash. In any event, the concept of deferring payment, dependent on subsequent financial performance, is worthy of serious consideration. In the meantime it would be helpful for the public to have a greater understanding of the remuneration of management, such as the disclosure recommendations set out in the next chapter.

CHAPTER 13

The Irish State –
A Reluctant Bride

With the granting of the guarantee of €440 billion to the depositors and eligible bondholders the Irish State became fundamentally wedded to the banks, whose future prosperity, or lack of it, would directly impact Irish citizens and taxpayers. Before long Anglo Irish Bank and Irish Nationwide were nationalised, put into IBRC (the Irish Bank Resolution Corporation) and placed into windup. Following the recapitalisation of AIB, the State had a shareholding of over 99 per cent in it and its subsidiary EBS. Similarly, it came to own over 99 per cent of Irish Life and Permanent, selling off the insurance business in due course, while retaining Permanent TSB. That left only Bank of Ireland, in which the State already had a significant interest.

The Irish State found itself in this position not of its own volition. Prior to the crisis it had disengaged from banking as a matter of policy. In 1990 it had wound up Foir Teo, the State-owned rescue agency, which had spent large sums of money in the 1970s and 1980s attempting to rescue businesses which often had no viable future. In 2001 the Government had sold ICC and ACC, finally cutting its links with banking which had existed for nearly 70 years. Inevitably, politicians would come under pressure from sectional interests to persuade these banks to provide loans, where other banks would decline them. By 2001 there were many domestic and overseas banks competing for Irish business and the State was happy to leave the stage to them. Ironically, the acquirers of ICC and ACC, Bank of Scotland and Rabobank, were to withdraw separately from the Irish market in 2010 and 2013. But just because it was wedded to the banks did not mean that the State wished to play an active role in the marriage.

Hands-off Management

Operating in a global banking market, the State was well aware of the dangers involved in attempting to micromanage the banks, which it could do by exercising its shareholder power and consequently its ability to select bank boards. The public sector lacked the necessary expertise in any event and operated in a very different culture to that of the private sector. While individual politicians might well see the advantages of advancing the interests of their constituents, they realised the necessity of resisting political pressures to influence credit decisions.

The State did initially decide to nominate two public interest directors to each of the stricken banks. Often Government appointments to State-owned institutions are made on narrow political grounds, rewarding party friends, however lacking their apparent qualifications might be. In this case the candidates were drawn largely from those people with whom they were best acquainted, namely retired public servants and politicians, though some were not known as supporters of the ruling political parties.

The exact role of these public interest directors remains something of a mystery. Much political capital was made of the responsibilities of directors and the need to avoid conflicts of interest. Yet it is commonplace for banks to nominate directors to boards of subsidiary companies to represent the interests of the parent company, which does not cause undue problems in practice. In general, minority groups often seek board representation and can participate subject to restrictions governing conflicts of interests, such as declaring interests, withdrawing from certain discussions or abstaining from voting, when appropriate.

Having guaranteed many of the major liabilities of the banks the State had enormous interests to protect and could have been expected to demand rapid reform. But the Government chose a more hands-off approach. In 2013 it was revealed that the Minister for Finance had provided no formal brief to these directors, had minimal contact with them and in general did not receive formal reports from them, so it is not clear how they were to represent the public interest. Maybe, like the former Taoiseach, Eamon de Valera, they were expected to look into their own hearts to discover what the public interest in any given situation was.

Following the crisis the banks did not hurry to dismiss senior executives. Governor Honohan indicated that keeping in position the management who had made the bad decisions prolonged the tendency to remain in denial about the problem. In 2011 the Department of Finance advertised for people to act as bank directors. Also the Central Bank decided to check out the credentials of senior bank managers. By December 2012 senior figures were obliged to complete a questionnaire concerning their fitness and probity to hold their positions and submit it to the Central Bank for approval. Several bankers resigned their posts around this time. The Central Bank's role was to try to ensure that any appointment made was a safe pair of hands.

The upshot of these moves meant that seven years after the crisis broke there are a number of new faces on bank boards. Many of them are British and male, who for a variety of reasons had the time available to serve on Irish bank boards. However, fundamentally the appointments rest with the boards themselves, subject to a veto by the Central Bank on grounds of fitness or probity. As indicated earlier, the Bank of Ireland tended not to appoint directors with unknown views for fear of upsetting the cohesiveness of the board. Whether or not such a policy has resulted in like-minded people, who can be relied on not to rock the boat, being appointed to bank boards remains to be seen.

Light Touch Regulation and Regulatory Capture

In the Honohan Report both the Central Bank and the Financial Regulator came in for serious criticism for their conduct prior to the crisis. 'Light touch' had been considered the appropriate means for conducting business, but light touch could quickly deteriorate into no touch. As a result of the Inspectors' Report into NIB, certain senior figures were disqualified from acting as directors by the courts after the Director of Corporate Enforcement initiated proceedings, but this was exceptional. Where banks were found to have overcharged their customers, they were obliged to refund the money involved. But prosecutions were non-existent and any white collar criminals had little to fear.

Complicating the situation is the disagreement amongst regulators as to how they should perform their function. The US has favoured a rules-based approach, where strict rules are enforced by an army of supervisors. The alternative is an approach based on broad principles, favoured in the EU, where guidance is provided but considerable discretion is permitted in the interpretation of these rules, thereby allowing a high degree of self-regulation. While the debate continues, it must be stated that neither approach can be held up as a role model in the recent financial crisis.

Achieving an international consensus on banking rules proved difficult, given the power of strong bank lobbies. The relevant financial authorities met periodically in Switzerland to set down rules, obliging banks globally to maintain certain minimal levels of capital and thereby creating a level playing field. The first Basel Agreement in 1989 laid down certain capital requirements, but was generally considered to be too crude in weighting risks. The second agreement in 2004 attempted to deal with the shortcomings of its predecessor, but allowed the banks considerable freedom in measuring risk with their own risk models. Perversely, it indirectly encouraged them to take risks off their balance sheets through securitisation, thereby fuelling the subprime property bubble. The third agreement, still to be implemented, aims to increase equity capital requirements. Confidence was shaken in the effectiveness of stress testing, since too many banks which passed the tests failed shortly afterwards in 2008. But even if stress tests prove to be more rigorous, many gaps remain in the system. No consensus has emerged on other important issues, such as limitations on proprietary trading or breaking up banks which are considered to be too large to fail, or even the scope of the required regulation.[1]

Under light touch regulation the markets were presumed to penalise miscreants, thus avoiding the necessity for intervention by regulators. In Ireland fines were rare, though a fine of €3.25 million was imposed on the Quinn Group in 2008 for misuse of insurance company assets, while Sean Quinn was fined €200,000 personally.[2] Again, shortly after the creation of the bank guarantee, INBS was fined €50,000 for trying to use the guarantee to generate deposits in London in a move which infuriated UK competitors. But these were rare exceptions. In the UK, by way of contrast, the Financial Services Authority levied an average of £14 million on financial institutions between 2002 and 2007, followed by £27 million over the next eighteen months.

Light touch regulation was by no means unique to Ireland. Around the world it was discovered that the public servants in the regulatory authorities were ill equipped to challenge the highly paid bankers they were expected to regulate. Relationships were based on collaboration, rather than conflict, which could easily turn into surrender by the regulators. Indeed, many commentators considered that in effect the regulators had been captured by the banks and other financial institutions.

In the aftermath of the crisis this was to change, as the regulatory authorities began to flex their muscles, albeit somewhat belatedly. In the US the authorities have imposed multibillion dollar fines on banks which behaved recklessly during the sub-prime mortgage boom, including a $13 billion settlement with J.P. Morgan Chase for misrepresentations to investors in 2008/9. In 2014 Bank of America settled similar claims with a fine of $16.6 billion, the largest fine ever imposed on any single company by the US authorities. The UK is considering the introduction of criminal penalties for bankers and deferring payment of their bonuses for up to ten years, so that they can be clawed back in the event that the bank requires support from the State. Light touch regulation has given way to serious sanctions.

Stiff fines for misdemeanours should provide a starting point for imposing stronger regulation, but may not be sufficient to root out malpractices. Nor will accepting a few sacrificial lambs found guilty of breaching regulations. Where there has been widespread abuse, such as the selling of payment protection insurance, it is important to discover the real reasons for such behaviour. The activity generated substantial profits and persisted for a long period. It remains unclear why senior management did not act to correct the abuses earlier. In such circumstances the Regulator could institute some form of 'cultural audit' to see if the banks' systems, especially rewards, encouraged such behaviour. If so, management should be obliged to deal with the problem by changing the systems which encourage malpractice.

Making the Marriage Work

It may not have been the wish or intention of the Irish Government, but as a result of the guarantee to depositors and other creditors, the State was wedded inextricably to banking. The State is involved on several different fronts. First, it had to introduce and enforce a new form of financial regulation. Secondly, it needed to manage NAMA to minimise the losses on its loan book. Thirdly, it has to oversee the liquidation of IBRC and the disposal of its loan book, either to external investors or to NAMA. Fourthly, as a Government, it needs to restore the damaged reputation of Ireland in international markets after leaving the bailout and to raise funds on long-term capital markets. The banks in their turn rely heavily on the Central Bank and ultimately the Government. The Central Bank acts as lender of last resort, arranging funding through the ECB. The banks are also large holders of Government bonds and have a strong vested interest in seeing interest rates remain at low levels. There exists therefore a strong mutual interest in ensuring that the relationship works.

Its starting position after the crisis has been problematic, since the Financial Regulator did not appear to command the respect of the banks, which had disregarded its reports into their lending. The behaviour of Anglo Irish Bank, in particular, as evidenced by the tape recordings between senior management figures, indicated a total lack of respect for the authorities. The initial challenge is to re-establish the authority and independence of the Financial Regulator. Beyond that it must tackle the decline in the performance standards of the individual banks and restore confidence in the system.

The work practices within the Central Bank in the past were also questionable, since many employees enjoyed unusually short working hours. Its staffing had been strengthened, as it sought to establish a new working relationship with the fragile banking sector. The Financial Regulator now has clear reporting lines under the aegis of the Central Bank, so there is no blurring of responsibilities. Since the State now guarantees deposits up to €100,000 it must ensure that banks do not fail in the future and impose yet further burdens on the taxpayers. Given recent history, it would be unwise to rely on the management of the banks to conduct their affairs without rigorous regulation and close supervision to ensure both compliance and high standards of performance.

The banking sector continues to pose serious problems for the efficient operation of the economy. It has been pressed by the Central Bank, on behalf of the Troika, to make inroads into resolving the mortgage arrears issue. The Central Bank also wants to see credit flowing again to SMEs, where the two pillar banks, AIB and BoI, have allocated a modest amount of funds for this purpose, but some other banks remain somewhat reluctant to do so in practice, whatever their official statements. Yet progress has been disappointingly slow on both fronts. Exhortations from the Central Bank seem to carry less weight than those of their counterparts in other jurisdictions, such as the UK. Overall, the profitability of the banks may suffer from the banking levy announced in the 2013 National Budget and the increase in DIRT, which may lead to some loss of deposits.

While the Central Bank has been trying to impose tighter regulation, there has been some opposition from the banking sector, which naturally resists efforts to restrict their freedom of action. John Bruton, president of IFSC Ireland and a former Taoiseach, has repeatedly called for a rein on regulation, claiming that excessive regulation is driving banks out of the country.[3] But not long ago the country was denounced in the US as the 'Wild West of Capitalism' and its reputation badly besmirched as a result. In 2007, the collapse of the German Depfa Bank subsidiary in the IFSC drew much criticism on the Irish regulatory authorities. Although the Irish taxpayer was not saddled with the cost, the country might not be as fortunate next time if a bank, under the ambit of the Financial Regulator, were to fail. There is no alternative to greater regulation if Ireland is to regain its traditional good reputation. It is the responsibility of the Government to ensure that it has the necessary powers to fulfil its role effectively.

The way NAMA and IBRC conduct their affairs will also impact the future of Irish banking. If recalcitrant developers are seen to escape without repaying their loans, and after a short period undergoing bankruptcy proceedings in a friendly jurisdiction return to do business in Ireland still enjoying a high lifestyle, there will be public outrage and a determination by those struggling to deal with mortgage payments to emulate them. Wealthy oligarchs can afford to pay for professional advice as to how best to distance their assets through transfers to family members or offshore trusts in jurisdictions where it is difficult or impossible to follow their footsteps. If Government Ministers are seen to condone such action, or simply wring their hands, protesting their impotence to act, they will be storing up problems for the banking system.

Another way the Government can help is to pursue any bankers and others who they believe have breached criminal law. A start has been made in 2014 with the prosecution of three former directors of Anglo Irish Bank for offences connected with advancing loans to purchase the bank's own shares, even if it resulted in no custodial sentences. Frequently the case is made that the country has neither the laws nor the skills to pursue white collar criminals. What it must, at least, show is a will to tackle the matter with a sense of urgency. There would be an understandable sense of outrage if after a long period the courts were to dismiss cases on the grounds of delay, or that the defendants could not receive a fair trial in Ireland. Above all, if the country is not seen to be tough on crime, it is difficult to see how it can regain the confidence of the electorate or international financiers.

There is a limit to the ability of the Irish regulatory authorities' ability to solve the banking problems of the country. Economic recovery depends also on the Government's success in addressing its fiscal difficulties and renewed growth in the wider global economy, in addition to the banks' success in reforming themselves. But it remains a vital part of the jigsaw, since without effective regulation confidence is unlikely to return and recovery will be stalled. So Government must ensure that banks are in future run for the benefit of depositors and shareholders, rather than management. One way to achieve this end is to monitor closely the pay and bonuses of senior management.

Salary Disclosures

The disclosure of management remuneration in the Irish private sector has long been opposed by strong vested interests, with the consequence that less information is generally available than in neighbouring countries, such as the UK. For many years it has been mandatory there to disclose the remuneration of individual directors in companies, whether listed or not. In private companies it is difficult to interpret the profits produced in any given year without an appreciation of the size of directors' remuneration. It may suit family-owned businesses to take out all the profits by way of bonuses or conversely take nothing out, where they take their rewards from other businesses. The aggregate figure is of little assistance, since one individual may receive the lion's share, bringing friends on board for a nominal reward, thereby making the average look reasonable.

Opposition to such disclosure was based on spurious grounds. It was claimed that pay was a private, confidential matter and that shareholders need only consider that the aggregate figure was reasonable. However, if shareholders are expected to elect a director to the board, it would seem sensible to know the price of his or her services. The other argument advanced was that it was a dangerous security issue and that directors on high salaries might become kidnap victims of terrorists. This is fanciful, since kidnappers need victims with access to cash, rather than highly paid executives, and therefore aim their sights on businessmen, such as supermarket tycoons. When in recent years listed companies did disclose the remuneration of individual directors, there were some surprisingly high figures, previously hidden in an aggregate number. But for many years it had been impossible to discover how much the CEO was paid in a bank, such as INBS, since his remuneration was aggregated with that of another director.

During the Celtic Tiger era, as described in Chapter 12, the pay of senior bankers rose to levels which many outsiders found difficult to justify in the light of the disastrous performance of the banks. The Government reacted by placing a cap on the pay of bankers, ignoring their protestations. Of course, it is not just the pay of directors that should be monitored, since it would be an easy matter for the CEO to resign from board membership and therefore keep private his or her rewards. The pay of senior executives, other than directors, should also be kept under review for any organisation in receipt of State assistance, a matter which has recently attracted considerable public interest in the light of the disclosure of the remuneration packages for certain senior executives in the charity sector. Whether or not the new bank boards will be less generous than their predecessors remains to be seen, but their policy should be transparent.

A simple way to achieve transparency would be for each bank to disclose the total remuneration of its executives earning more than €100,000 in bands of, say, €20,000, with the number in each band. This would not show the names of those involved, thus preserving their privacy, while allowing the public to judge the reasonableness of the pay policy. This type of information has been made available in the National Treasury Management Agency (NTMA). Shareholders could then judge for themselves whether or not the general level of rewards for management was excessive.

It appears that the culture of greed, an obsession with large bonuses and a disregard for the long-term interests of shareholders all played a key role in creating the banking crisis. But it was also enabled by a failure of regulation worldwide to control the excesses, driven by a misguided faith in market forces to promote the common good. The inevitable question arises as to what should be done to fix the mess and ensure that it is never repeated.

PART FOUR:

Devising Solutions – The Rugged Road Ahead

CHAPTER 14

Ethical Banking – A Necessity or a Contradiction in Terms?

Many commentators have questioned whether banking can ever be constrained by ethical considerations. Certainly the image of banking and bankers in particular has suffered enormous damage in the recent financial meltdown. For many people it seems that wrongdoers can escape with fortunes, while shareholders and the public are left to pay the price. But cynical despair is surely not the remedy.

In the past I had often discussed with colleagues at the IMI the possibility of running a course on business ethics, but it never materialised. The general conclusion was that the people you would like to attend would absent themselves on the basis that they had no need for it. The likelihood was that you would only be preaching to those already converted, who in general ran their businesses by high ethical standards.

I did, however, have occasion to address the issue of ethics and banking, when Chartered Accountancy Ireland asked me to contribute an article on the subject for one of their publications.[1] My conclusion was that ethics have always been fundamental to the financial services industry. Indeed, the word 'credit' is derived from the Latin word *credo*, meaning 'I trust'. Without trust it is difficult to manage credit. Without credit it is difficult to carry out trade. And without trust a fractional reserve banking system cannot survive, if all depositors can demand the withdrawal of their deposits simultaneously. Trust and confidence have always been at the heart of the financial system.

Ethical Successes – Socially Responsible Investing and Microfinance

There have been developments in parts of the financial system where ethical considerations have brought about change in the way business is transacted.

For years some investors have decided against purchasing shares in businesses which did not meet their ethical standards. Socially Responsible Investing (SRI) attempts to combine financial returns with the social good. To this end it seeks to identify such businesses which are ethically unacceptable and exclude them from the portfolio. The list of industries varies from institution to institution, but typically armaments and tobacco are ruled out, as are gambling and pornography. Others might eliminate companies which fail to protect adequately workers' rights, exploit third world suppliers or seriously damage the environment. Alcoholic beverages and genetic engineering still generate considerable debate.

Drawing boundaries is by no means easy in practice, as I have discovered with others on a committee struggling to decide what is unacceptable. A case can be made against almost any company or industry on some grounds. If pornography is banned, does this imply that newsagents which stock the magazines must also be banned? If people condemn some of the activities of Government does this mean that their bonds should be blacklisted? Any workable policy needs to have a threshold level of significance for the objectionable activity, say 10 per cent of turnover. I listened to pleas for the exclusion of CRH, the Irish multinational building supplies group, on the grounds that it had a small minority holding in an Israeli cement company, one of whose customers used its product to build a dividing wall in Jerusalem, which was deemed offensive to some observers. This would seem a rather tenuous connection and insufficient to exclude the share.

Once the policy is established, implementation is relatively straightforward. There is plenty of software available to identify offending businesses. It also encourages shareholder activism, since problems can be taken up with the relevant organisation and explanations sought. Shareholders can also vote against resolutions over such issues as directors' remuneration, if they find the proposals objectionable. The ultimate remedy is, of course, to sell the investment. Investment banks have in fact benefited from the movement to SRI, since they have created and sold ethical funds. Such funds include investments compliant with Sharia law for Muslim clients, and 'green' funds for investors particularly concerned with environmental issues. So, the question arises, if ethical considerations can determine investment strategy, why can they not be extended to other aspects of banking?

Another successful application in the world of banking has been the introduction and dissemination of microfinance, particularly in the third world. Microfinance, providing credit and other financial services to the poor, has enormously grown as a sector of banking in recent years. For many years the very poor were of no interest to bankers. Many were illiterate, so entering into contracts was problematical. They usually could provide no security and the chance of default was high. Above all, it was uneconomic to manage very small loans, especially if there was no branch in the area. So the field was left to moneylenders who charged usurious rates of interest and adopted heavy handed tactics to enforce repayment.

Microfinance owes its origin to an enterprising professor of economics in Bangladesh, Muhammad Yunus.[2] In 1976 he visited a poor village and found that the industrious women, wholly dependent on traders who provided the materials and to whom they sold their bamboo products, were shamefully exploited, leaving them with almost no profit. Professor Yunus personally provided a loan, the equivalent of $27, spread between 42 families. The loan was to be repaid with a small amount of interest when they were able to afford it. His confidence in them was well founded and the loan, along with many later ones, was duly repaid with interest.

In due course Professor Yunus managed to get further funding from a bank to expand this small scale banking to the poor, but was obliged to guarantee each loan personally. Run on the principles of a mutual society, his students would enter a village and seek out women who were in need of financial support. This entailed overcoming religious and cultural opposition in a Muslim society based on 'purdah', where women were not used to handling money. The loans were made for small items of capital equipment and working capital, usually repayable over a year with weekly repayments. Each borrower formed a support group from five other women to solve any problems.

The project was named Grameen, meaning rural, and ran on the principles of discipline, unity, courage and hard work. It was an enormous success with a dedicated staff, heavy local participation and less than 1 per cent bad debts. In 1977 it was able to expand as an autonomous branch of the State-owned Agricultural Bank. The following year it expanded into a new poor area near the capital, Dhaka. Within ten years of its creation, Grameen was to become a fully independent bank with the backing of the Central Bank. Ten years later it had lent over $10 billion.

Grameen has gone from strength to strength. It has been replicated in over 50 countries, particularly in Africa, Asia and Latin America. But it has also been introduced to more advanced countries, such as the US and Europe. Professor Yunus and Grameen Bank were jointly awarded the Nobel Peace Prize in 2006, 30 years after the first small loans. Grameen has found many imitators and is now available in over 100 countries. Microfinance is available in Ireland under an EU programme. If a credit scheme driven by the social good can be so successful that it wins the Nobel Peace Prize, surely there is space for an ethical policy in banking.

Irish Frailties and Moral Lapses

I had always naively believed that peer pressure would act as an effective break on unethical behaviour. When bankers and professional people congregate informally in their clubs, topical matters in the public domain may be discussed. Few bankers would care to draw the opprobrium of friends or colleagues for behaviour deemed to be unethical. However, it now seems that at least in some banks profit pressure was a more effective motivator than peer pressure.

The many scandals emerging from Irish banking over the last 40 years have been summarised in Chapters 2 and 10. First, there was reckless lending which brought about the downfall of many small banks over the years. Secondly, there were the conspicuous failures of control at AIB over its ICI insurance subsidiary and later its rogue trader in the US. Thirdly, there was the overcharging of customers, particularly at AIB and NIB. Fourthly, there was the defrauding of the taxpayer at all or nearly all banks in the competition for deposits. Fifthly, there were the secret rewards for senior management at AIB through its Faldor activities. And finally, there was virtually a total collapse in standards resulting in 'Ponzi lending' in the recent property bubble.

How were such catastrophic lapses allowed to happen in what the public believed to be a conservatively managed industry? The answer seems to lie in a change of culture, vividly illustrated by the shocking revelations contained in the *Irish Independent* tapes of conversations among senior managers at Anglo Irish Bank. Underlying this was the relentless drive for ever greater profits and bonuses. This end appeared to justify any means, which on occasions could lead to serious breaches of the law or, at the very least, highly unethical behaviour. Undoubtedly this was not uniquely an Irish problem, but was endemic in the industry, particularly in the investment banks. In the UK the public were shocked by stories of money laundering, rigging of the key LIBOR interest rate and mis-selling products to customers. Banks and regulators may wish to believe that such practices have ceased, but many others believe that the greed driven by the enormous potential rewards still occurs. A serious moral vacuum still seems to exist in at least some elements of banking, where the condemnation of the misdeeds of the 'Bangsters' remains muted.

While bribery and backhanders are illegal and wrong, sometimes it may prove difficult to draw up reasonable, comprehensive rules in practice. One practical application of the particular culture of any business is what it permits as reasonable expenses for entertaining customers. 'Soft commission', where a service is provided for free in the expectation that it will lead to business, is often a difficult area to police. Providing company research from brokers to financial institutions is acceptable, but what about providing expensive computer software? Banks should and often do have strict rules as to what is permissible.

Where is the boundary between entertainment and backhanders? Most people find invitations to sporting fixtures in corporate boxes at Croke Park or the Aviva stadium acceptable, but what about taking customers to the US to watch the Ryder Cup, as AIB did in 2008, while other customers were obliged to cut back their overheads? The budget for entertainment at Anglo Irish Bank was recently disclosed as €3.4 million per annum.[3] This covered extravaganzas to watch Formula 1 races, trips on the Orient Express and the drinks bills of executives' weekends in Portugal while visiting exotic night clubs. People do not need to be prudish to object to the lavish corporate entertaining, the likes of which existed in London during the boom years, as outlined in Chapter 9. What is acceptable in any organisation depends on the set of values inherent in its particular culture.

Moral Leadership – Clerical Viewpoints

It might be expected that clerics would generally provide moral leadership and ethical advice. This could not be said of the chairman of the traditionally conservative and ethical UK Co-operative Bank, the Reverend Paul Flowers, whose personal life shocked the British public and caused many to question how he could have ever been a suitable person as chairman. In 2013 he was photographed, waving wads of banknotes, as he purchased illicit drugs, for which he was later convicted, so as to engage in sexual orgies.[4]

A respected senior banker who addressed current problematic issues in banking was Stephen Green, a recent CEO and Chairman of HSBC, who subsequently became a senior British Government minister. As an ordained priest in the Church of England, he would seem well qualified to tackle problems of morality. In his book he ranges widely around history, geopolitics, literature, philosophy, religion and economics. Ultimately, he comes down in favour of capitalism, despite its obvious flaws, as the best way to improve material human wealth.[5]

It is, however, one thing to advocate high standards of behaviour, but another to see that they are upheld throughout the bank. While Green was Chairman, the bank was accused of money laundering for drug dealers and terrorists, an accusation which was vigorously denied. Subsequent inquiries did establish that money laundering had occurred during his tenure as CEO and Chairman. In due course his successor admitted that money laundering controls, particularly in Mexico, should have been stronger and more effective; also the bank had failed to spot and deal with unacceptable behaviour.[6] The bank was duly fined $1.9 billion by the US authorities.

A warning was given by an expert on derivatives and risk, Catherine Cowley. She pointed out the dangers in derivatives in 2006 because, while they contained quantified benefits, they also contained unquantifiable risks, which could destabilise economies.[7] She attributed the problem to lack of transparency and complexity, together with the dynamic nature of the products which can spill into other markets. It was compounded by the market structure and the moral hazard of volatility, whereby the financial sector can generate more business and make bigger profits if assets have a volatile price. She believed that the problem was too important to be left to a small group of technical experts and should be a matter for public debate. Her views, which were an important contribution to the understanding of risk, did not receive the attention they deserved when she changed her career. She subsequently became a nun and now teaches Christian Ethics.

Subsequently, the Archbishop of Canterbury, Justin Welby, a member of the Banking Standards Commission and a former oil industry executive, deplored the 'culture of entitlement' which exists in parts of the City of London in which the ethos seemed to disconnect from what people saw as reasonable in the rest of the world. Certainly when bankers are questioned about their remuneration, the arrogant claim to 'entitlement' is often the response. This may mean that they have been granted generous employment contracts designed for a more prosperous era, which may include dubious clauses containing guaranteed bonuses and golden hand-cuffs. But to the rest of the world these aspects no longer seem reasonable. Similarly, the smug claim of 'because I am worth it' may fail to convince. Many onlookers hold bankers responsible for the very considerable destruction of shareholder value which oc-curred in 2007/8 and the bailout by the State to keep the financial system intact. Bankers' remuneration should be adjusted to fit this new reality, rather than being based on some unjustified mystique.

The Dubious Sales Culture

One aspect of banking which has attracted adverse criticism is the whole selling culture and the bonuses it generates. I gained some experience from National Irish Bank, where the Australian par-ent bank placed a strong emphasis on sales and insisted that every employee from the CEO downwards had at least some training in the basics of salesmanship. My own experience of cold calling was dispiriting when the company finance director on my first call stat-ed that he had been visited by six banks in the last three months and asked how was ours any different. Without being able to of-fer cheaper finance, the assurance of better customer service rang somewhat hollow. As the sales culture took hold, it was not always appreciated by customers. I was told by one manager of a custom-er coming into the branch carrying a placard indicating that he did not wish to buy any products, but merely wished to deposit cash. The later experience of the bank in product innovation in deposits did indeed prove attractive to customers who wished to evade tax, but ultimately destroyed the reputation of the bank.

Many commentators in the UK have deplored the sales culture which has developed there and led to serious mis-selling of prod-ucts.[8] There have been complaints about the selling of pensions and endowments in the past, but more recently the focus has been on payment protection insurance (PPI) and interest rate swaps. PPI was designed to help customers meet their financial obligations in the event that they lost their jobs. But many policy holders found that when they came to claim, the small print contained clauses which prevented them from doing so. In Ireland, too, PPI policies were mis-sold and the banks were obliged to refund €25 million to their customers. Those who bought interest rate swaps, believing that they would protect them from rising interest rates, suddenly found themselves liable for large payments when rates fell. The risks of the new products simply had not been adequately explained to customers who often were financially unsophisticated.

The nature of retail banking had undergone a massive change. Automation and increased competition had made traditional branch banking lending and deposit taking relatively unprofitable. Many branches were closed and replaced by an impersonal service from a remote centre. To reach profit targets staff were urged to take a larger share of the customers' wallets. This required selling them new products which may not have suited their needs. Often customers did not realise they were being sold products, but thought they were being given sensible financial advice which they traditionally expected from their banks. Those who sold the products, on the other hand, were well rewarded by commissions and bonuses.

As time went on some of the new products, such as PPI, accounted for an alarmingly high percentage of bank profits. But it was to end badly when complaints of mis-selling were upheld and the banks became liable for massive compensation claims. New scandals emerged around money laundering and the rigging of LIBOR interest rates, which further disillusioned the public with the prevailing banking culture. There have even been suggestions that businesses have been unnecessarily collapsed to generate fees and allow a bank to acquire properties cheaply. The reaction of the public has been a mixture of anger and contempt, as they sought to deal with the problems created by the enormous expansion of credit fuelled by the banks during the boom. Cynicism grew, particularly as senior banking offenders have not yet ended up in jail.

The scandals occurred at least partly because the nature of banking had fundamentally changed. In the 1980s banks placed a strong emphasis on building up a strong and enduring relationship with their customers. Subsequently the focus switched to short-term profits and generating the products and transactions to achieve this end. Relationships with customers were deemed less significant, as banks were judged by the 'bottom line', which earned the managers their bonuses. The culture became endemic, as managers imposed challenging performance targets on their subordinates. The risks inherent to the reputation of the bank were overlooked and its future placed in jeopardy. By changing the emphasis from relationship banking to transaction banking, driven by ruthless selling, the banks forfeited the trust of their customers, which would inevitably take time to restore.

A Banking Charter

Globally little seems to have changed in the way bankers behave since the banking crisis broke. Bonuses are still high on Wall Street. While the $32.9 billion bonus pool in 2007 has not been equalled, it was only reduced to $18 billion in the disastrous 2008 year and in 2012 was back to $20 billion, despite the enormous reduction in the number of jobs. Scandals periodically surface, ranging from reckless trading in derivatives to serious breaches of the laws in the countries in which they operated.

In 2012 the respected J.P. Morgan Chase lost $6 billion in the enormous, notorious London 'whale' trade, paying a $920 million fine for its troubles, since the transaction had not been adequately reported and disclosed. The CEO had his bonus halved to $10 million. Criminal charges are pending against two former traders, while the reputation of bankers in general remains besmirched. In 2014 Credit Suisse agreed a $2.6 billion settlement for assisting US citizens to evade taxes, while Barclays was fined for manipulating the price of gold. In the same year BNP pleaded guilty to violating US sanction laws involving Sudan, Cuba and Iran while agreeing to pay a fine of $8.9 billion. Global banks appear to have simply disregarded the law in a manner and to an extent that many law abiding citizens find deeply disturbing. Nor can this be blamed on a few rogue traders, acting in isolation. In many cases the issue was known to and condoned by senior management, as they conducted their business in pursuit of profit.

It seems that banks in many different countries continue to be driven by greed and the desire to generate short-term profits, often irrespective of the damage inflicted on their reputations and the substantial fines they might incur when they are caught. The enormous fines which have been imposed on the banks seems in no way to reduce the expectations for large bonus payments. Mis-selling products to customers, money laundering, sanction breaking and the rigging of financial benchmarks should all have been outlawed by senior bank management. But often they seem to have been either ignored or condoned. To judge by the events of the last few years it is far from obvious that the culture which existed before the financial crisis has fundamentally changed.[9]

To restore trust and confidence the public needs to be convinced that the banks are taking action and that the excesses of recent history will not be repeated. Integrity, competence and best practice should not be lost in the search for profits. It is easy to pay lip service to ethical behaviour, but much more difficult to put the principles into practice. Professions such as medicine, law and accountancy control the conduct of their members through entry requirements and a disciplinary process. Those who breach standards may face expulsion. Although qualifications may exist in sectors such as retail banking and security analysis, banking lacks mandatory entry examinations and cannot terminate membership of individuals who may breach ethical codes of conduct. It is left to the regulatory authorities of the State and the courts to exclude from further employment any bankers found guilty of misconduct.

Banks are well aware of the importance of high standards of behaviour and often pay lip service to the principle. The Irish Banking Federation launched a Code of Ethics in the year 2000. The principles of integrity, confidentiality, professionalism and compliance were stressed as being fundamental. The chairman of the IBF who launched the document was the CEO of Anglo Irish Bank, Sean Fitzpatrick. Irish banking seems to have lost sight of some of these lofty ideals during the property bubble, failing to implement its professed standards.

A start might be made by laying out standards of behaviour in some form of charter, though this will not succeed without showing that it will be rigorously enforced from the board downwards. This would necessitate penalising management for any serious breach of the charter. Here are a few of my suggestions for new standards:

1. Always treat all stakeholders, especially customers, Government and employees, fairly, respectfully, professionally and with integrity.

2. Ensure that all transactions stand up to ethical scrutiny.

3. Refrain from selling customers products which are not in their best interests.

4. Align remuneration policies with overall strategic direction, discouraging individuals from behaving antisocially for personal gain.

5. Admit mistakes and encourage more open discussions at all levels.

6. Ensure that no misleading public statements are made.

7. Restore traditional prudent lending values and advance credit where appropriate.

8. Identify all major risks and operate effective controls.

9. When detected, report any serious criminal offences at any level to the relevant external authority.

10. Adopt and apply to banking a version of the Hippocratic Oath: 'Above all, do no harm to society'.

Without some form of behavioural changes, such as those set out in this charter, it will be difficult for the public to believe that bankers will not succumb to moral hazard and cause a further banking crisis in due course. If practices more usually associated with share pushers and bucket shops become accepted in Irish banking, the future for the industry is bleak indeed. A manifesto encompassing appropriate reforms is considered in greater detail in Chapter 18. Ethical banking is a necessity, not simply an option for the restoration of confidence.

CHAPTER 15

International Banking Reform – The Glacial Pace of Change

Bystanders to the banking industry might expect that over six years after the fall of Lehman Brothers that many reforms would have been introduced into the world of international banking. Previously, in the years following the Great Crash of 1929 the world of US banking was fundamentally reformed with the passing of the Glass-Steagall Act and the development of the Federal Reserve Board, which provided relative stability for the next 70 years. This time, however, they would be disappointed because in reality, despite many proposals, little progress has been achieved in practice in recent years.

As early as 2010 it became clear that Wall Street had enormously increased its influence over American politicians, who bought into the free market philosophy and were reluctant to impose change on an industry which was famous for advancing its own interests. Politicians, who included many former bankers amongst their ranks, welcomed their financial contributions. Following the failure of Lehman Brothers in 2008, the US Government felt obliged to intervene to save the banking system and prevent another possible Great Depression. It did so by investing funds at highly subsidised interest rates, while failing to impose strictures on management such as it commonly insisted for third world countries facing banking crises. The largest banks were considered to be too big to be allowed to fail. These bankers, believing that, if necessary, they would be bailed out in future are vulnerable to moral hazard and may well be tempted to indulge in reckless risk taking again. So a further financial meltdown cannot be ruled out.[1]

Little Progress to Report – Must Try Harder!

Some changes which have occurred in the past five years are for the worse.[2] Risk seems to be more concentrated in a few financial behemoths than formerly. Incredibly, banks have actually grown bigger, particularly in the US, despite the numerous calls to reduce their scale in order to prevent a recurrence of the 'too big to fail' syndrome. These banks have the benefit of an implicit State guarantee, which allows them to raise funds more cheaply than their competitors while presenting them with the opportunity to take enormous risks. The difficulties of Fannie Mae and Freddie Mac in the US compounded the problems in the US mortgage market. At the time they accounted for 60 per cent of the market, but subsequently their share has grown to over 90 per cent.

Another worrying feature has been the continued growth of the shadow banking system, which is beyond the control of the regulatory authorities and has grown for that very reason, so that hedge funds and others may ply their trade without external supervision. The authorities believe that they can monitor these institutions rather better than before, but big risk positions still exist, especially in the rarefied atmosphere of derivatives.

Experimentation continues in the world of central banking, but this can lead to undesirable side effects, such as increasing inequality. The main policy change has been the use of QE or 'quantitative easing', whereby central banks effectively print money on an unprecedented scale in an attempt to keep interest rates down and encourage spending to restore economic growth. The result has benefited the asset-rich wealthy elite, including bankers. The Bank of England estimate that 40 per cent of the benefits of QE accrue to the top 5 per cent of the population.

Lastly, those responsible for the crash have not been prosecuted. Unlike the US Savings and Loans crisis in the 1990s, when almost 2,000 financial professionals were convicted, little effort has been made to prosecute culprits this time, other than fraudsters such as Bernard Madoff, who had managed to steal $65 billion from investors. When banks have been found to be guilty of rigging markets or other breaches of acceptable conduct, the organisations have had to bear severe fines, but the human perpetrators have usually escaped serious punishment. Some bankers may have lost their jobs, but they generally left with generous termination arrangements, including large pensions. Such are the rewards for failure!

Perhaps the lack of progress is not surprising. Bankers are expert in blocking change which they perceive not to be in their best interests. They object to anything which might reduce their scale or their independence. Regulatory changes can be damned as adding to the cost of lending and thus inhibiting economic recovery. Financial penalties, such as the financial transaction, or 'Tobin', tax, are strongly opposed on the basis that they would destroy the 'level playing field', since some major financial centres will refuse to introduce them. Ultimately, where their rewards are at risk, the banks simply threaten to relocate to a tax haven or just a more accommodating country, taking many jobs with them. When the proposal was made to limit bonuses to one year's salary, they responded by promising to increase salaries to protect their 'entitlements'.

Five Possible Routes to Progress

If meltdown is to be avoided in future, radical reform is required, rather than minor tinkering with the rules. While a number of proposals have been advanced, it is by no means certain that any of them will be implemented globally.[3]

1. Make bankers bear more of the risks personally

Investment banks in the US traditionally operated as limited liability partnerships until the 1990s, when they sought to bring in outside capital through stock market flotations. Many commentators believe that this caused them to place a greater emphasis on short-term profits and greater risk taking. Certainly personal liability can be a deterrent to recklessness. When the City of Glasgow Bank failed in 1878, the majority of its shareholders were pursued to bankruptcy. The oldest fully owned family bank in the world, the London-based C. Hoare & Co, is run cautiously as a partnership, lending only 40 per cent of its deposits and paying out minimal dividends.

Whatever the real and potential advantages of unlimited liability, any reform in this direction is most unlikely. There is little incentive to turn back the clock and bankers would find personal liability an unwelcome burden in a culture where downside risks can be referred back to Governments in time of crisis for support. More progress, however, might be made if directors realised that they could be prosecuted under criminal law for providing false or misleading information.

2. *Make bankers poorer – cancel or limit their bonuses*

Bankers have earned considerable public odium for their large pay packets and especially their hefty bonuses, which continue to be paid internationally, even as massive fines are imposed on banks and fresh scandals emerge. Given that the bonus system seems to have contributed to excessive risk taking, there must be a strong case for its reform, if not abolition of bonuses altogether. The EU proposes to limit bonuses to twice their salaries from 2014. The payment of annual bonuses in cash is dangerous, when the eventual profits are uncertain. A more sensible method might be to pay them either in shares, which could not be sold for a number of years, or loan stock which could only be redeemed when it is clear that no losses have been incurred.

However popular they might be to the general public, restrictions on bonus payments will be strongly resisted by banks. They claim that many bankers are highly mobile and are likely to leave if they do not receive their 'entitlements'. But too often bankers have received enormous financial rewards when their performance has been poor or, at best, indifferent. To date the profession has appeared impervious to public opinion.

3. *Make banks smaller*

Although smaller banks might face higher costs when raising capital, they can fail without threatening the future of the entire system. One way would be to restrict their geographic scale, so that they become regional banks, which have traditionally existed in the US. The most popular European model is the Savings banks in Germany, the *Sparkassen*, of which there are more than 400, demonstrating how to lend professionally in the downturn. They encourage local savings and support family businesses, the so-called *Mittelstand*, which have been the mainstay of German economic growth.

Smallness and geographic restrictions of themselves, of course, do not guarantee prudence, as some of their peers have demonstrated. The seven German *Landesbanken*, which are essentially regional wholesale banks, have experienced low levels of profitability, but also have not all managed to avoid the problems of US subprime lending. British Building Societies, such as Northern Rock, have strayed in their search for growth. Spanish *Cajas*, small local banks which traditionally were minimally regulated, were heavily exposed in the national property bubble. Nor could all large banks disappear. Multinationals require sophisticated international services unlikely to be found in small regional banks. Nevertheless, some reversal of the trend to globalisation in banking might make the system more secure.

Another way that banks could become smaller is to set out in advance what should happen if they get into difficulties. In 2010 the Financial Stability Board of the G20, which is coordinating global financial reform, decided that banks should make 'living wills' which will set out how they could be shut down or stabilised in a crisis. To date progress has been slow, so it is currently difficult to see how their activities might be reduced should such a crisis arise.

Restrictions on size are unlikely to be welcomed by the large banks, which now dominate the industry. Scale is associated with power. It would be likely to reduce bonuses when remuneration comparisons are made with successful small banks. The most fundamental reform of all in the US, namely the reintroduction of legislation along the lines of the Glass-Steagall Act, separating retail and investment banks, would reduce the size of banks, but would almost certainly meet strong resistance from powerful vested interests with close political connections.

4. Make banks take less financial risk

Many commentators believe that the problems of the banks lie with their excessive financial gearing. Equity frequently amounts to only 1.5/2 per cent of financing, the balance being borrowed in some shape or form. The Basel III regulations for international banking propose to increase this figure to a minimum of 3 per cent. Two academic economists argue that this figure is totally inadequate and should be increased to 30 per cent, reverting back to levels which existed over a century ago.[4] When banks are highly geared they believe themselves to be either explicitly or implicitly guaranteed by the State. Accordingly, they may take on excessive risk in search of higher profits.

Despite the theoretical advantages of high levels of equity, any such major decrease in financial gearing would be difficult to achieve. Banks historically have earned returns on equity of 15 per cent or more. If they were required to increase their equity tenfold, it might prove impossible to raise further equity. Already there is widespread opposition to the Basel III proposed increase in equity.

5. Make bondholders take more of the risks

An alternative to more equity from shareholders is equity from bondholders. This entails issuing hybrid financial instruments which are part bond and part equity. Convertible contingent liability bonds, known as 'Cocos', are issued and act as bonds, unless something happens which converts them into equity. The usual trigger point is the dropping of Tier 1 Capital below a certain percentage, or the share price reaching a certain figure. They can boost equity in time of trouble by changing bondholders into shareholders and taking on more risk.

UK banks such as Lloyds have already issued 'Cocos', but they are seen as only part of the solution. It is feared that hedge funds could react by short selling the equities when trigger points are reached, thereby negating much of the benefit. More radical measures are needed to restrict short selling in falling markets, which can become self-fulfilling, thereby creating a meltdown in a time of crisis.

The Uncertain Future of Capitalism

As the situation in financial markets has deteriorated, concern has spread for the future of the current capitalist model. The present model owes its origins to the laissez-faire values of the Thatcher era in the UK and the Reagan presidency in the US. It abhors Government interference and believes that management will act in the best interests of the shareholders, if left to their own devices and duly incentivised to do so. Yet, as shown in Chapter 11, this may not be the case, as Alan Greenspan was to discover. In the extreme case, focusing solely on short-term profits and rewards, while neglecting the interests of other stakeholders such as customers, creditors, employees and Government, can lead to the collapse of businesses and ultimately the economy.

As explained in Chapters 8 and 9, banking has evolved towards casino capitalism in the pursuit of short-term profits. Increasingly, the focus has switched from seeking deposits and advancing loans to making bets, often of a vast and complex nature, in proprietary trading through the use of the bank's own capital. Unfortunately, their neglect of the inherent risks, while failing to protect the interests of depositors, customers, employees and regulators, led to the financial crisis. The rewards of senior management relative to average employees have massively increased, while the shareholders have seen the destruction of their wealth. For many bystanders the system appears to be dysfunctional, unfair and dubiously legitimate, as the taxpayers and wider public have been obliged to bail out the banks.

In many countries it is alleged that a perverted form of 'crony capitalism' has emerged, where a golden circle of oligarchs wield the real power. Religious leaders and a wide range of commentators increasingly question the legitimacy of the current capitalist model, criticising the rising levels of inequality, regulatory failures, rewards for failure and lack of bank credit, together with wider concerns about bank management and high unemployment. Pope Francis has denounced unfettered capitalism as a new tyranny, condemning the enormous inequality of incomes and wealth which accompany it. Such fundamental criticisms of the system indicate that radical reform is required, if the system is to survive.

In an era of limited economic growth and widespread austerity, the policy of 'quantitative easing' through the central banks' printing of money has been called into question. Some commentators have predicted a sudden total collapse of the current system. One such recent view foresees China rejecting settlement of debts in dollars and the end of the dollar as a reserve currency. The dollar has become the central currency in world trade, but if confidence is lost in it as a store of value it could rapidly lose another feature of money, namely, being a medium of exchange. If such a scenario were to occur, global trading could be curtailed, leading to the collapse of the international monetary system and general economic chaos.[5]

Another writer in the past painted a particularly gloomy outlook for the system:

> The owners of capital will stimulate the working class to buy more and more expensive goods, houses and technology, pushing them to take more and more expensive credits, until their debt becomes unbearable. The unpaid debt will lead to the bankruptcy of the banks, which will have to be nationalised.[6]

This scenario cannot be summarily dismissed in Ireland of today, given the high levels of personal borrowings generated during the Celtic Tiger era. The prediction was made almost 150 ago by Karl Marx. His solution, which he had described as the 'spectre haunting Europe' in 1848, was the advent of the Communist State. Support for communism has, however, waned since the collapse of the USSR and the spread of capitalism to Eastern Europe. Even in China, where the old communist order has not totally disappeared, the behemoth, opaque State-owned banks would rarely be held up as role model for others to follow.

Until recently economists largely ignored the distribution of wealth and income, focusing instead on growth. While economic growth was strong, the tide lifted all boats, albeit some much higher than others. But in an era of low growth and concern about inequality in the recession, the subject has returned to the forefront of research. A recent best-selling study by a French economist traces an increase in inequality throughout all countries, but particularly the US, during recent years. With the advent of the 'supermanager' in most countries income inequality has grown, benefiting especially the top 1 per cent. Inequality in the distribution of wealth is even more extreme. He attributes it to the fact that the return on capital has exceeded the rate of economic growth, which is set to continue. Although some of the figures have been contested, the book has precipitated a whole new debate to the issue of growing inequality globally.[7]

As concerns have grown about inequality, serious reservations have been expressed as to whether the neoliberal approach is a suitable model for less developed countries.[8] As well as questioning the reality of businesses being run purely for the benefit of transient shareholders, the efficacy and desirability of such a goal is considered dubious. Free trade brings more benefits to advanced economies then those in early stages of development, while the free movement of capital can create financial crises. Modern capitalism appears to have done little to solve the problems of poverty, unemployment, low growth, energy conservation, global warming or hyperinflation in many parts of the third world. An alternative system of State capitalism, whatever its theoretical disadvantages, is preferred in many countries.[9]

Since the advent of the global financial crisis harsh criticisms have been levelled at the US version in particular, questioning whether it can any longer be considered a suitable role model for others to emulate.[10] Just as American military might falters so too bystanders wonder if the US economic system is truly a gobal panacea. The enormous inequality of income and wealth give rise to serious social problems, while the dream of social mobility remains unavailable to most of the underclass, as many work long hours for the minimum wage with low job security. CEOs, on the other hand, often earn several hundred times the average wage and can depart on generous terms, even when they fail and are sacked. The country meanwhile has lost much of its manufacturing base, while remaining excessively focused on property and finance. It struggles to generate many high level skills and to provide for an aging population with a massive pension burden.

In Europe less faith was traditionally placed in the pure market model than in the US, but this less extreme system faltered and severe problems within the euro have indicated that a new model of regulation is required to support the currency and reconcile conflicting national aspirations. Considerable dissatisfaction too exists in the UK with the overall state of the capitalist model there.[11] A new paradigm may emerge in due course, but this is likely to take many years, particularly where strong vested interests exist that are opposed to changes which might affect them adversely. Evolution is more probable than revolution. In the interim, uncertainty in financial markets and the future of the entire system, as well as the poor outlook for economic growth, has spread fear and damaged confidence globally.

Any reform of the financial system must address the dysfunctional elements in banking, since the banking system lies at the heart of capitalism. In these circumstances the banks might be well advised to reform themselves and try to regain the confidence of the public before matters are taken out of their hands.

Groping for a New Form of Capitalism

While the demise of the 'Washington Consensus' has left an enormous void in the economic underpinning of capitalism, it is difficult to predict confidently what the shape of the system might be in the future. Some pundits expect it to be transformed into something totally new, while others, in particular bankers, hope for and predict virtually no change. Any radical new way will need much debate and will need to be able to confront the powerful interests defending the status quo. While unsurprisingly no comprehensive alternative has yet been developed, some interesting ideas have emerged from the fields of economics, journalism, financial regulation and politics.

A Nobel Laureate economist, Joseph Stiglitz, produced a highly critical analysis of the crisis in the US and castigated the Governmental response. Low interest rates and lax regulation led to the property bubble and the country living beyond its means. The market mispriced and misjudged risk, leading to a failure of the banking system. The response of the US Government had been fundamentally flawed, based on an inadequate fiscal stimulus and bailing out the banks at enormous cost in a manner which lacked transparency, but cheated the taxpayer. The policies did little to sort out the problems of banks being overleveraged and too big to fail, but permitted bankers to return to massive bonuses and dividends.[12]

The solution needed to be the creation of a new capitalist order, founded on more rigorous regulation of banks and a changed role for the State, which should generate full employment and a stable economy while providing social protection and insurance, preventing exploitation and promoting innovation. The whole discipline of economics required reform in the light of market failures. The country was facing a moral crisis and needed to reconsider its true values. Above all, there could be no return for the US to the old system centred on a discredited 'Washington Consensus'.

An eminent UK journalist, Anatole Kaletsky, sees capitalism adapting and evolving in order to avoid a repetition of the meltdown of 2007/8. The first era of capitalism was the golden age of imperialism, which stretched from the end of the Napoleonic Wars through the First World War and ended in the great crash of 1929. There then followed a Keynesian Age, where Governments intervened to provide full employment. This in turn gave way to a third version in the Thatcher/Reagan era, which was based on market forces and minimal regulation by the authorities. A new form is bound to evolve, given the enormous cost of the recent crash, but it remains unclear exactly what shape it will take.[13]

Two other journalists from *The Economist*, John Micklethwait and Adrian Wooldridge, also see four revolutionary elements, which have contributed to the current state of capitalism. The first was the birth of the Nation State in the seventeenth century, followed by the rise of the Liberal State in the nineteenth century and the growth of the Welfare State in the twentieth century. The challenge is now to reinvent the State, so that it provides an appropriate range of services in an efficient manner through a fourth revolution. For their role models, however, they look not to America or the UK, but to Singapore and Sweden, as well as selective aspects of China, India and Brazil.[14]

The Chairman of the disbanded UK Financial Services Authority, Adair Turner, has argued that the system of economic liberalism, which preceded the crisis, produced neither market efficiency nor stability. Its growth policy did not necessarily result in increased human welfare, but definitely resulted in greater inequality. A new system in a world of great instability and uncertainty should not rely on risk measurements, which do not stand up to scrutiny when bubbles burst. Light touch regulation should give way to regulation which focuses on avoiding economic setbacks, since they are accompanied by unemployment and heavy social costs.[15]

A prominent businessman and former Minister in a UK Labour Government, David Sainsbury, has set out his views as to the role the State might perform in future. The State should not attempt to take over the functions more efficiently performed by the private sector, which is better attuned to the needs of the market place. It nevertheless should perform an important enabling role to ensure that financial and labour markets operate efficiently, that corporate governance of companies and businesses is effective, that world class systems of innovation exist and that education and training systems produce highly skilled workers.[16]

It is unlikely that the enormous growth in markets brought about by globalisation can be reversed. But, in view of the widespread criticisms of the system, the era of the 'Great Moderation', with its economic growth and prosperity which accompanied the abundance of credit, will disappear for a long time. The 'Washington Consensus' which was founded on light touch regulation and non-interference with markets has broken up and cannot be restored. If, as Alan Greenspan discovered, bank management cannot be relied on to act in the best interests of their shareholders, then more stringent regulation is required. Exactly how this could be achieved, however, remains uncertain, particularly given the need to reduce the size of the public sector and eventually balance national budgets. The bright new financial system – for all its talents and rich rewards – had failed the test of the marketplace, as Paul Volcker remarked in 2008. Risk management will inevitably be required to play a more central role.

If capitalism is to undergo any major changes, as outlined above, Ireland can have little influence in guiding the direction and pace of change. But it will be obliged to adapt to the new system, if it is to prosper. As a country Ireland has traditionally looked more to Boston than Berlin for its role models. Perhaps with the US brand of capitalism badly damaged after the subprime banking crisis, Europe could provide more suitable solutions.

Swedish Rhapsody

Banks in Ireland and elsewhere might usefully learn from the example of Sweden. Following deregulation in the 1980s, Swedish banks relaxed their credit standards. I remember being surprised at their generosity in providing facilities for a small Irish subsidiary. In the mortgage market they increased their exposure from a traditional 75 per cent to 90 per cent of cost. The resulting property bubble burst and Swedish banks faced a major crisis in 1991-2. The Government stepped in and took over the bad loans, guaranteed depositors and other creditors, before nationalising several banks in much the same way as Ireland was to do almost 20 years later.

There was, however, one bank which required no assistance then, in 2008/9, or subsequently – Svenska Handesbanken. For 25 years this bank has been ranked at or near the top of the Swedish banking league, measured in terms of financial performance. It remains decentralised in style with 96 per cent of credit decisions taken at branch level, rather than head office. But what distinguishes it most of all is its approach to rewarding and motivating staff.

In 1970 an eminent economist, Jan Wallender, was appointed CEO and, being familiar with the hazards of forecasting, abolished the traditional budgeting system in an act that was to start a movement of 'Beyond Budgeting', which was to spread slowly in Scandinavia and eventually further afield. But the success of the bank was believed to be the result of the collective contribution of the employees. While bonuses were abolished, they were replaced by a profit sharing scheme. The bank's profits were compared with those of their Swedish peer group and one-third of the profits in excess of the peer group average were placed in a separate foundation for the benefit of employees. About 90 per cent of the foundation's funds are invested in the shares of the bank. Each employee from the most junior to the most senior receives the same allocation. However, no employee is allowed to draw on the fund before reaching the age of 60.

This egalitarian, deferred profit sharing scheme has proved a great success. Based on the usual financial comparisons the bank outperformed its peer group in every year except one. Employees are believed to be motivated by the long run success of the bank, rather than meeting short-term sales targets. Its overall performance record speaks for itself. Despite its obvious merits, it does not seem to have found many imitators in banking, where management claim they must pay large bonuses to attract and retain key staff, but the model has the support of the British Government as an example for industry in general.

Implications for Ireland

Ireland cannot remain unaffected by changes in the wider banking field. To some extent it has adopted most of the five possible routes to progress outlined above. It has set limits to bankers' remuneration. The banks have become smaller as their international activities have been mostly sold, so that they now operate almost exclusively domestically on the island of Ireland. Those banks still lending have been recapitalised and have been submitted to international stress testing. Bank of Ireland, AIB and Permanent TSB have all issued convertible contingent capital notes. The only route not tried is to make bankers personally liable. Few wealthy individuals would relish providing unlimited liability in financial services, particularly in light of the experience of Lloyds' Insurance 'Names' in the 1990s. Its effectiveness in any event is open to question, given the recent success of some large borrowers in distancing their assets when pressed for payment.

Ireland is, of course, a very small country in the global banking market. As such it can have relatively little influence over changes introduced to banking worldwide. Inevitably, it must succumb to changes emanating from global or European sources, where new rules were introduced in 2014. Powerful banks globally may block changes, which might have merit by threatening to relocate their activities to block new regulations or taxes, such as controls over derivative trading or the introduction of a financial transactions tax, as advocated by the economist Professor Tobin. Such decisions will be made elsewhere and Ireland could suffer competitive disadvantages by attempting to conduct an independent policy.

The country's small size severely restricts its freedom of action, but does not provide an excuse for inaction or for a failure to negotiate with the EU the detailed terms of any changes which could adversely affect the country. Given its inherent present weakness and recent track record it can no longer set itself up as a model for others to follow, as it did at the height of the Celtic Tiger era. It may find itself operating under a new form of capitalism in due course. If and when it does, it will need to adapt to whatever new regulations accompany it.

In the short term Irish banks must accede not only the traditional restrictions imposed by the Irish Central Bank, but also the capital requirements of Basel III and the diverse regulations of the European Central Bank. Future changes need to be considered within the confines of this immediate context unless, of course, Ireland decides to abandon its membership of the Eurozone or default on its debts. If any Irish Government were to embark on such a radical policy change, the consequences would be very profound for Irish banking. It is therefore time to examine the options currently available to the State.

CHAPTER 16

Challenges and Options for Ireland

The Irish public does not need to be reminded that the country is facing difficult times. After a series of severe budgets austerity fatigue has set in and in 2014 voters have expressed their displeasure in both local and European elections, generating calls for a more populist agenda. It is therefore timely to examine the current situation and the options which lie ahead, as Ireland has finally emerged from the Troika recovery programme and received copious general praise from abroad for its achievements to date.

Eurobonds or Euro Shackles?

In the mid-1990s I was working with a large Ukrainian bank, which was moving towards the full adoption of the capitalist model. At lunchtime a young man came to me looking for advice. He had earned $500 cash, which he kept at home, but wanted to know what to do with it. Naturally I told him to deposit it with a bank. He responded with horror, asking me why he should lend his hard earned money to a bank. He was, of course, technically correct, though I had never really thought of a deposit as a risky loan to a bank. I quickly recovered and told him that I meant an international bank, such as Citicorp. Again he recoiled in horror, asking me if I did not know that the Government had levied all foreign bank deposits the previous year. I realised that, in view of my lack of relevant experience, I was unfit to advise him and told him so. What I should have also realised was that a similar problem could arise in any troubled economy, including the EU, as Cyprus would prove almost 20 years later. Sadly, I had missed the opportunity to benefit from a real life Ukrainian education.

Ireland is a member both of the EU and the Eurozone area. As such it is bound by rules and regulations, not necessarily of its own choosing. By joining the euro, it had already lost control over its monetary policy. While the country has now emerged from the Troika programme, it has inevitably lost a further element of its sovereignty, since its budgetary fiscal targets are still set in consultation with the Troika. As is often stated, the country remains reliant on the kindness of strangers. The classical approach to economic recovery is to restore competitiveness through the devaluation of its currency, a course adopted by Iceland. However, this approach is ruled out for Ireland by membership of the Eurozone.

A complicating factor is that the Eurozone does not act like a full currency union. The European Central Bank is very different from the Federal Reserve Board in the US, having a narrower remit with a focus on avoiding inflation, a legacy from Germany's experience of hyperinflation under the Weimar Republic. The Fed considers both control of inflation and tackling unemployment. In particular, the Eurozone lacks a common fiscal policy, since all countries remain free to set their own taxes. More significant still is that, while some preliminary steps have been taken, there is currently no banking union, which means that there is no ready solution when banks in any one country run into difficulties.

Ireland was told that no bank should be allowed to fail and that it was not acceptable that the bondholders should bear losses. Accordingly, the Irish Government felt obliged to guarantee all depositors and certain bondholders, when one large bank in particular was facing a funding crisis, while confidence in the market was severely strained. Although bonds on the market were trading at a discount which reflected the risk of default, their owners, which included many hedge funds, received a windfall bonus when they were redeemed in full on maturity. The German institutions, which provided much of the funding for the Irish property bubble, similarly incurred no material loss. A former Finance Minister and EU Commissioner has claimed that initially the ECB reacted favourably to burning bondholders, but relented under pressure from French and German banks.[1]

When the Cyprus crisis arose in 2012, the rules were changed so that bondholders and large depositors lost substantially there. The Irish Government would like to see the issue of eurobonds, guaranteed centrally, which would transfer the liability away from Ireland in recognition of the fact that the Government guarantee benefitted the EU institutions. Instead of eurobonds, however, at present the country has euro shackles, which bind it to a policy of economic austerity for the foreseeable future. While Ireland has reasonable grounds to feel badly treated, it seems that the Irish taxpayer has been and will continue to be left to shoulder the burden.

Following the successful exit from the Troika programme Ireland received a welcome boost to its reputation and its ability to manage its own finances. However, the country is still dependent on raising international capital, which could be withdrawn at any time if markets were to lose confidence in the Irish recovery. In Budget 2015 the Government proclaimed the end of austerity in the light of a forecast of renewed economic growth. But many independent commentators, including their own Irish Fiscal Advisory Council, consider such a change of policy to be premature. The economy remains vulnerable to shocks, whether caused internally arising from banking weakness or externally from general Eurozone difficulties, deriving from countries such as Spain and Italy in an environment of weak economic growth, while further afield geopolitical uncertainties in Eastern Europe and the Middle East cast a long shadow which could upset any international economic recovery.

There are some promising signs in the property market with a significant lift in prices, especially in Dublin, attracting overseas investors back into the market. While the rating agencies have improved their ratings so that Ireland is no longer sub-investment grade and has reduced its cost of borrowing, nevertheless favourable sentiment is dependent on continued economic success. The bond markets continue to wield considerable power over the economy. It is no wonder that an aide to President Clinton once jested that, if he were ever reincarnated, he would wish to return to life as the bond markets, so that he could terrify everyone. The question to be answered is whether there is any way that Ireland can escape from a prolonged period of relative austerity, as the public yearns for another Celtic Tiger.

Leave, Default or Remain in the Euro?

Periodically suggestions have been made that Ireland should leave the euro. But just as political parties in Greece have rejected such a move as a solution to their problems, so have Irish political parties. It is one matter to laud the freedom that such a major step would have for exchange rate policy, but quite another to suggest departure. The consequence would be to create massive confusion and uncertainty. Since no country has yet left the euro, it is difficult to predict exactly what the consequences might be. As a minimum, since all debts are designated in euros, creditors would demand settlement in euros or enter into litigation which could drag on for years.

Whatever new currency might be created to replace the euro would need to be protected on world capital markets. No political party so far has suggested re-joining the sterling area, so presumably some form of new Irish punt would be required. This would be likely to lead to higher interest rates and capital controls. Such a situation would probably upset many US multinationals which have located in Ireland to be within the Eurozone and to export to the EU. Any increase in the number of such countries withdrawing operations from Ireland could have catastrophic consequences for employment. Ireland is a small open economy, reliant on export markets, so any trade restrictions could be extremely serious. If any other country were to leave the single currency, the costs should become clearer. In the meantime, any such move by Ireland would be at very high risk indeed. Even the suggestion that such a move was being considered could badly damage confidence and curtail any economic recovery.

Another suggestion made is that Ireland should default on its debts, and indeed a study has been made of the consequences of such an act.[2] The consequences of default are difficult to predict for Ireland. A controlled default with the consent of the EU, such as

Greece has tried, would leave the country free to write down Government debt. This would cause great hardship for holders of this debt, in particular pension funds and banks, which might well be forced into insolvency. The country would be forced out of world capital markets for a number of years and the cost of Government borrowing would rise inexorably. The length of time the country might be locked out of capital markets is a matter for conjecture, but it is worth pointing out that Soviet Russia was excluded for 69 years after defaulting in 1918. The mortgage market would probably freeze up. At an early stage Government services would be halted, as they were briefly in the US in late 2013, when the threat of default loomed. For a small open economy, such as Ireland, to be locked out of international capital markets for a prolonged period could bring about severe hardship, while the Government would lack muscle in any negotiations to return.

The EU might well decline to sanction any default, since Ireland is regarded as the best example of recovery through austerity in Europe and permitting it to default could lead to contagion in Spain, Portugal and Italy. In any event there is a significant risk that a controlled default could degenerate into an uncontrolled default, as confidence in the system collapses. An uncontrolled default, such as Argentina experienced in 2001/2, led to economic chaos. Government revenues collapsed, State assets had to be sold at knocked down prices and civil order broke down. Savings were wiped out, while unemployment and inflation rose. Litigation by disgruntled creditors continued for years. There was a run on the banks, multinationals profiteered from the forced privatisations, but great and long lasting hardship and poverty was visited on most of its citizens. It did not reach a general agreement over its debts with its creditors until 2014. Even then dissident bondholders cased further disruption to its capital markets, demanding repayment in full and precipitating a further default. It would be a very brave person who would advocate such a policy for Ireland or act in a way which could risk such an outcome.

Calls for Ireland to leave the euro and default have become less common since the country exited the troika programme, but have not entirely disappeared.[3] The example of Iceland, as discussed in

Chapter 3, showed that devaluation does not necessarily provide a quick fix to a country dealing with a banking collapse. Given the dangers inherent in either leaving the Eurozone or defaulting, particularly in view of its dependence on foreign direct investment and its fragile banking system, Ireland has little room for manoeuver.

Historically, banking crises and property market collapses around the world have been closely followed by a considerable period of recession, accompanied by high unemployment and rising Government borrowings. Membership of the euro eliminates the possibility of devaluation or inflation as policy options. Countries seeking bailouts seldom welcome the terms imposed by their creditors. Some, like Dubai, may be fortunate to be rescued by a friendly neighbour, Abu Dhabi. But Ireland had no real alternative to help from the troika, however unpleasant or inequitable the terms on offer may seem. It can only seek to renegotiate the terms, when the opportunity presents itself.

Although the country has managed to exit the bailout programme the EU restraints on budgetary policy remain and Ireland, however much it might protest, is stuck in the EU austerity straitjacket, unless and until the straps are loosened. If, of course, the EU were to relax its stance on budgetary rules and introduce quantitative easing the position could change dramatically. In the meantime, Ireland has little option but to continue with its policy of relative austerity, however unpopular and politically difficult that may prove to be, while simultaneously negotiating with its creditors as best it can. Such an opportunity could arise with the refinancing of its IMF loans by borrowing from global capital markets, or if the EU were to seek changes which would require Irish consent. While some relaxation of austerity became possible with buoyant tax revenues in 2014, it would be unwise to abandon the policy of fiscal rectitude on a unilateral basis.

Mortgage Arrears – the Politicians' Quandary

The key to the banks' profitability lies with the necessity to provide for further loan impairments, particularly in relation to domestic mortgages. As the recession in Ireland deepened, mortgage arrears have steadily climbed. In mid-2013 mortgages with arrears in excess of 90 days accounted for over 12 per cent of all mortgages. A large part of this increase can be attributed to loss of employment and hardship, including extra charges and taxes, under the austerity programme. Many householders, especially those who took out large mortgages shortly before the top of the housing boom, fell into negative equity, when falling property values meant that the loans outstanding exceeded the value of the property. Banks and consumer groups disagree on the extent of strategic defaulting, where borrowers elect not to reduce their loans in the hope that they can reach an acceptable settlement.

For a long period after the collapse of the market there was a phony war between banks and borrowers. Consumer legislation had inhibited the banks from pressing too hard those in arrears, but in any case they did not wish to repossess a large volume of houses. Eviction has historically been a very emotive topic in Ireland, while vacant properties have often proved to be difficult to manage or sell. If they did manage to establish market values, it would inevitably crystallise losses and so lead to extra loan provisioning. Many banks were also slow to realise security on buy-to-let properties, although landlords could expect less public sympathy than an impoverished ordinary householder. In 2013 the State introduced new insolvency legislation, while the Central Bank pressed the banks to address the problem and come to sustainable settlements with customers in arrears.

Political leaders face something of a dilemma. Many politicians have traditionally sided with the small person against the large institution, since obtaining relief for distressed borrowers might well generate votes. But forcing banks to incur greater losses and raise further capital to fund them would lead to a serious economic problem in the longer term. Politicians also have often sought to create short-term employment by stimulating the construction industry, paying particular attention to a strong building lobby. But while such jobs may prove to be temporary, the damage caused by a fresh unsustainable property bubble could be more enduring.

The temptation to take a short-term view is probably aggravated by the particular form of proportional representation, which underpins the electoral system. The only other country in the world to adopt a similar single transferable vote system is Malta, where politics is a part time occupation. In Ireland, with its large multi-seat constituencies, there is considerable competition between members of the same party to capture a seat, leading to populist promises by individual politicians which are difficult to fulfil. Governments tread on a perilous tightrope when trying to reconcile the desires of their constituents and maintaining the stability of the banking system.

Given the continuing problems of the economy and the constraints imposed by membership of the Eurozone, it is difficult to see any easy solution. A diverse group of economists, writing in 2010, concluded that policy should focus on restoring competitiveness, raising employment levels, attracting foreign direct investment and resolving the banking crisis to avoid Ireland remaining in a long lasting recession.[4] While some modest progress has been made in improving competitiveness, limited progress has been achieved on the remaining issues during the last three years.

Eternally optimistic politicians often believe that they can spot the green shoots of recovery whenever any favourable news breaks, but unfortunately the return to strong, sustained economic growth remains elusive. Time and again economic forecasts have been revised downwards. In 2014, some pundits again saw favourable signs and some modest recovery in the property market. International investors have shown an increased interest in Irish commercial property, while Dublin residential properties have found buyers, despite the low level of bank finance available. The improved sentiment is helpful, but much still depends on the return of economic growth internationally, which in turn depends on factors beyond Ireland's control. One eminent economist has suggested that any recovery is likely to be U-shaped, rather than V-shaped.[5] If this proves correct, Ireland's eventual recovery will be slow.

The New Competitive Framework

One major hurdle facing the State is the absence of a healthy level of competition in the banking sector. Bank of Scotland, which had acquired ICC, withdrew from the market in 2010, while Rabobank, which had acquired ACC, announced its withdrawal in 2013. Danske Bank then announced its withdrawal from personal and small business banking. Ulster Bank remains a troubled part of a struggling group, RBS, and is set to contract its branch network after disposing of non-core assets and downsizing its operations. While it remains committed to the Irish market with an emphasis on SME lending and consumer finance, given its weak position it is unlikely to be a major threat to the two market leaders, though it could become an element of a third banking force.

The Government policy is to have at least two 'pillar banks', especially in the field of lending, but currently of domestically-owned banks only Bank of Ireland is not Government-controlled, since AIB is over 99 per cent owned by the State. It looks as though Irish banking is now conducted by a duopoly with two banks having a market share of 80 per cent or more. Permanent TSB remains weak with a substantial tranche of loss making tracker mortgages. Having failed the 2014 ECB stress test, revealing a capital shortfall of €845 million, it will seek new funds from the market. Another limited source of longer-term finance for SMEs may come from the Government's launch of its Strategic Banking Corporation of Ireland.

In 2014 clouds remain on the horizon for the banks, even though all banks, except Permanent TSB, passed the ECB stress tests. During the year sentiment has improved, but it is still possible that problems could re-emerge with stuttering economic growth. Since 25 European banks failed the test, they are seen as more stringent than their 2008 predecessors. But some commentators fear that they may prove inadequate to restore economic growth or deal with sovereign default. One well-known economic commentator, who correctly forecast the property downturn, predicted a new crisis for Irish SMEs when the extent of their property-related loans becomes apparent during the stress tests.[6]

The problem of a lack of real competition amongst banks willing and able to lend remains. While a ray of hope may come from AIB'S unilateral cut of its variable mortgage rate shortly after the stress tests, competition is generally muted. On the wider front, credit unions compete with banks, but that sector is not without problems, as evidenced by the difficulties of the large Newbridge Credit Union. KBC, the Belgian bank, has expressed an interest in opening branches, while the South African bank, Investec, has announced its intention to enter the domestic mortgage market. Any new competition would be most welcome for consumers.

It may be that increased competition in Irish banking will not emanate from the present banks or new entrants, but rather from the shadow banking sector. A rapidly growing sector in both the UK and the US is peer-to-peer (P2P) lending.[7] Borrowers and lenders are matched directly on lending platforms, usually by means of auction. Given the low cost base of such a business attractive rates can be offered to borrowers, while lenders, both large and small, can receive interest rates considerably in excess of the miniscule rates available from banks. Naturally, this business is in its early stages of development, is unregulated and provides no guarantee to depositors, but it could yet pose genuine competition to banks, saddled with their heavy cost base.

Certainly the present credit crunch is inhibiting a return to growth. Consumers and small businesses are all too aware of the difficulty of obtaining finance, and certainly not on what they consider to be reasonable terms. Naturally, customers and banks will disagree on what constitutes reasonable terms. Banks wish to restore margins in terms of interest spreads and can be selective in lending their limited available funds. Stuck with negative margins on tracker loans, they must increase interest rates elsewhere. Customers, on the other hand, may still retain unrealistic expectations, based on the free availability of consumer credit and 'Ponzi' loans advanced during the property bubble when banks distributed credit with gay abandon.

Judging by a very small overdraft I was offered recently, margins have already been expanded. I was offered a small overdraft with an interest rate of 11.85 per cent, but, if the limit were exceeded it would attract an additional 12 per cent. Since deposits are paid around 1 per cent, this would offer a generous double digit margin to the bank, certainly much higher than when they offered 3 per cent to depositors, lent out at 6 per cent and expected to be out on the golf course at 3.00 pm.

The concern of the State must be that in a banking duopoly the pillar banks will exploit customers in their efforts to restore their stability. Gouging customers through excessive charges and high interest rates could create major problems for industry, especially the struggling SME sector, as well as further burdening the consumer, who is currently struggling to pay increased taxes and charges. A more acceptable way to put their houses in order is to look at their costs anew with a view to securing a cost base more suited to their reduced role and the current economic situation. The Central Bank in 2013 reported that bank lending was lower and interest costs remain high, despite cuts in the European Central Bank's base rate. Nor is it by any means clear that banks have adopted proper credit criteria. In 2013, the EU suggested that there were signs that some banks continue to provide unsecured credit to highly indebted borrowers without adequately checking out their creditworthiness.

The Need for Strategic Cost Reduction

The initial focus of banks to the crisis was to focus on their balance sheets and, in particular, to ensure that they had adequate capital to survive. Eventually, they gave their attention to reducing costs. Even before the crisis the branch networks were coming under scrutiny. Advances in technology, especially since the introduction of ATMs, enabled customers to perform many services without the assistance of staff. Indeed, customers sometimes preferred to queue at ATMs rather than use empty staff counters. Branch rationalisation was the inevitable consequence and the crisis has served to accelerate the process.

Nevertheless, further cost cutting needs to be undertaken to restore profitability. Head office structures were designed for an age when banks had international ambitions. Now they need to be examined again in light of the banks' reduced circumstances and retrenchment to domestic business. The large head office buildings, which once exuded confidence, now seem curiously out of place, symbolising the extravagance of an earlier era.

For years banks have measured their cost/income ratios and benchmarked them with their peers. But this is a very crude tool. INBS had a low cost/income ratio, but lacked the control systems and management to run a rapidly growing institution. Frequently, cost reduction is approached as part of a budgetary exercise. Departments may succeed in reducing costs in the short term, but find that they gradually return over time. Unfortunately, most costing systems, designed for budgetary purposes, rarely provide assistance in the pursuit of radical cost savings. Crude cost reduction undertaken in an emergency can do serious damage to future business and in any event prove not to be sustainable.

Twelve years ago IMI research indicated that the number one item on the agenda of CEOs was cost reduction, a somewhat surprising finding during a time of prosperity. I set about trying to establish how leading companies set about major cost reduction projects. After running three conferences on the theme, working jointly with a colleague who had an operations background, we published a book explaining how to set about reducing costs in a strategic manner.[8]

Usually the process starts with a strategic review, taking care to safeguard products or services valued by customers. This is followed by a benchmarking exercise with peers or industry leaders to establish target costs. A cross functional team is set up to analyse the situation and establish options. Finally, the decisions are taken and a detailed implementation plan worked out, since this is crucial to its success.

Twelve years ago banks were intent on growth, so often cost reduction was very much a secondary issue. In an era of retrenchment cost reduction is fundamental to survival. Inevitably, banks now face additional costs in complying with new regulatory requirements. Increasing charges to customers may seem an easier route to profitability, but has distinct limits in a time of recession. Most other businesses have been forced along a cost reduction route by the recession and the credit crunch. Banks have little option now but to follow their example. As they struggle to avoid raising additional equity capital, they would be well advised to return to their traditional ways of managing risks conservatively and keeping a tight rein on costs.

Despite the continuing clamour for a full explanation of the financial crisis, Ireland has been slow to analyse the role of the banks into what went wrong. While the Oireachtas inquiry is in train it is by no means clear that it will produce the desired outcome within a reasonable timeframe, in view of the various restrictions placed upon it. Unfortunately, without a comprehensive and credible answer, it is difficult to be sure that the country can avoid a further crisis in the current challenging economic climate. The Irish people, suffering from austerity fatigue, need to be provided with the answer quickly and be reassured that the necessary reforms are in hand.

CHAPTER 17

Understanding the Real Causes
of the Debacle

Irish banking in 2014 languishes in an unhappy position amongst the very weakest banking systems in the world, according to the World Economic Forum. Despite some recent improvement the environment remains generally unfriendly with low economic growth, high unemployment and strained Government finances. In an uncertain world the banking system is vulnerable to shocks, whether from the unpredictable forces of globalisation or internal sources. In the words of the old joke, if you want to get there, you should not be starting from here. But this real difficulty provides no excuse for a failure to address the underlying problems.

The Responsibility for the Mess

At the outset of the book I stated that I would try to discover the real causes of the financial crisis and why a traditionally successful team performed so poorly. Most of the explanations to date have focussed on the mistakes of the referee (the Financial Regulator) and the grounds staff (the Government), with some adverse comments on the linesmen (the auditors and rating agencies). While acknowledging their contribution to the problem, the various reports still fail to explain the chronic deterioration in the team's performance (the banks).

Another analogy is a motorway pile up, the worst in living memory, in which there were numerous fatalities and serious injuries. Disappointingly, no flashing lights had been put in place by the independent experts who were monitoring the individual vehicles. The drivers of the cars initiating the pile up, who had emerged almost miraculously unscathed, attributed the cause of the accident to unprecedented bad weather, allied to the fact that the motorway was poorly designed for the high volume of traffic. They insisted that there was no need for changes in driving regulations or their enforcement. On investigation it transpired that these drivers had been enjoying a long party, where they had overindulged. They were driving recklessly at high speeds and were actually competing in a race with each other, where they expected and indeed felt entitled to be well rewarded for a fast finish in recognition of their much vaunted driving skills.

Bankers' attitudes and self-belief change little over the ages. The collapse of Overend Gurney, a leading British bank, mentioned in Chapter 3, was attributed to greed, ambition and an overwhelming sense of self-confidence, compounded by a refusal to admit its mistakes or the imminence of disaster. No Irish banker today was alive at the time, since the failure occurred almost 150 years ago, yet it must be said that all these features abounded in the demise of the Celtic Tiger, however often they may be denied by the banks or their spokesmen.

Arthur Schopenhauer, the German philosopher, famously proclaimed that truth passes through three stages. First, it is ridiculed. Secondly, it is violently opposed. Thirdly, it is accepted as self-evident. On national radio in 2008 I had attributed the financial crisis to bad lending by the banks in the property bubble.[1] Less than a week later, after the announcement of the bank guarantee, the same radio chat show hostess challenged Ireland's best known and highest paid bank chairman, Sean Fitzpatrick, on the matter.[2] He strongly denied reckless lending, instead ascribing the problem to liquidity difficulties on the wholesale market. Years later some banks made a grudging admission to some mistakes without clarifying exactly what they were, who was responsible or why they were made. It should now be accepted as self-evident, thus opening the way to real reform.

Doubtless the forthcoming Oireachtas political inquiry will examine the circumstances surrounding the issuing of the State guarantee and whether it would still have been made, if the recklessness of the banks' lending were known at the time. I, however, have no reason to revise my initial opinion expressed in 2008 that the banks have only themselves to blame, but will now attempt to justify it, based on the analysis provided throughout this book. But first the banks' own explanations need to be scrutinised to see if they are valid, help to understand the crisis or provide a way forward to provide a better form of banking.

Dismissing the Spurious Defences and Feeble Excuses

In the aftermath of the collapse of Lehman Brothers in the US and the provision of the €440 billion guarantee of the banks' liabilities by the State, nobody could deny the existence of a crisis in Irish banking, even though few participants or commentators at the outset appreciated the gravity of the problem. How did the banks defend their role?

> *1. Bankers ascribed the problem to an international liquidity crisis, arising from the disappearance of wholesale markets, since nobody knew where the toxic US subprime assets were held. The State guarantee would free up liquidity and enable banks to lend to businesses again.*

An immediate crisis was indeed caused by the failure of the interbank market, but the more fundamental reason was the international market's concern over the impact of the domestic property boom on the solvency of the Irish banks. The bankers' argument was quickly refuted, as Irish banks became insolvent, requiring nationalisation for some and enormous financial support for others. Yet even after the injection of substantial capital into the banks the flow of credit did not return to Irish SMEs.

> *2. The banks denied imprudent lending and reckless risk taking. They believed in the robustness of their systems*

220

and the adequacy of their controls, protesting their innate prudence. Nobody could reasonably have foreseen the extent of the global downturn in the property market.

The measure of the low quality of their lending is that the enormous book of loans transferred to NAMA carried an average discount of almost 50 per cent. Certain independent economists did indeed forecast a serious property downturn for which they were roundly denounced by the banks. The banks' faith in a 'soft landing' constituted a serious managerial misjudgement on their part. Too often they answered their critics with an attitude of aloofness and arrogance, rather than apology.

3. The banks blamed Government policy and lack of proper regulation. Government policy was to encourage the construction industry, which provided important employment and underpinned economic growth. Banks could reasonably compete with each other in the market for loans, provided the Central Bank did not intervene to restrict national levels of credit.

Successive Governments did provide budgetary incentives to assist the construction sector, but banks undertook their own analysis of the industry and should have set prudent limits to their exposure on an individual basis. To profess that they might expand their loan book excessively, unless prevented by outsiders, is to admit to gross professional incompetence and shameful irresponsibility.

The time for the banks to take responsibility for the mess candidly is long overdue. An examination of the major factors in the debacle should make it self-evident.

Revealing the Real Explanation

1. A vast property bubble developed in Ireland from around the year 2000.

Coming on the back of a period of soundly-based economic growth, only a few commentators recognised it as such at the time and their views were generally ignored. Politicians and others had a strong vested interest in sustaining the boom in the short run, but at some stage it had to burst in common with all other such bubbles over the ages, both in Ireland and elsewhere. Regulators worldwide had difficulty in recognising peaks in the cycle and so as a matter of policy often did not intervene, relying unwisely on market forces to price property efficiently. The US subprime property crash in 2007 led to a loss of confidence in property markets globally, thereby triggering a downturn in Ireland, but could not be blamed for the crisis.

2. Property cycles are driven by expansions and contractions of credit, which the Irish banks failed to control.

The unwise granting of credit on a large scale leads to an inflation of property prices. Traditional lending is designed to ensure the payment of interest and repayment of capital over a reasonable period. 'Ponzi' lending relies solely on the rise of property values to service borrowings. Both domestic and overseas banks operating in the Irish market abandoned traditionally prudent standards in reckless competition for business. In particular, they ignored the dangers inherent in permitting high gearing by developers and householders. When the downturn came they resorted to wishful thinking in forecasting a 'soft landing' for the property market.

3. The conventional checks and balances associated with risk management in banks failed to operate.

Conventional internal procedures and credit committees failed to enforce traditional controls. In general it appears that after years of strong economic growth senior bankers had a poor understanding of basic risks and failed to manage them as a consequence. Neither did risk managers, nor high level risk committees, restrict the excessive exposure to the property market in general and undue concentration on a small number of developers. Similarly, externally neither auditors, regulators, nor rating agencies identified the problems or, if they did, their warnings were ignored. Boards did not encourage their members to challenge fundamentally the strategy of the banks and took refuge in 'groupthink'. The failure of these checks and controls resulted in reckless mismanagement of critical risks by the banks.

4. Inappropriate funding was raised to finance the rapid growth of loan books.

Due to the scale of the commitments, funding from domestic sources proved insufficient to cover the requirements. Consequently, banks were obliged to source funds from overseas, particularly in Germany, through the interbank market, mainly on a short-term basis. While they could have raised equity during the boom period by way of rights issues through the stock market, they chose not to do so. When the inter-bank market froze up in the aftermath of the subprime crisis banks suffered severe liquidity problems. They sought the assistance from the State on the basis that the problems were short term in nature, but in reality some perceptive creditors were concerned at their property exposure and the adequacy of their capital to fund losses.

5. During the Celtic Tiger era the banks had undergone a profound change of culture and the values by which they operated.

To some extent this transformation was influenced by changes in the industry globally, in particular the rise of investment banking. As older bankers retired there were fewer people who had experienced an economic downturn or subscribed to traditional values. The importance attached to protecting depositors' funds and serving their customers' needs received lip service, but declined in importance relative to the pursuit of short-term profits, which increasingly banks perceived to be the measure of their success. Investors, stock markets and the press greeted rapid growth of profits enthusiastically, rather than focusing on the management of risks or the creation of longer-term shareholder value. The banks reacted to these pressures and expectations of continuous rapid growth by expanding their loan books aggressively at a rate that could not be sustained indefinitely.

6. Profits in banks are difficult to measure, mainly because of the problem in establishing appropriate reserves for the impairment of loans and to a lesser extent other complex financial instruments.

Sometimes in the past banks were permitted to defer recognition of losses in times of crisis, such as the problems which global banks experienced in loans to Latin America during the 1980s. The relevant accounting standard stipulates that loan impairments should only be made on the basis of losses incurred. Under such a convention banks have had and continue to have considerable flexibility in recognising losses in their accounts, enabling them to hide the seriousness of their difficulties. If impairments are considered to be complex and subjective, the fundamental establishment of measuring bank profits is totally unsatisfactory. Whether or not Irish banks have transgressed in applying the standard is a matter for the courts.

7. The rewards policies, and in particular the insidious bonus culture, had a significant bearing on how bankers behaved and their attitude to risk.

Investment bankers internationally have often enjoyed enormous remuneration packages compared to their peers in other industries. Sometimes they justified the generous rewards by the profits they generated and an element of job insecurity. Despite the massive destruction of shareholder value and mismanagement of risk, bankers often still claimed them as an entitlement and expected to receive large rewards, even when the profit performance was poor. Their attitude seems to be based on a perverse and inflated opinion of their own worth. Where large bonuses were granted on the basis of reported profits, which deferred the recognition of losses, a financial incentive existed for management to accept business which could lose money in the longer term. Where bonuses led to increased pensions, the incentives were even more dangerous. Bonuses also encouraged a sales-driven culture where unscrupulous individuals could subordinate the interests of customers to their own personal financial welfare.

8. The initial reaction of most Irish bank boards to the crisis was ill-judged and not credible, denying misman-agement while accepting the support of the State.

Banks were slow to make changes to senior management, which the Governor of the Central Bank believed prolonged their tendency to remain in denial about their problems. Although the State did appoint directors to represent the public interest, it did not attempt to play a central role in the management of the banks. Some banks may have believed that they were too big to be allowed to fail, following the precedent set by Continental Illinois in the US 20 years earlier. After the failure of Lehman Brothers and the liquidation of IBRC, this belief could not be sustained for all banks, nevertheless BoI and AIB might reasonably consider that it could now apply to them. So moral hazard can still persist and reasonable changes may encounter stout resistance.

9. Banking is not a profession with the ability to enforce codes of behaviour through a unified governing body.

Professions such as medicine, law and accountancy restrict membership through examinations and can discipline their members for breaches of ethical standards. While many Irish retail bankers are members of the Institute of Bankers and have passed its examinations, other senior figures, particularly investment bankers, arrived by different routes and may or may not have any professional qualification. Internationally there have been numerous complaints about bankers' behaviour, including disregard for their customers' best interests, excessive risk taking and the manipulation of key market data. Globally it appears that neither individual banks, nor the industry collectively, have managed to eliminate wrongdoing and protect its reputation. In the absence of effective self-regulation banks have been subjected to extensive external regulation and have incurred hefty fines for various misdemeanours, but concerns over bankers' conduct persist.

The Consequences of Mismanagement

The financial crisis has left deep scars in the Irish economy, which will not be healed easily:

1. The most obvious result of mismanagement has been the collapse or near failure of most Irish banks.

This development should not have come as a surprise, since for some time they had exhibited most of the classical sighs of business failure. They had failed to foresee the bursting of the property bubble and had developed a highly risky exposure to the sector. They had overtraded and lacked proper controls. Having neglected to raise equity during the boom period, they were excessively borrowed and too heavily reliant on overseas funding in the interbank market. They completely destroyed or severely depleted their shareholders' wealth and have cost the Irish taxpayer €65 billion to date. Ireland, like Iceland, had developed an excessively large financial sector relative to the economy, which could not cope with a serious market downturn.

2. The banks' problems were spread to the Irish public through the granting of the €440 billion guarantee in September 2008.

While its creator hailed it as a cheap solution to the problem, in fact it turned into one of the most expensive bailouts ever. In relative terms the guarantee, which equated to €100,000 per head of the population, was much higher than schemes in other countries, such as the US or the UK. The decision to introduce the guarantee was made quickly during a crisis, when relevant information about the gravity of the problems was not available or fully understood. Whether a cheaper solution might have been found in consultation with the ECB over a longer time period remains a matter for conjecture. The upshot has been that the decision benefited overseas institutions by avoiding any Irish bank failure, while imposing the entire cost on the Irish people.

3. The banking system has become dysfunctional, being unable to supply adequate credit to business, particularly those in the SME sector.

With the winding up of two banks and the withdrawal of several overseas banks from the market, there is an unhealthy lack of competition between banks. The future depends heavily on the continued health of the two 'pillar banks', BoI and AIB, the latter being almost wholly owned by the State. The banking collapse led in turn to a serious economic and national budgetary crisis. Economic recovery and a return to full employment are seriously hampered by a lack of credit for the SME sector, as banks reduced their lending.

4. The public has been dismayed at the inequity inherent in the outcome to date.

Powerful property developers, some of whom have been technically declared bankrupt, seem to enjoy a much better lifestyle than most members of the public. Due to the opaque nature of NAMA and its lack of transparency, it is not known what deals were made with the individual developers, but suspicions abound that they were not treated as harshly as ordinary members of the public when seeking to renegotiate their mortgages with their banks. As the liquidators of IBRC dispose of their loan portfolio at a discount to the face value of the loans, there seems to be ample scope for those borrowers to reach settlements which provide for large write offs of debt, while providing the new loan holder with a quick profit. The solution seems to entail the greatest transfer of wealth since the foundation of the State at the expense of the taxpayer.

5. Bankers have rarely been popular in the past, but today their reputation in Ireland and globally has reached an all-time low level.

Many citizens, holding them in contempt, would like to see senior bankers loaded into tumbrels and carted off to the modern equivalent of the guillotine, as aristocrats were during the French Revolution. At the higher echelons the term 'banker' often seems inseparable from 'greedy', as they have successfully avoided the hardship visited on others during the recession. Their actions did much to create the global meltdown, yet many of those responsible held on to their well paid jobs, while others departed on generous terms. The 'Occupy Wall Street' movement may be strongest in the US, but has found imitators around the globe, including Dublin.

> *6. The way that the public now regard and treat their bankers in Ireland and elsewhere has serious implications for the proper operation of the system.*

The fact that they did not manage their businesses effectively, and could not continue to provide credit in a meaningful way, has cast serious doubts as to their professional competence, which results in a general loss of confidence. But the way bankers have protected their own interests, while accepting enormous financial support, exacerbates the problem. Globally they have also sold products which did not fit the customers' needs, while earning hefty commissions for so doing. They stand accused of dishonestly manipulating key interest rates, such as LIBOR, together with other ethical breaches of behaviour, such as money laundering, assisting with tax evasion and persistent taking of enormous risks. Bankers as a breed seem for many people to be self-serving, as well as avaricious, expecting generous rewards even when they fail to perform professionally. Consequently, they can no longer be trusted by a disenchanted and disillusioned public. This loss of trust led to a damaging loss of confidence, since banking is founded on trust and confidence.

The Priority for the Future – Restoring Confidence

Ireland has fared worse than most countries due to the severity of its banking crisis. Given the extent of the mismanagement of the banks, the public has good reason to lose confidence in them. Restoring confidence and trust must take priority in rebuilding the system, but is unlikely to happen of its own accord. A 2014 survey by Ernst & Young showed that consumer confidence in their banks was growing in many countries around the world with a third of them reporting an increase over the previous year. But in Ireland confidence and trust had decreased by 62 per cent, while the level of complaints and dissatisfaction with how their problems were handled were amongst the highest anywhere.[3]

Some deposits have been taken overseas and if banks are to retain their deposit base it is vital that the public have confidence in the system. An unregulated shadow banking system is developing as a competitive threat to established banks. Internationally, reforms to the industry have proceeded with glacial speed, attracting widespread opposition from banks when they perceive their interests being adversely affected. In such circumstances it would be naive to expect salvation to arrive from global or even European changes in the industry.

Without radical reform there is no guarantee that banks will not again resort to reckless competition for business, which was evident in the lending of both domestic banks and the subsidiaries of oversea banks. Unfettered competition, which was advocated by most independent commentators, has not served the country well. The remaining banks need to find a better balance between profits and risk management, while placing less emphasis on short-term results. Meanwhile, regulators must take a more proactive role and ensure that banks do not succumb to moral hazard, while insisting that proper controls are installed and reforms are implemented. This should include a review of the rewards system and the incentives for bankers to take undue risks, which could destabilise Irish banking.

The alternative is for Irish banks to undertake reform of their own volition. This would necessitate not only restoring their financial health by ensuring that they are adequately capitalised, needing no further support from the public purse, but also changing the way they conduct their business to demonstrate that they are worthy of public trust and confidence. In short, they need to change their culture and values by which they conduct their business, explaining clearly the new ethos to their shareholders and customers. Only if banks are seen to embrace and deliver radical changes as quickly as possible, can the first steps be taken on the long rugged road ahead to restore confidence.

CHAPTER 18

A Manifesto for Reform

Embarking on a path to restore trust and confidence presents a daunting undertaking. It is easy for banks to pay lip service to any proposed changes, many of which cannot be reasonably opposed, adopting the ideas as part of a public relations exercise. But profound cultural change is notoriously difficult to implement in organisations with deeply embedded practices and beliefs. Responsibility for bringing about the changes must lie with the senior bank management, backed up by the full support of the board. Sceptical staff will watch the actions, as well as the words, of senior managers to ascertain if real changes are intended. Here are some ideas, most of which have been mentioned already in the text, about how banks should relate to the outside world and manage their affairs internally:

Six Guiding Principles

1. Become truly accountable to all stakeholders.

If banks wish to be believed by those stakeholders to whom they are accountable, more candour and transparency are vital. Stakeholders are not limited to shareholders, but include customers, depositors, staff, the Financial Regulator and the tax authorities. Clear and concise reports on risk, remuneration and social responsibility in the annual report would be of great assistance. Senior management need to take full responsibility for past mistakes and show that appropriate action has been taken to avoid any repetition of them. It is not the low level officials in the branches who were responsible for the problems of Irish banking, though they often bear the brunt of customers' wrath over what happened and their inability to provide traditional levels of service and credit. Banks must also convince the public that they will not succumb to moral hazard in the expectation of further bailouts.

2. Change the way bankers treat their customers.

It has often been stated in the past that the overriding objective of banks is the protection of depositors' funds. This noble goal needs to be emphasised again, which means a more traditional attitude to prudence and risk taking. Customers should not be treated as targets to be sold bank products, while advice given to them should be both professional and impartial. Unfavourable feedback from customers should result in corrective action, thereby conducting business on mutually beneficial terms. I have suggested that banks should adopt a charter, setting out core principles to be observed and the values to be guarded, but, if this is to be more than a cynical exercise of 'spin', such a charter must be strictly enforced from the top and offenders at any level duly sanctioned.

3. Check that all public communications are accurate and carefully considered.

The credibility of bank management was damaged by reassurances regarding the adequacy of bank capital and the payment of future dividends. The public traditionally had accepted that such statements were reliable and that management were in full control of the situation. Similarly forecasts of a 'soft landing' were proved incorrect. Particular care is required to ensure that neither shareholders nor customers are misled by any opinion released by the bank, however innocently it is made. 'Spin' or wishful thinking can be no substitute for accuracy, if stakeholders are to accept at face value statements issued by the banks in future.

4. Ensure that all transactions stand up to ethical scrutiny.

The litany of scandals over the years has inevitably damaged the public's trust and confidence in the banks. Dishonesty or misleading customers in any aspect of banking is totally unacceptable and perpetrators should never be protected. Overcharging customers or selling them inappropriate products must not be allowed to recur. Greater care needs to be observed in the launching of new products to ensure that their distribution is not abused in the search for profit. Whistleblowers should be encouraged to disclose any improprieties, rather than being suppressed, as is often the case in Ireland. Full transparency in all dealings would provide the appropriate starting point in the challenge to regain public confidence.

5. Abandon the excessive emphasis on short-term profits.

The creation of shareholder value is not achieved by promoting short term profitability at the expense of prudent risk management. Bank profits are difficult to measure precisely in the short run, due to the difficulties in establishing appropriate levels of provisions for loan impairment. Treated in isolation the worship of short term profits and return on equity can prove to be a false god. In these circumstances attempting to emulate competitors reporting strong short term earnings can be a recipe for disaster. While a return to profits is a necessary short term objective, in future a much greater emphasis should be placed on strategic goals and adherence to high standards of performance in terms of quality and prudence. The operation of staff rewards in terms of pay and promotion should reflect these values.

6. Adopt a policy of open discussion for issues at all staff levels.

The banks have been criticised for their herd mentality collectively and the development of groupthink internally. Bank boards do not have a monopoly of wisdom in addressing difficulties and finding solutions. Staff must not be discouraged from voicing dissent openly to any proposals. Stifling dissent resulted in policies not being subjected to appropriate scrutiny and challenge. Individuals should be encouraged to express their views without fear of sanctions. Problems should always be discussed freely at all levels from the board downwards.

Five Major Challenges for the Board

Bank boards need to manage their affairs differently, so that there can never be a repetition of the mistakes of the past. They must devise strategies suitable for their present situation and communicate these ideas to their stakeholders clearly. This constitutes a formidable challenge, since they lost considerable credibility when they attempted to explain the reasons for the crisis initially. The Governor of the Central Bank is on record as stating that the slowness of changes to bank boards aggravated the problems.

1. Ensure that the bank is adequately capitalised.

It is a necessary, but not sufficient, condition that banks are seen to have adequate capital to trade and to lend, where appropriate. The fact that, with the exception of Permanent TSB, all of the Irish banks passed the ECB stress tests was a welcome development, removing a major uncertainty for the sector. But international regulators require the largest global banks to increase their capital substantially by 2019 and smaller banks may soon face similar demands. To restore confidence shareholders want a return to dividend payments, accompanied by a return to prudent lending growth against a backdrop of conservation of capital.

2. Restrict the activities and geographic spread of the bank.

Growth is no longer the ultimate strategic goal and Irish banks have no particular expertise in servicing overseas markets. Banks have now returned to their Irish roots and have no reason to expand beyond this base for the foreseeable future. Geographical aspirations to trade in England, America or elsewhere are now largely irrelevant. It is a time to return to the basics of banking. Activities, such as much of the proprietary trading, which is risky and ties up precious capital should be discontinued. Customer feedback, however, should be sought for any reduction in the level of customer services through the branch network.

3. Institute sound risk management in all aspects of banking.

Banks need to return to the basics in terms of risk taking, rather than casino-style betting. The banks also need to understand why the controls, which existed prior to the financial crisis, failed to operate effectively when they were most needed, permitting an excessive exposure to the property market. Prudent risk management is not simply a box-ticking exercise or cataloguing every conceivable risk in the annual financial statements. Risk managers need to be granted the necessary authority and resources to fulfil their function at the highest level in banks. Boards should monitor exposures to ensure that risks are carefully managed, while internal audit should undertake detailed checks at all levels. Any proposal to improve profitability should be assessed in the light of the risks entailed. Sound risk management entails tighter control systems, but need not lead to a stultifying bureaucracy and slow decision making.

4. Introduce a more equitable gender balance in senior management.

Banking for many years has been a predominantly male preserve on boards and amongst senior management. While the legal and accounting professions changed radically over recent years, encouraging female entrants, Irish banking remained largely impervious to these social changes. It is certainly arguable that this deficiency contributed to the reckless macho risk taking during the bubble. In London and New York women appear to play a greater role in senior banking positions than in Dublin. Irish banking could certainly benefit, not only in senior executive management but also at board level, by a stronger representation of suitably qualified women.

5. Do not promise excessive returns to shareholders.

Banks should manage the expectations of shareholders and not make themselves hostages to fortune. Domestic banks can no longer provide the means to rapid national economic growth, whether it is in Ireland or Iceland. Excessive growth in lending was simply overtrading, which resulted in grave solvency problems and horrendous risk taking. Unrealistic expectations as to future earnings and dividends need to be tempered by reality. Future growth should be related more closely to the growth rate of the economy. While this may result in a smaller financial sector, it should be stronger and more robust than it has been in recent years.

Five Tasks for Immediate Action

Unfortunately, time is not on the side of the banks. A number of issues facing them in the post-crisis world need to be resolved quickly. Lack of progress in some areas has given rise to public frustration. Where banks have denied the existence and seriousness of the problems, it is difficult to believe that they have been effectively resolved.

1. Deal with the problem of loan repayment arrears promptly and fairly.

Banks need to engage in a meaningful way with customers experiencing difficulties, as the Financial Regulator has repeatedly urged. This necessitates engaging fully with the new insolvency laws. To date some banks have been slower to react than others, while the policy of debt write offs varies enormously. Loans need to be restructured, writing off irrecoverable debts, where appropriate. Postponing the issue simply masks the necessity for making proper provisions. The problems have been compounded by a high level of personal lending in addition to mortgage finance. Cases need to be treated on an individual basis in a fair and consistent manner. Strategic defaulting, however, cannot be tolerated, especially by large customers.

2. Restore traditional lending standards.

Banks must return to prudent lending to the extent that their capital base enables them. They have been castigated for their failure to provide credit to support Irish SMEs, which was a fundamental reason for the injection of capital by the State. They must again advance funds on reasonable terms to businesses, which can offer a satisfactory prospect of repayment. Without an adequate flow of funds to SMEs it is difficult to see a restoration to sustainable economic growth or the desired reduction in unemployment, since SMEs provide most of the private sector jobs. To achieve this goal banks must ensure that all personnel concerned in the advancing of loans and approval of credit are proficient in the basic principles of credit and their application.

3. Train and retrain staff to perform all services professionally.

If professional standards are to be restored, this necessitates a thorough examination of what went wrong, making the appropriate changes in systems and personnel. Fundamental to this goal is an assessment of the values taught at every level to bankers, so training is a critical ingredient for change. Responsibilities and duties should be stressed, rather than entitlements and rights. Traditional training practices need to be reviewed, since reliance on internal training and professional exams failed to prevent the growth of 'Ponzi' lending. Budgetary constraints should not lead to any lack of professionalism in the way service is provided to customers.

4. Adopt suitable remuneration policies.

It has been shown that the rewards system has a direct impact on the way managers at all levels behave. The bonus culture encouraged excessive risk taking. Bankers around the world seem to believe that they are entitled to large rewards for what they perceive as their unique skills. Yet they seem reluctant to reduce their rewards or accept the blame when they can be shown to have destroyed most of the wealth of their shareholders. Governments have capped pay in an effort to deal with the vicious spiral of increasing levels of remuneration, while European banking guidelines will introduce further restrictions. Basic salaries need to be kept in line with comparable positions in other industries, while any variable pay tied to long-term profitability and kept at a level which does not promote antisocial behaviour. Incentives should be more centred on shares, rather than cash, and any cash bonuses should not be released until longer-term targets have been met.

5. Embark on a programme of strategic cost reduction.

Banks can return to profit either by raising their income from higher charges, by reducing their costs or a combination of both approaches. In a recession with consumers severely squeezed, there is limited scope for increasing charges. These charges, along with cost-to-income ratios, should be benchmarked against those imposed by their peers in other countries. Almost certainly costs will need to be further reduced to return to a satisfactory level of profit. This should not be achieved by a mindless slash and burn activity, but rather by a more considered approach which takes advantage of changes in technology and modern cost reduction techniques. Since staff pay constitutes such a large element of costs in banking, inevitably the overall cost of labour, including perks, must come under scrutiny. Head office costs need examination also to ensure that they provide value for money.

It may be that progress has been made by some banks in addressing these problems, but it is far from obvious that all banks have embarked on a path of radical reform. Certainly the annual reports devote considerably more space to issues such as risk management and remuneration policy, but whether the cultural transformation necessary to implement the changes effectively has occurred remains to be proved. If and when major improvements can be demonstrated, then it should be possible to make progress in restoring public confidence, which can be lost quickly, but inevitably can only be regained slowly over time. In view of the credibility of some bank statements made in the recent past, carefully worded and politically correct reports of themselves may not persuade the public that all is now well.

Five Ways Regulators Can Help

The office of the Financial Regulator lost much public respect during the banking crisis, when, if it was not a victim of 'regulatory capture', the office seemed insufficiently independent in its handling of the problem. While a lack of staff in the boom cannot justify regulatory failures, employee numbers have been significantly increased and a change of approach has been promised under the new management. The office needs to re-establish its independence and its authority, while ensuring that banking restores traditional standards. It can assist banking reform in the way it conducts its business.

1. Deal firmly with banks and resist calls for 'light touch regulation'.

It would seem from the published tape recordings of senior management in Anglo Irish Bank that the Central Bank was treated with minimal respect in their effort to obtain a substantial loan, which they believed could not be repaid. When problems were uncovered in bank lending there seemed to be little determination to ensure that matters were promptly sorted out. The damaging charge that Ireland was the 'Wild West' of capitalism must be refuted once and for all. For the public, domestically and internationally, to regain confidence in the way banks are run, it must be made clear that the Central Bank is on top of the situation and will not tolerate any breaching of its rules and regulations. Light touch regulation has been challenged internationally and has no place in Ireland's banking future. The fragile Irish banking system needs a mixture of good governance, appropriate reporting and workable sanctions for those who breach the rules.

2. Set a strict cap on the exposure of banks to the property sector.

'Ponzi' lending to builders and developers lay at the heart of the property bubble. Memories can be short and a repetition of the explosion of credit must be avoided the next time confidence returns to the sector. Realistic, prudent limits need to be set to curtail the banks' exposure to the property sector as a whole and to subsectors, such as speculative building. In the past loose definitions allowed banks to disguise the full extent of their true exposure to the sector. It will always be tempting for banks to grow their loan books quickly by making large loans for property and construction, rather than advancing more challenging credits to other sectors. A cap could supplement prudent limits on loans to individual house buyers relative to their income and the value of the property. The financial crisis has demonstrated the foolishness of relying on the wisdom of bank management to limit this particular risk without close supervision.

3. Ascertain the root causes for breaches of ethical behaviour by banks.

When banks are found to have breached fundamental codes of behaviour, such as happened in the sale of payment protection insurance to its customers, heavy fines must be imposed on them. This of itself may prove insufficient to prevent a repetition, based on the feeble excuse that the bank was only copying its competitors. Nor would the dismissal of a few scapegoats necessarily achieve this end. The Regulator should institute some form of 'cultural audit' on any offending institution to establish what systems and procedures gave rise to the misdemeanour. In particular, the impact of the rewards system should be examined to establish whether it contributed to the problem. Based on these findings the Regulator could force management to address the root cause by changing its systems.

4. Set up an Irish Banking Standards Review Council.

In the absence of a professional banking body to enforce operational standards, the Financial Regulator needs to fulfil this role. One approach, proposed recently in the UK, is to set up a council funded by the banks, as an independent champion to monitor improvements. This body would be designed to complement the regulatory function and would operate in a style similar to the Advertising Standards Authority. If the changes have already taken place, as some bankers may claim, the council could give independent verification of the improvements. It should meet once a year and publish a report outlining progress made, while naming and shaming offending institutions. In the UK it is a voluntary body to which most leading banks have signed up, but if it meets opposition from the banks it could be made mandatory for Irish banks to participate.

5. Make information public about bankers' remuneration.

Alan Greenspan discovered to his horror that banks did not always act in the best interests of their shareholders. Since bonuses were a factor in creating the problem, they must be closely monitored. As part of a policy of greater transparency, there should be more detailed disclosure of what remuneration levels are, leaving outsiders to judge whether or not they are excessive. Simple aggregates or averages are insufficient. An analysis of pay over, say, €100,000 in brackets of €20,000 should be disclosed with the number of recipients in each category. The information could be extended to cover pensions of former employees. This publicity should act as some block on remuneration committees increasing rewards without strong underlying performance.

Five Ways Government Can Help

The Irish Government has found itself centre stage in the banking crisis, performing both regulatory and ownership roles. Many onlookers at home and abroad will take a keen interest in its actions to restore confidence in the system. While its skill in managing the public finances has a major bearing on the recovery of both the economy and the banks, it can also help the image and reputation of Irish banking in various other ways:

1. Pursue relentlessly major borrowers in arrears to repay their loans.

Most large loans have been transferred into NAMA, which is a Government-controlled institution. If the property oligarchs are permitted to distance their assets through special trusts and the use of offshore tax havens with tight secrecy rules, the public will be rapidly disenchanted. It would be manifestly unfair if wealthy and powerful individuals were to be forgiven loans, while the ordinary householders suffer through an era of austerity. Since IBRC has been placed into liquidation and its loan book is being auctioned off, there must be fears that deals will be made by the new owners of the loans to forgive substantial amounts of debt in order to make a quick profit. There would be very real anger if the developers who did much to cause the crisis were seen to re-emerge relatively unscathed after a short period in bankruptcy.

2. Prosecute promptly those who have broken criminal law.

The Government must uphold the national reputation outside the country. Much frustration has been voiced in public about the absence of prosecutions during the five years after the crisis broke. In 2014 a limited start was made when the State finally brought to court a case against three former directors of Anglo Irish Bank in connection with advancing loans to purchase its own shares. But no custodial sentences were handed down, which did little to allay public cynicism about white collar crime. Wherever else there are cases of suspected criminal malpractice the State must take appropriate action, as happened with Breifni O'Brien, who misused investors' funds. If the country is perceived to be lax in dealing with white collar crime, it will be difficult to regain confidence internationally. The charge of crony capitalism is unpleasant and can only be rebutted by firm action. It would indeed be disastrous if, when cases eventually come to court, they are rejected on the basis that those charged cannot receive a fair trial in Ireland or that undue delay has damaged the case.

3. Establish a clear role for public interest directors.

When the Government guaranteed the liabilities of the banks in 2008 it appointed two directors to the boards of each of the stricken banks. Five years later, in 2013, it was revealed that the Minister for Finance had provided no brief for these directors, had minimal contact with them and rarely received any reports from them. If they are to act as the national guardians, they themselves and the public need to understand how their duties are to be performed. The State has a strong vested interest in the banks through its shareholdings, as well as the guarantee, so it must endure that its interests are properly protected. Presumably they should not be expected to advance short-term electoral considerations. Nevertheless, in view of the historical performance of bank boards, it would be wise not to rely exclusively on them to protect the interests of their shareholders.

4. Strengthen the independence of auditors and non-executive directors.

Ireland can do little to improve the effectiveness of rating agencies, but it can influence the two other guardians of shareholders' interests – the auditors and non-executive directors. To be effective in checking the excesses of management they must be, and be seen to be, totally independent. Codes of best practice exist for good governance, but these may not always be observed in practice. The independence of both auditors and non-executive directors would be enhanced if their term of office were restricted to a maximum of five years. Similarly, auditors should be precluded from accepting consultancy work from audit clients or being appointed their liquidators. Such practices could be enforced if they were to be embodied in company law.

5. Set up an effective inquiry into the causes of the crisis.

The Government has set up to a public inquiry into the causes of the crisis. Certainly there are serious limitations to the powers of such a body, since it cannot compel witnesses to attend and cannot make adverse findings against individuals, and there are concerns that it could prejudice certain criminal prosecutions. Nevertheless, Ireland's banking collapse was more serious than those occurring in other countries, which have conducted helpful enquiries. A well run investigation, conducted professionally, should result in recommendations for real reforms which should at least diminish, if not eliminate, the chance of another systemic crisis in the future. If, on the other hand, it is conducted badly, it could degenerate into mere political grandstanding ahead of an election and achieve little.

How Accountancy Bodies Can Help

There are many things which would be helpful, if initiated by European or global agencies to reform banking, such as a re-examination of laws separating retail and investment banking and the capital required for the different activities. Unfortunately, it is difficult for a small country such as Ireland to influence such events, especially where strong vested interests and powerful lobbies oppose change. Nevertheless, although such a task may require cooperation of professional bodies outside of Ireland, accountancy bodies need to reassure the public regarding the professional conduct of its members in key areas:

1. Establish clear accounting standards for loan impairments.

One key issue requiring clarity is the accounting standard in connection with loan impairment. It is impossible for a bystander to pass an informed judgement on the adequacy of any particular bank audit without access to unpublished information and vast resources. But, particularly when the principle of prudence is no longer central to the issue, it seems that banks in general have had considerable scope to defer recognition of losses. It is most unsatisfactory if provisions for loan impairment are both complex and subjective, since auditors are limited then in their ability to insist on higher levels of impairment than the bank proposes. For the financial accounts of banks to be of real value to stakeholders, this situation needs to be rectified. The new accounting standard issued by the International Accounting Standards Body in July 2014, which is binding in Ireland and in more than 100 countries outside the US, should help address the problem, but much will depend on how it is interpreted when it is eventually implemented.

2. Clarify the role and responsibilities of external bank auditors.

The public has seen large banks collapse or find themselves in severe difficulty in a short space of time. Reading the usual lengthy audit reports, preceding the crisis, it is not obvious that any serious problems existed. Firms of accountants are paid substantial fees to conduct their audits, which pin the responsibility for the accounts on the directors. While it must be accepted that an audit report which instigates a run on the bank is undesirable, if all banks are given clean reports every year the whole purpose of the audit comes into question. Auditors must be seen to be truly independent of the banks, which would be helped if they are changed on a regular basis. There exists currently a gap between the expectations of the public and the reality of what is possible for auditors to do. The reader of bank accounts and the wider public have a right to know what can be expected from external auditors.

How the Wider Public and Individual Shareholders Can Help

The public too has a role to play in the new banking world. Since ultimately they are paying for the banking crisis through higher taxes, involuntary emigration and austerity, they are entitled to protect their interests. They can and should actively make their views known through shareholders, the press and their public representatives, giving a sense of urgency to the necessary changes.

1. Insist on banking reform.

The banks need the public to buy their services. While in the short term some banks may have minimal capacity to lend, they need the deposits from as many sources as possible. The present banks cannot prosper without the confidence of the public and would not welcome a loss of business to new banking entrants or shadow banking institutions. The public must insist on the reform of the banking system, as outlined above. They should ensure that the bank boards are fully aware of their wishes through the public interest directors and not tolerate any arrogant dismissal of their views or requests.

2. Press the State to safeguard the interests of shareholders and the wider public.

As outlined above, the State has important functions to perform. At least initially there was a reluctance to prosecute suspected offenders and progress towards an official Oireachtas inquiry has been pitifully slow. The banks themselves possess considerable lobbying strength, which they use to good effect in opposing greater external regulation or changes which might adversely affect their independence. Persistent lobbying of politicians by members of the public should help concentrate minds. Ultimately, the public can make its views known through the polling booth, if those responsible for the debacle are seen to benefit at the expense of the public, while politicians defer resolute action.

3. Encourage shareholder activism, especially for institutional shareholders.

Small shareholders rarely have the time, expertise or numerical weight to bring about major changes in listed companies. Institutional shareholders, on the other hand, are much better positioned to perform this task and usually will at least obtain an audience, due to their voting power, either on an individual or collective basis. Traditionally, Irish institutional shareholders have played a relatively passive role and nearly always have endorsed management proposals. Indeed, by pressurising management for ever increasing returns they unwittingly contributed to the whole problem of short-termism and reckless risk taking. Now, however, as their counterparts in London and New York seek to influence events, Irish institutions should not find themselves left behind. They can act as guardians of shareholders' interests, particularly in matters such as management remuneration and incentives.

A Plea for Positive Action

It is always easy to defer resolute action, hoping, like Mr Micawber of Dickensian fame, that something will turn up. Perhaps the much heralded official Oireachtas inquiry will surprise the public and provide policies to lead the country forward, or maybe the various court cases will help the public understand who was responsible for the problems and lead to changes which will prevent a recurrence. Others simply believe that nothing will ever change, so that any initiative is doomed to fail. But neither masterly inactivity nor cynical despair are likely to produce satisfactory solutions.

Ideally, the banks would initiate radical reform themselves, but progress to date, six years after the granting of the State deposit guarantee and the nationalisation of Anglo Irish Bank, provides little support for such optimism. They have refrained from taking responsibility for the debacle, while pressing for the return of bonuses. Globally the industry has successfully resisted external interference, despite the continuation of serious trading scandals. Where banks do not appreciate the necessity to change the way in which they operate and the values they espouse, deeply rooted cultural change is improbable.

Many parties have a valid vested interest in seeing the return to a rejuvenated and robust banking system. The Government needs to protect the financial stability of the State and restore economic growth. The Financial Regulator, having discovered that banks do not always act in the best interests of their shareholders, needs to prevent further banking failures and oversee the return to sensible business and consumer credit. The professional bodies must ensure ethical behaviour of their members. A disenchanted public, weary of paying for the mess with their taxes, needs the proper provision of banking services.

Banking reform, however, is too important to be left solely to the banks to introduce if confidence in the system is to be restored at the earliest possible time. All relevant parties must insist that it takes place to serve the wider public interest. While some progress may have been achieved, much more needs to be undertaken. Neither carefully worded platitudes in the annual financial statements, nor assertions by well remunerated spin doctors that matters are in hand and that the banks must be left to manage their own future without external guidance, provide genuine reassurance.

The starting point must be a wide-ranging debate to identify the major problems and the possible solutions. The long suffering Irish public can reasonably expect no less. This book has attempted to outline the reasons for the financial cataclysm from the perspective of the banks. To this end it has delved into the fields of banking, economics and accountancy before exploring the more obtuse fields of ethics and culture. To the extent that this contributes to opening up a discussion on the changes needed and overdue in banking, it will have served its purpose.

APPENDIX

A Lending Checklist

Twenty Key questions devised by the author from his banking experience

A. *The Borrower*

1. Is the legal entity of the borrower fully understood?
2. Is the borrower considered trustworthy?
3. Does the borrower possess the competences required for the project?
4. Has the borrower sufficient management depth?

B. *The Business:*

1. Who are the main customers and competitors – present and future?
2. Are both the financial and management accounts credible?
3. Are controls adequate (cash, credit, working capital)?
4. Can the business be downsized in trouble?

C. *The Credit:*

1. Is the real purpose fully understood and acceptable?
2. Has total funding been properly assessed?

3. Is the borrower making an appropriate contribution?
4. Should the risk be shared with other lenders?

D. Repayment:

1. Are conservative, comprehensive cashflow projections available?
2. Are all contingent liabilities covered?
3. Are all other repayment commitments known?
4. Does current trading support the projections?

E. Terms:

1. Do drawdown conditions minimise the risks?
2. Do continuing covenants allow for full monitoring and control?
3. Is the security adequate to cover the known risks?
4. Is the overall margin acceptable on a risk/reward basis?

Endnotes

Introduction

1. Report of the Inspectors Appointed (Under Section 8 of the Companies Act 1990) to Investigate the Affairs of National Irish Bank Limited and National Irish Bank Financial Services Limited, Mr Justice Blaney and Tom Grace FCA, 23 July 2004.

2. 'The banks have only themselves to blame', *Sunday Tribune*, 21 September 2008,

3. 'Banks that step out of line should pay the ultimate price', *Sunday Tribune*, 5 October 2008.

4. The Irish Banking Crisis – Regulatory and Financial Stability Policy, A Report to the Minister of Finance by the Governor of the Central Bank, 31 May 2010.

5. A Preliminary Report on the Sources of Ireland's Banking Crisis, Klaus Regling and Max Watson, May 2010

6. Misjudging Risk: Causes of the Systemic Banking Crisis in Ireland, Report of the Commission of Investigation into the Banking Sector in Ireland, March 2011.

7. 'Restoring Confidence in the Irish Banks', Tim McCormick, *Accountancy Ireland*, June 2009.

8. *The Bankers: How the Banks Brought Ireland to its Knees*, Shane Ross, Penguin Ireland, 2009.

9. *The Fall of the Celtic Tiger and the Euro Debt Crisis*, Donal Donovan and Antoin E. Murphy, Oxford University Press, 2013.

Chapter 1: The Irish Financial Crisis Revisited

1. Global Competitiveness Surveys 2008/9 to 2012/13, World Economic Forum website.

2. *Irish Times*, 9 July 2010.

3. *Irish Times*, 20 January 2011.

Chapter 2: Weaning the Celtic Tiger

1. In the case of Ireland GNP statistics can be misleading, due to the considerable impact of multinational companies which repatriate their profits. GDP or Gross Domestic Product is considered by many to be a better guide.

2. *Ireland and the Global Question*, Michael O'Sullivan, Cork University Press, 2006.

3. *Something Rotten: Irish Banking Scandals*, Simon Carswell, Gill and Macmillan, 2006.

4. *All in a Life: An autobiography*, Garret FitzGerald, Gill and MacMillan, 1991.

Chapter 3 Lessons from Overseas Banking Failures

1. 'A Crash to Remember', Geoffrey Elliott, *The Spectator*, 30 September 2006.

2. *The Fall of Northern Rock*, Brian Walters, Harriman House, 2008.

3. *The Crunch: How greed and incompetence sparked the credit crisis*, Alex Brummer, Random House, 2008.

4. *Rogue Trader*: Nick Leeson with Edward Whitley, Warner, 1997.,

5. *Can You Trust Your Bank?* Robert Heller and Norris Willatt, Weidenfeld and Nicolson, Part 2, 1977.

6. *Meltdown Iceland*, Roger Boyes, Bloomsbury, 2009.

7. 'History of the 1980s – Lessons for the Future, Chapter 4, The Savings and Loan Crisis and its Relationship to Banking,' Study by the FDIC Research and Statistics, 1995.

8. 'History of the 1980s – Lessons for the Future, Chapter 7, Continental Illinois and Too Big to Fail,' Study by the FDIC Research and Statistics, 1995.

9. 'History of the 1980s – Lessons for the Future, Chapter 5, LDC Debt' Study by the FDIC Research and Statistics, 1995.

10. *Inventing Money: The Story of Long Term Capital Management and the Legends Behind* it, Nicholas Dunbar, Wiley, 2000.

Chapter 4: Alchemy and the Calculation of Bank Profits

1. Anglo Irish Bank website.

2. *Anglo Republic: Inside the Bank that Broke Ireland*, Simon Carswell, Penguin Ireland, 2011.

3. *Irish Times*, 23 July 2010.

4. *Irish Times*, 6 August 2010.

5. The main relevant international accounting standard is IAS 39, which was adopted in 2005.

6. The Turner Review – a Regulatory Response to the Global Financial Crisis, Turner Lord, Financial Services Authority, March 2009.

Chapter 5: *The Seven Deadly Sins – The Route to Insolvency*

1. *Corporate Collapse: The Causes and Symptoms*, J Argenti, McGraw-Hill, 1976. Also *Corporate Financial Distress and Bankruptcy*, Edward Altman, 2nd Edition Wiley, 1993. *Corporate Financial Crisis in Ireland*, Edward Cahill, Gill and MacMillan, 1997.

2. First published as 'Business Failure – the Seven Deadly Sins', Tim McCormick, *Accountancy Ireland*, December 2009. The examples of Lehman Brothers and Anglo Irish Bank were included in Chapter 18, 'Strategic Cost Reduction – how to cut costs without killing your business', Tim McCormick and Dermot Duff, Chartered Accountants Ireland, 2012.

3. *How the Mighty Fail*, Jim Collins, R. H. Business Books, 2009.

4. The first stage is hubris, born of success, which corresponds to pride and neglect of change. The second is undisciplined pursuit of more, which resembles overtrading. The third is denial of risk and peril, which usually leads to over-borrowing. The fourth is grasping for salvation or taking the big risk. The last is irrelevance or death, where an attempt can be made to restore controls. Throughout management suffer from delusion, which may result in creative accounting, when trying to disguise the performance downturn.

5. *Greed and Glory on Wall Street: The Fall of the House of Lehman*, Ken Auletta, Penguin, 1986 recounts this collapse.

6. *A Colossal Failure of Common Sense: The Incredible Story of the Collapse of Lehman Brothers*, Larry McDonald, Ebury Press, 2009.

7. *Too Big to Fail: Inside the Battle to Save Wall Street*, Andrew Ross Sorkin, Penguin 2010.

8. *Irish Times*, 6 August 2010.

9. *Banksters: How a Powerful Elite Squandered Ireland's Wealth*, David Murphy and Martina Devlin, Hachette Books Ireland, 2009.

10. *The Bankers: How the Banks Brought Ireland to its Knees*, Shane Ross, Penguin Ireland, 2009.

11. *The Fitzpatrick Tapes: The Rise and Fall of One Man, One Bank and One Country*, Tom Lyons and Brian Carey, Penguin Ireland, 2011.

12. *Breakfast with Anglo*, Simon Kelly, Penguin Ireland, 2010.

13. *RTÉ News* 19 December 2008.

14. *Irish Times*, 19 November 2010.

15. *Irish Times*, 14 June 2013.

16. *Making it Happen: Fred Goodwin, RBS and the Men Who Blew up the British Economy*, Iain Martin, Simon and Schuster, 2013.

17. *Shredded: Inside the Bank that Broke Britain*, Ian Fraser, Birlinn, 2014.

Chapter 6: Riding the Celtic Tiger

1. *Extraordinary Popular Delusions and the Madness of Crowds*, Charles Mackay, Wiley, 1996 (first published 1841).

2. This is an amplification of the Kindelberger model, which distinguishes five elements in a cycle: Displacement, Euphoria, Mania, Distress and Revulsion. See: *Manias, Panics and Crashes: a History of Financial Crises*, Charles Kindelberger and Robert Aliber, 5th edition, Wiley, 2005.

3. *The Great Crash*, J.K. Galbraith, Penguin, 1961.

4. *Irrational Exuberance*, Shiller Robert, Princeton, 2000.

5. *The Big Short*, Michael Lewis, Penguin, 2011.

6. *Stabilizing an Unstable Economy*, Hyman Minsky, McGraw Hill, 2008.

7. *Madoff: The Man Who Stole $65 Billion*, Erin Arvedlund, Penguin, 2009.

8. *The Origin of Financial Crises: Central banks, Credit Bubbles and the Efficient Market Fallacy*, George Cooper, Random House, 2008.

9. *The Fall of the Celtic Tiger*, Donal Donovan and Antoin E. Murphy, Oxford, 2013.

10. Taoiseach Bertie Ahern in 2006, quoted in *The Economist*, 17 February 2011 and speech to ICTU on 4th July 2007.

11. 'The Irish Credit Bubble,' Morgan Kelly in *Understanding Ireland's Economic Crisis: Prospects for Recovery*, Eds: Stephen Kinsella and Anthony Leddin, Blackhall, 2010.

12. *Ship of Fools*, Fintan O'Toole, Faber and Faber, 2009.

13. *Who Really Runs Ireland?* Matt Cooper, Penguin Ireland, 2009.

14. *The Big Lie*, Gene Kerrigan, Transworld Ireland, 2012.

15. *Ireland's House Party*, Derek Brawn, Gill and MacMillan, 2009.

16. *The Bankers: How the Banks Brought Ireland to its Knees*, Shane Ross, Penguin Ireland, 2009.

Chapter 7: The Fundamental Rules of Lending

1. See *Business and Finance*, 13 September 1990 and the *Sunday Tribune*, December1990.

2. The 20 'C's of Credit: Basic Considerations the Banks Overlooked,' Tim McCormick, *Accountancy Ireland*, August 2009.

3. *The Builders*, Frank McDonald and Kathy Sheridan, Penguin Ireland, 2008.

Chapter 8: How Contagion Spreads Risk

1. *Frozen Assets: How I Lived Iceland's Boom and Bust*, Armann Thorvaldsson, Wiley, 2009.

2. *Meltdown: The End of the Age of Greed*, Paul Mason, Verso, 2009.

3. See chapter 17, 'Strategic Cost Reduction,' Tim McCormick and Dermot Duff, Chartered Accountants Ireland, 2012.

4. *The Tipping Point*, Malcolm Gladwell, Abacus, 2006.

5. *Infectious Greed: How Deceit and Risk Corrupted the Financial Markets*, Frank Partnoy, Henry Holt, 2003.

6. See: *Bad Money: Reckless Finance, Failed Politics, and the Global Crisis of American Capitalism*, Kevin Phillips, Penguin, 2008.

7. *The Age of Turbulence*, Alan Greenspan, Penguin, 2008.

8. *Fool's Gold: How Unrestrained Greed Corrupted a Dream, Shattered Global Markets and Unleashed a Catastrophe*, Gillian Tett, Abacus, 2010.

9. *The Black Swan: The Impact of the Highly Improbable*, Taleb Nassim Nicholas, , Penguin, 2007.

10. *The Quants: How a Small Band of Maths Wizards Took over Wall Street and Nearly Destroyed it*, Scott Patterson, RH Business Books, 2010.

11. *More Money than God: Hedge funds and the Making of a New Elite*, Sebastian Mallarby, Bloomsbury, 2010.

12. *The Alchemy of Finance*, Soros George, Wiley, 1987.

13. *The New Paradigm for Financial Markets*, George Soros, Public Affairs, 2008.

14. The Turner Review – a Regulatory Response to the Global Financial Crisis, Turner Lord, Financial Services Authority, March 2009.

15. *The Bankers*, Chapters 8 and 9, Shane Ross, Penguin Ireland, 2009.

Chapter 9: Retail and Investment Banks – Two Conflicting Cultures

1. *The Big Bang*, William Kay, Weidenfeld and Nicolson, 1986.
2. *All Change in the City*, Margaret Reid, MacMillan, 1988.
3. *The Financial Revolution*. Adrian Hamilton, Penguin, 1986.
4. *Liar's Poker*, Michael Lewis, Hodder and Stroughton, 1989.
5. *F.I.A.S.C.O. – Blood in the Water on Wall Street*, Frank Partnoy, Profile Books, 1997.
6. *The Greed Merchants*, Philip Augar, Penguin, 2006.
7. *The Accidental Investment Banker*, Johnathan Knee, Oxford, 2006.
8. *How I Caused the Credit Crunch*, Tetsuya Ishikawa, Icon, 2009.
9. *Binge Trading: The Real Inside Story of Cash, Cocaine and Corruption in the City*, Seth Freedman, Penguin, 2009.
10. *Cityboy*, Geraint Andersen, Headline, 2008.
11. *The Wolf of Wall Street*, Jordan Belford, Hodder and Stroughton, 2008.

Chapter 10: Competition in Ireland's Unique Banking Culture

1. *Back from the Brink: 1000 Days at Number 11*, Darling Alistair, Atlantic Books, 2011.
2. *Irish Times*, 2 September 2011.
3. *Irish Times*, 12 November 2010.
4. *Open Dissent*, Mike Soden, Blackhall, 2010.
5. *Hubris: How HBOS Wrecked the Best Bank in Britain*, Ray Perman, Berlin, 2012.
6. *The Ansbacher Conspiracy*, Colm Keena, Gill and MacMillan, 2003.
7. Report of the Inspectors Appointed (Under Section 8 of the Companies Act 1990) to Investigate the Affairs of National Irish Bank Limited and National Irish Bank Financial Services Limited, Mr Justice Blaney and Tom Grace FCA, 23 July 2004.
8. *The Great Irish Bank Robbery*, Liam Collins, Mentor, 2007.

Chapter 11: Shareholders or Management First?

1. Evidence to Congress, 24 October 2008.
2. *The Age of Turbulence*, Alan Greenspan, Penguin, 2008.
3. *The Road to Serfdom*, Friedrich Hayek, Routledge, 1944.

4. *Free to Choose*, Milton and Rose Friedman, Pelican Books, 1980.

5. *This Time is Different – 8 Centuries of Financial Folly*, Carmenn Reinhart and Kenneth Rogoff, Princeton, 2009.

6. *The Managerial Revolution*, James Burnham, Pelican, 1945.

7. The usual approach is through the Capital Asset pricing Model (CAPM). This is based on the cost of debt + the equity risk premium+ the riskiness of the particular stock relative to the market. The equity risk premium is based on stock market returns over a long period. Research is needed to see whether it and the relative stock riskiness (or 'BETA') have been affected by recent stock market turmoil, particularly in the financial sector.

8. Examples of such approaches are Economic Value Added (Stern Stewart and Co), Cashflow Return on Investment (Braxton, Deloitte Touche), Equity Cashflows (Marakon), Free Cashflow (Rappaport/Alcar) and Return on Invested Capital (McKinsey).

9. *Valuation: Measuring and Managing the Value of Companies*, Ch 13, Tom Copeland, Tim Koller and Jack Murrin, McKinsey and Co, Wiley, 1990.

10. *The Value Imperative*, James McTaggart, Peter Kontes and Michael Mankins, Free Press, 1994.

11. *Finance for Executives*, Gabriel Hawawini and Claude Viallet, International Thompson Publishing, 1999.

Chapter 12: The Rewards System and the Insidious Bonus Culture

1. *The Greed Merchants*, Phillip Augar, Penguin, 2006.

2. *Freud in the City*, David Freud, Bene Factum Publishing, 2006.

3. *Confessions of a City Girl*, S. Suzanna, Virgin, 2009.

4. *The Collapse of Barings: Panic, Ignorance and Greed*, Stephen Fay, Arrow, 1996.

5. *How John Rusnak lost AIB $691 million*, Siobahn Creaton and Conor O'Clery, Gill and Macmillan, 2002.

6. See 'The Folly of Rewarding A, While Hoping for B', Steven Kerr, *Academy of Management Journal* 18, 1975.

7. Report of the Inspectors Appointed (Under Section 8 of the Companies Act 1990) to Investigate the Affairs of National Irish Bank Limited and National Irish Bank Financial Services Limited, Mr Justice Blaney and Tom Grace FCA, 23 July 2004.

8. *Crisis – Cause, Containment and Cure*, Thomas Huertas, Palgrave Macmillan, 2010.

9. *Something Rotten: Irish Banking Scandals*, Simon Carswell, Gill and Macmillan, 2006.

10. *The Bankers*, Ch 10, Shane Ross, Penguin, 2009.

11. *Fingers: The Man who Brought Down Irish Nationwide and Cost us €5.4 billion*, Tom Lyons and Richard Curran, Gill and MacMillan, 2013.

12. 'Inside Irish Nationwide', Richard Curran, RTÉ, 11 February 2013.

Chapter 13: The Irish State – A Reluctant Bride

1. *The Problem with Banks*, Lena Rethel and Timothy Sinclair, Zed Books, 2012.

2. *Citizen Quinn: A Man, an Empire and a Family*, Gavin Daly and Ian Kehoe, Penguin Ireland, 2013.

3. *Irish Times*, 11 May 2013 and 18 September 2013.

Chapter 14: Ethical Banking – A Necessity or a Contradiction in Terms?

1. 'Ethical Banking: Reasonable Expectation or Impossible Oxymoron?' Tim McCormick, published in *The Business Compass*, Chartered Accountants Ireland, 2011.

2. *Banker to the Poor: The story of Grameen Bank*, Muhammad Yunis with Alan Jolis, Aurum, 1999.

3. *Sunday Independent*, 13 October 2013.

4. *Mail on Sunday*, 17 November 2013 and 12 January 2014, and Brummer, cited 9 below.

5. *Good Value: Reflections on Money, Morality and an Uncertain World*, Stephen Green, Allen Lane, 2009.

6. *Daily Telegraph*, 18 July 2012.

7. Interview with Chris Blackhurst, *The Tablet*, 11 April 2009.

8. 'Bankers: Payback Time', BBC 2, 22 May, 2013.

9. *Bad Banks: Greed, Incompetence and the Next Global Crunch*, Alex Brummer, Random House, 2014.

Chapter 15: International Banking Reform – The Glacial Pace of Change

1. *13 Bankers – the Wall Street Takeover and the Next Financial Meltdown*, Simon Johnson and James Kwak, Vintage, 2011.

2. 'Insane Financial System Lives on Post-Lehman', Gillian Tett, *Financial Times*, 13 September 2013.

3. '5 Bitter Pills', Patrick Jenkins, *Financial Times*, 13 September 2013.

4. *The Bankers' New Clothes*, Anat Admati and Martin Hellwig, Princeton, 2013.

5. *The Death of Money: The Coming Collapse of the International Monetary System*, Rickards James, Portfolio Penguin, 2014.

6. *Das Kapital*, Karl Marx, 1867.

7. *Capital in the Twenty-first Century*, Piketty Thomas, translated by Arthur Goldhammer, Redknapp Press, 2014.

8. *23 Things They Don't Tell You about Capitalism*, Ha-Joon Chang, Penguin Books, 2011.

9. 'The Rise of State Capitalism,' *The Economist*, 21 January 2012.

10. *How the West Was Lost*, Dambisa Moyo, Penguin, 2012.

11. 'The Crisis of Capitalism', *Financial Times*, 9-14 January 2012

12. *Freefall: Free Markets and the Sinking of the Global Economy*, Joseph Stiglitz, Penguin, 2010.

13. *Capitalism 4.0: The Birth of a New Economy*, Anatole Kaletsky, Bloomsbury, 2010.

14. *The Fourth Revolution: The Global Race to Reinvent the State*, John Micklethwait and Adrian Wooldridge, Allen Lane, 2014

15. *Economics after the Crisis: Ends and Means*, Turner Adair, MIT Press, 2012.

16. *Progressive Capitalism: How to Achieve Economic Growth, Liberty and Social Justice*, David Sainsbury, Biteback Publishing, 2013.

Chapter 16: Challenges and Options for Ireland

1. 'The Poisoned Chalice, Ray MacSharry', in Brian Murphy, Mary O'Rourke and Noel Whelan, editors, *Brian Lenihan*, Merrion Press, 2014.

2. *What if Ireland Defaults*, Eds Brian Lucey, Charles Larkin and Constantin Gurdgiev, Orpen Press, 2012.

3. *Plan B – How leaving the euro can save Ireland*, Cormac Lucey, Gill and MacMillan, 2014.

4. *Understanding Ireland's Economic Crisis: Prospects for Recovery*, Eds Stephen Kinsella and Anthony Leddin, Blackhall, 2010.

5. *Crisis Economics: A Crash Course in the Future of Finance*, Roubini Nouriel and Mihm Stephen, Penguin, 2011.

6. UCD Lecture, Professor Morgan Kelly, quoted in *Irish Times* 10 March 2014.

7. 'Peer-to-peer lending – Banking without banks', *The Economist*, 1 March 2014.

8. *Strategic Cost Reduction: Cutting Costs Without Killing Your Business*, Tim McCormick and Dermot Duff, Chartered Accountants. Ireland, 2nd edition 2012.

Chapter 17: Understanding the Real Causes of the Debacle

1. 'This week in the papers', RTÉ 1, 28 September 2008.

2. 'The Marian Finucane Show', RTÉ 1, 4 October 2008.

3. 2014 Global Banking Survey, Ernst and Young, quoted in the *Irish Times*, 17 March 2014.

Selected Further Reading

Admati, Anat and Hellwig, Martin, *The Bankers' New Clothes*, Princeton, 2013.

Andersen, Geraint, *Cityboy*, Headline, 2008.

Argenti J., *Corporate Collapse: The Causes and Symptoms*, McGraw-Hill, 1976. .

Arvedlund, Erin, *Madoff : The Man Who Stole $65 Billion*, Penguin, 2009.

Augar, Philip, *The Greed Merchants*, Penguin, 2006.

Auletta, Ken, *Greed and Glory on Wall Street: The Fall of the House of Lehman*, Penguin, 1986.

Belford, Jordan, *The Wolf of Wall Street*, Hodder and Stroughton, 2008.

Blaney, Mr Justice and Grace, Tom, *Report of the Inspectors Appointed (Under Section 8 of the Companies Act 1990) to Investigate the Affairs of National Irish Bank Limited and National Irish Bank Financial Services Limited*, 23 July 2004.

Boyes, Roger, *Meltdown Iceland*, Bloomsbury, 2009.

Brawn, Derek, *Ireland's House Party*, Gill and MacMillan, 2009.

Brummer, Alex, *The Crunch: How Greed and Incompetence Sparked the Credit Crisis*, Random House, 2008.

Brummer, Alex, *Bad Banks: Greed, Incompetence and the Next Global Crunch*, Random House, 2014.

Burnham, James, *The Managerial Revolution*, Pelican, 1945.

Cahill, Edward, *Corporate Financial Crisis in Ireland*, Gill and MacMillan, 1997.

Carswell, Simon, *Something Rotten: Irish Banking Scandals*, Gill and Macmillan, 2006.

Carswell, Simon, *Anglo Republic: Inside the Bank that Broke Ireland,* 2011.

Chang, Ha-Joon, *23 Things They Don't Tell You about Capitalism,* Penguin, 2011.

Collins, Jim, *How the Mighty Fail,* Random House, 2009.

Collins, Liam, *The Great Irish Bank Robbery,* Mentor, 2007.

Cooper George, *The Origin of Financial Crises: Central banks, Credit Bubbles and the Efficient Market Fallacy,* Random House, 2008.

Cooper, Matt, *Who Really Runs Ireland?* Penguin Ireland, 2009.

Copeland, Tom, Koller, Tim and Murrin, Jack, *Valuation: Measuring and Managing the Value of Companies,* McKinsey and Co, Wiley, 1990.

Creaton, Siobahn and O'Clery, Conor, *How John Rusnak Lost AIB $691 Million,* Gill and Macmillan, 2002.

Daly, Gavin and Kehoe, Ian, *Citizen Quinn: A Man, An Empire and A Family,* Penguin Ireland, 2013.

Darling, Alistair, *Back from the Brink: 1000 Days at Number 11,* Atlantic Books, 2011.

Donovan, Donal and Murphy, Antoin E., *The Fall of the Celtic Tiger and the Euro Debt Crisis:* Oxford University Press, 2013

Dunbar, Nicholas, *Inventing Money: The Story of Long Term Capital Management and the Legends Behind It,* Wiley, 2000.

Fay, Stephen, *The Collapse of Barings: Panic, Ignorance and Greed,* Arrow, 1996.

FDIC Research and Statistics, 'History of the 1980s – Lessons for the Future,' 1995.

Fraser, Ian, *Shredded: Inside the Bank that Broke Britain,* Birlinn, 2014.

Freedman, Seth, *Binge Trading: The Real Inside Story of Cash, Cocaine and Corruption in the City,* Penguin, 2009.

Friedman, Milton and Rose, *Free to Choose,* Pelican Books, 1980.

Freud, David, *Freud in the City,* Bene Factum Publishing, 2006.

Galbraith, J.K., *The Great Crash,* Penguin, 1961.

Gladwell, Malcolm, *The Tipping Point,* Abacus, 2006.

Green, Stephen, *Good Value: Reflections on Money, Morality and an Uncertain World,* Allen Lane, 2009.

Greenspan, Alan, *The Age of Turbulence,* Penguin, 2008.

Hamilton, Adrian, *The Financial Revolution,* Penguin, 1986.

Hawawini, Gabriel and Viallet, Claude, *Finance for Executives*, International Thompson Publishing, 1999.

Hayek, Friedrich, *The Road to Serfdom*, Routledge, 1944.

Heller, Robert and Willatt, Norris, *Can You Trust Your Bank?* Weidenfeld and Nicolson, 1977.

Honohan Patrick, Governor of the Central Bank, 'The Irish Banking Crisis – Regulatory and Financial Stability Policy', A Report to the Minister of Finance by 31 May 2010.

Huertas, Thomas, *Crisis: Cause, Containment and Cure*, Palgrave Macmillan, 2010.

Ishikawa, Tetsuya, *How I Caused the Credit Crunch*, Icon Books, 2009.

Johnson, Simon and Kwak, James, *13 Bankers: The Wall Street Takeover and the Next Financial Meltdown*, Vintage, 2011.

Kaletsky, Anatole, *Capitalism 4.0: The Birth of a New Economy*, Bloomsbury, 2010.

Kay, William, *The Big Bang*, Weidenfeld and Nicolson, 1986.

Keena, Colm, *The Ansbacher Conspiracy*, Gill and MacMillan, 2003.

Kelly, Simon, *Breakfast with Anglo*, Penguin Ireland, 2010.

Kerrigan, Gene, *The Big Lie*, Transworld Ireland, 2012.

Kindelberger, Charles and Aliber, Robert, *Manias, Panics and Crashes: A History of Financial Crises*, 5th edition, Wiley, 2005.

Kinsella, Stephen and Leddin, Anthony, editors, *Understanding Ireland's Economic Crisis: Prospects for Recovery*, Blackhall, 2010.

Knee, Johnathan, *The Accidental Investment Banker*, Oxford, 2006.

Kontes, Peter and Mankins, Michael, *The Value Imperative*, James McTaggart, Free Press, 1994.

Leeson, Nick with Whitley, Edward, *Rogue Trader*, Warner, 1997.

Lewis, Michael, *Liar's Poker*, Hodder and Stroughton, 1989.

Lewis, Michael, *The Big Short*, Penguin, 2011.

Lucey, Brian, Larkin, Charles and Gurdgiev, Constantin, editors, *What if Ireland Defaults*, Orpen Press, 2012.

Lucey, Cormac, *Plan B: How Leaving the Euro Can Save Ireland*, Gill and MacMillan, 2014.

Lyons, Tom and Carey, Brian, *The Fitzpatrick Tape: The Rise and Fall of One Man, One Bank and One Country*, Penguin Ireland, 2011.

Lyons, Tom and Curran, Richard, *Fingers: The Man Who Brought Down Irish Nationwide and Cost Us €5.4 Billion*, Gill and MacMillan, 2013.

Mackay, Charles, *Extraordinary Popular Delusions and the Madness of Crowds,* Wiley, 1996 (first published 1841).

McDonald, Frank and Sheridan, Kathy, *The Builders,* Penguin Ireland, 2008.

McDonald, Larry, *A Colossal Failure of Common Sense: The Incredible Story of the Collapse Lehman Brothers,* Ebury Press, 2009.

Mallarby, Sebastian, *More Money than God: Hedge Funds and the Making of a New Elite,* Bloomsbury, 2010.

Martin, Iain, *Making it Happen: Fred Goodwin, RBS and the Men Who Blew up the British Economy,* Simon and Schuster, 2013.

Mason, Paul, *Meltdown: The End of the Age of Greed,* Verso, 2009.

Micklethwait, John and Wooldridge, Adrian, *The Fourth Revolution: The Global Race to Reinvent the State,* Allen Lane, 2014.

Minsky, Hyman, *Stabilizing an Unstable Economy,* McGraw Hill, 2008.

Moyo, Dambisa, *How the West Was Lost,* Penguin, 2012.

Murphy, Brian, O'Rourke, Mary and Whelan, Noel (editors), *Brian Lenihan,* Merrion Press, 2014.

Murphy, David and Devlin, Martina, *Banksters: How a Powerful Elite Squandered Ireland's Wealth,* Hachette Books Ireland, 2009.

Nyberg, Peter and others, 'Misjudging Risk: Causes of the Systemic Banking Crisis in Ireland', Report of the Commission of Investigation into the Banking Sector in Ireland, March 2011.

O'Sullivan, Michael, *Ireland and the Global Question,* Cork University Press, 2006.

O'Toole, Fintan, *Ship of Fools,* Faber and Faber, 2009.

Partnoy, Frank, *F.I.A.S.C.O.: Blood in the Water on Wall Street,* Profile Books, 1997.

Partnoy, Frank, *Infectious Greed: How Deceit and Risk Corrupted the Financial Markets,* Henry Holt, 2003.

Patterson, Scott, *The Quants: How a Small Band of Math Wizards Took over Wall Street and Nearly Destroyed Tt,* RH Business Books, 2010.

Perman, Ray, *Hubris: How HBOS Wrecked the Best Bank in Britain,* Berlin, 2012.

Phillips, Kevin, *Bad Money: Reckless Finance, Failed Politics, and the Global Crisis of American Capitalism,* Penguin, 2008.

Piketty, Thomas, translated by Arthur Goldhammer, *Capital in the Twenty-first Century,* Redknapp Press, 2014.

Regling, Klaus and Watson, Max, 'A Preliminary Report on the Sources of Ireland's Banking Crisis', May 2010.

Reid, Margaret, *All Change in the City*, MacMillan, 1988.

Reinhart, Carmenn and Rogoff, Kenneth, *This Time is Different: 8 Centuries of Financial Folly*, Princeton, 2009.

Rethel, Lena and Sinclair, Timothy, *The Problem with Banks*, Zed Books, 2012.

Rickards, James, *The Death of Money: The Coming Collapse of the International Monetary System*, Portfolio Penguin, 2014.

Ross, Shane, *The Bankers: How the Banks Brought Ireland to Its Knees*, Penguin Ireland, 2009.

Roubini, Nouriel and Mihm, Stephen, *Crisis Economics: A Crash Course in the Future of Finance*, Penguin, 2011.

S. Suzanna, *Confessions of a City Girl*, Virgin, 2009.

Sainsbury, David, *Progressive Capitalism: How to Achieve Economic Growth, Liberty and Social Justice*, Biteback Publishing, 2013.

Shiller, Robert, *Irrational Exuberance*, Princeton, 2000.

Soden, Mike, *Open Dissent*, Blackhall, 2010.

Sorkin, Andrew Ross, *Too Big to Fail: Inside the Battle to Save Wall Street*, Penguin 2010.

Soros, George, *The Alchemy of Finance*, Wiley, 1987.

Soros, George, *The New Paradigm for Financial Markets*, Public Affairs, 2008.

Stiglitz, Joseph, *Freefall: Free Markets and the Sinking of the Global Economy*, Penguin, 2010.

Taleb, Nassim Nicholas, *The Black Swan: The Impact of the Highly Improbable*, Penguin, 2007.

Tett, Gillian, *Fool's Gold: How Unrestrained Greed Corrupted a Dream, Shattered Global Markets and Unleashed a Catastrophe*, Abacus, 2010.

Thorvaldsson, Armann, *Frozen Assets: How I lived Iceland's Boom and Bust*, Wiley, 2009.

Turner, Lord, *The Turner Review – a Regulatory Response to the Global Financial Crisis*, Financial Services Authority, March 2009.

Turner, Adair, *Economics After the Crisis: Ends and Means*, MIT Press, 2012.

Walters, Brian, *The Fall of Northern Rock*, Harriman House, 2008.

Yunis, Muhammad with Jolis, Alan, *Banker to the Poor: The Story of Grameen Bank*, Aurum, 1999.

Index